MW01042097

DISCARD

PREBIND AWAKENING TO ANIMAL VOICES
9780001457140
BRUNKE
DB

Awakening
to
Animal
Voices

A Teen Guide to Telepathic communication with All Life

Dawn Baumann Brunke

STATION LIBRARY
BLDG 298 E ST
PSC BOX 8009
CHERRY POINT NC 28533

Bindu Books
Rochester, Vermont

Bindu Books
One Park Street
Rochester, Vermont 05767
www.InnerTraditions.com

Bindu Books is a division of Inner Traditions International

Copyright © 2004 by Dawn Baumann Brunke

All rights reserved. No part of this book may be reproduced or utilized in any form or by any means, electronic or mechanical, including photocopying, recording, or by any information storage and retrieval system, without permission in writing from the publisher.

Library of Congress Cataloging-in-Publication Data
Brunke, Dawn Baumann.
   Awakening to animal voices : a teen guide to telepathic communication with all life / Dawn Baumann Brunke.— 1st ed.
      p. cm.
   Includes bibliographical references.
   ISBN 0-89281-136-6
   1. Human-animal communication—Juvenile literature. 2. Extrasensory perception in animals—Juvenile literature. 3. Telepathy—Juvenile literature. I. Title.

   QL776.B782 2004
   133.8'9—dc22

                                                        2004003917

Printed and bound in the United States at Lake Book Manufacturing, Inc.

10 9 8 7 6 5 4 3 2 1

Text design and layout by Mary Anne Hurhula
This book was typeset in in Veljovic with Democratica and Critters as the display typefaces

For Alyeska, and for you.

contents

part one
Beginning the Journey

1

2

part two
seeking animal wisdom

part three
Deepening in Relationship

acknowledgments

Thanks to all the animals, of so many forms and species, who offered their insight and wisdom, humor and helpful collaboration in making this book a reality.

Thanks to the many humans, professional communicators and students alike, who shared their views, messages, and experiences. Special thanks to friends Tera Thomas, Penelope Smith, Rita Reynolds, Morgine Jurdan, Gretchen Kunz, Carole Devereux, and Kat Berard for extra assistance and support.

Thanks to manuscript readers Carol Baumann, Gretchen Kunz and Maya, Tera Thomas, Patricia Wade, and Katarina Werkmeister for excellent suggestions and words of encouragement.

Thanks to all the great folks at Bindu Books who help to create books of beauty and substance, especially Jon Graham, Jeanie Levitan, Peri Champine, and my editor, Laura Schlivek. Thanks also to my copy editor, Victoria Sant'Ambrogio, and to Mary Anne Hurhula for her playful and beautiful design.

Thanks to my parents, Richard and Carol Baumann, and my husband, Bob Brunke, for wholehearted support and love; to my daughter, Alyeska, never-ending source of joy, laughter, and inspiration; and to my very good pals Barney, Zak, Max, and Riza.

Introduction

The Door is Round
and Open . . .

We are the doorways through which life unfolds.

WU WEI, CHINESE SCHOLAR

This is a book of possibilities.

Maybe you'd like to learn to telepathically communicate with animals, or maybe you want to relate to your cat or parrot or horse in a deeper way. Maybe you're looking to find an animal guide who can show you a few things, or maybe you dream of a small golden toad and want to learn more. Maybe your beloved dog is dying and you want to know how to connect with her in her final days. Or maybe you're interested in discovering what it's like to see the world from an entirely different perspective—experiencing life through the eyes of a whale or dolphin, eagle, giraffe, or jaguar.

If any—or all—of these things are true, then this is the book for you. For in the following pages we will explore many new ideas and exciting ways of awakening to all the world's animal voices. We will share in the wisdom of the two-legged, four-legged, winged, and gilled alike—from spirit animals and guardians to mythic animals and human teachers, from dogs and cats and llamas and lions to ravens and sharks and flies and frogs.

A fundamental principle of this book is that there are limitless ways of being in the world. To explore this idea, we will look at a wide variety of techniques and tools—a rich tapestry of ways to see and feel and hear and touch and sense and be. There will be games to shake loose our thoughts, meditations to open our inner world, and hopefully some laughter and a good deal of fun along the way.

We begin the journey by recalling a time when humans and animals shared a common awareness and connection within the great web of life. Our ancestors were able to tap in to a universal language, communicating easily with animals and all aspects of nature. We, too, carry this ability within ourselves. So, if your most burning question is *Can I really talk with animals?* the answer is *Yes!* And that's not all. One of the great things about learning how to listen to animals is that you can't help but learn to listen to yourself, too. The process changes you in ways both inspiring and unforeseen.

We will investigate unusual encounters and magical meetings of the animal kind—those moments when an animal shows up in your life in just the right way, at just the right time. We will discover the ways of animal guides and teachers, look at the awe-inspiring ways that animal spirits, power animals, and totems visit our everyday lives as well as our visions and dreams, helping us in so many ways. We will visit the wonderfully creative world of dreams—of both humans and animals—and examine some of the treasures that come to us in the wee hours of the night.

We will deepen in relationship as well, looking at ways to heal with animals and be more present in our lives, especially during times of transition and death. We will develop skills to see animals and ourselves with new eyes and form partnerships in more meaningful ways. We will play with shifting the shape of our consciousness, viewing the world from wider, deeper perspectives, seeing through animal eyes, beholding the splendor of diversity, and so also seeing ourselves anew.

Behold, a sacred voice is calling you.
All over the sky a sacred voice is calling you.

BLACK ELK

Throughout these adventures, some of what you read may not make sense. And that, too, is often a fine and helpful thing. For always in our experiences we are planting seeds. By reading and playing with a variety of ideas and suggestions, we may be surprised to find that some of the things that do not fit now may be just what we need at a later time.

Did you know that yours is the first generation in a very long time to open the global connection with animals, nature, and the world at large in a more conscious and profound way? We live now in incredible times. As author, animal communicator, and teacher Penelope Smith notes, "My prediction is that by 2012 kids will be saying to their parents, 'You mean there was a time when people *didn't* communicate with animals?'" Or, as her beloved orange cat Sherman puts it, *"It's all progressing very rapidly. It's all getting much more relaxed. Humans are less uptight than they used to be."*

We all have brilliant gifts we bring to the planet, both as members of our own species and as spiritual individuals. As we share our talents and visions in appreciation, we celebrate the richness of our diversity, the many distinctive and exceptional ways we all have of seeing, sensing, understanding, and contributing to the world.

Maybe you, too, sense a deep connection, something longing to be birthed—but what is it and how does it come forth? How can you contact it and how can you become a vehicle of expressing your own special truth to the world?

I believe the call of our time is to awaken the individual gifts we came here to share and to give them voice in our world. Those are the things we desire deep within ourselves—those that ignite our enthusiasm, inspire our thoughts, encourage our dreams, and lead us to embrace the wonders of this little planet. Attuning ourselves to the deeper awareness that flows through all things, we begin to see

The important thing is not to stop questioning. Curiosity has its own reason for existing. One cannot help but be in awe when he contemplates the mysteries of eternity, of life, of the marvelous structure of reality. It is enough if one tries merely to comprehend a little of this mystery every day. Never lose a holy curiosity.

ALBERT EINSTEIN

all that is possible. We begin to accept the advice and wisdom and support that is so freely offered us from animals and the natural world. And so we begin to live with a sense of joy.

Most hopefully, this is a book about change in our world. It's about awakening not only to the voices of animals, plants, the earth, and other humans, but to our own brilliant voice within. It is to know that as we shine our clarity out to the world, we help to illuminate radiance in everyone.

This book is dedicated to my daughter, as it is to you. It's the type of book I wish I had read when I was much younger. I hope it offers you encouragement and the assurance of knowing that everything you need is right here, right now, before your eyes, within you, just waiting to be called forth.

My wish for you is that you consider the beauty, love, and wonder life has to offer you, that you choose your path based on what feels right and good and true to your soul, and that you trust yourself enough to shine what is most unique and magnificent about you to the world.

This is a book of possibilities. Let us begin . . .

The breezes at dawn have secrets to tell you.
Don't go back to sleep!
You must ask for what you really want.
Don't go back to sleep!
People are going back and forth
Across the doorsill where the two worlds touch;
The door is round and open.
Don't go back to sleep!

RUMI[1]

PART ONE

beginning
the journey

I

once upon
a time . . .

There was once a small boy, alone in the forest, who heard such a beautiful song. Following the sound, the boy discovered it came from a bird—the Bird of the Most Beautiful Song in the Forest. The boy brought the bird back to camp, for he wanted to feed the bird. The boy's father was annoyed at having to give good food to a mere bird, but the boy pleaded, and so the bird was fed. The next day, the boy heard the song and, once more, found the bird and brought it back to camp. The father was again annoyed, but the boy pleaded, and so the bird was fed. The third day—again the song! This time when the boy brought the bird back to camp, the father took the bird and told the boy to run along. And when the boy was gone, the father killed the bird. When the father killed the Bird of the Most Beautiful Song in the Forest, he killed the song, and with the song, himself. With the death of the bird and the song, the father dropped dead too, completely dead, and was dead forevermore.

"THE FOREST SONG OF THE PYGMIES,"
AS HEARD BY COLIN TURNBULL

---

*This story is slightly rewritten from "The Forest Song of the Pygmies," as heard by Colin Turnbull, as cited in Joseph Campbell, *The Way of the Animal Powers*, vol. 1 (London: Summerfield Press, 1983), 103; as noted from W. Bogoras, *The Chukchee*, Reports of the Jesup North Pacific Expedition (New York: Memoirs of the American Museum of Natural History, 1907), vol. 11, part 2, 450.

The Pygmies of the African rain forest tell this story. It is an old story that speaks of great loss: a bird, a father, a song, and more. The story reminds us of how we all long to hear the most beautiful song of the forest. And of how much we miss hearing this song.

Where is this forest, you might ask. If you were to venture into the forest, alone and quiet, might you find a similar bird?

Perhaps the Pygmies are not just speaking of *their* rain forest when they share this story but of a forest we all have inside ourselves. Perhaps it is a place we visit when we daydream or let our mind drift in imagination. Perhaps, like the young boy, we are filled with wonder when we suddenly hear the most beautiful song of our inner forest for the first time, and we are even more thrilled to discover that the bird who sings this song lives within us. Perhaps this most beautiful song is the secret of who we really are.

Stories, myths, legends, and folktales hold a powerful medicine that works to awaken us. It is so powerful, in fact, that a good story can touch and transform us in ways we may not even understand. And what is truly magical about these types of stories is that in order to benefit, we need do nothing but listen. As we listen, the essence of the story enters our ears, seeps down into our bones and our very being, until the medicine, the deeper magic of the story, unfolds within us.

We might think we are listening to a story about a boy and a bird, when really we are remembering a forgotten piece of ourselves. We are the boy and the bird. We are the forest and the father, too. When we tell or listen to a story such as this one, we are trying to remember. And so, we are on our way to finding ourselves once again.

When I began writing *Animal Voices*, my first book about animal communication, I hadn't yet actually talked to any animals. Instead,

Forget your old ideas.
Forget the lies they
told you.
Forget them all, and you
will begin to remember.
MARIANNE WILLIAMSON

I was interviewing professional communicators, asking them how this worked and how one could learn to connect with animals in such a way. I discovered many things that helped my mind to understand how talking to animals was possible, and yet . . . something was missing.

It wasn't until a flock of little brown birds showed up on the bush outside my office window one day that I experienced what it was like to talk with animals for myself. I was working on my manuscript at my computer when, from the corner of my eye, I saw the rush of birds onto the bush. Without a thought or plan, I put my hand on my heart, rose from my seat, and walked to the window. As I greeted the little birds in my mind, I heard their greeting in return! For me, this extraordinary event changed everything.

Why did the birds show up just then, and why did I notice them? What made me decide to talk with the birds? And how was it that I could hear them? Did everything I had learned from the communicators suddenly click and allow me to naturally open myself to the voices of the birds? I wasn't trying to do anything. Rather, it was as if a part of me that always knew how to communicate with animals suddenly awoke. I remembered.

A most remarkable thing also happened while working on this book. Maybe it will sound like a story to you, for the circumstances seem so unlikely, and yet it is true. I take it as encouragement of the finest kind.

While sitting at my computer, working on the final edits of this book, I came across a note from my editor. She pointed out that it would be good to share my own experiences, to tell you how I once was closed to the ability to talk with animals, and how a group of birds reminded me of my forgotten talents.

Just as I began to ponder what I might write, a group of birds

flocked to the bush outside my window. I could barely believe it! My eyes blinked, my heart raced, and I laughed out loud. Here was the same type of birds, coming in so much the same way, like some exquisite artistic flourish, like the echo of a memory, like a sign of something wonderful.

As before, I walked to the window, hand on heart, shaking my head in awe. Do you have a message, little birds? I asked. And this is what they had to say.

To You
The Birds on the Bush ~ Dawn Brunke

Our message is about hope and remembering. To you—all readers—we say, maybe you hope you can learn to talk to animals. We show up at just this time to say, yes, this is real. You truly can talk to animals. It is simply a matter of remembering what you already know.

We are birds who travel with the season, now on the lookout for food. But we also show up—and are noticed—when we are called. We alight on this bush as a remembering for your author, for her to recall what it felt like to hear us, to remind her of that first remembering. But our words also hold energy for you who are reading these words. Our message is time encoded, love encoded, designed to remind you of instances of greater remembering, too.

We are fast birds who flit from branch to branch, idea to idea, and here and now we bring you the gift of hope. We encourage you to know that you are participating in a great remembering. You are part of that awakening, and, as such, you are helping to awaken that great remembering in all beings. We come to you, through these pages, as creatures of beauty and light and love.

Before we try our hand at conversing with other creatures, we are going to start by opening our minds to new ideas. We'll take a new

Look about you. Take hold of the things that are here. Let them talk to you. You learn to talk to them.

GEORGE WASHINGTON CARVER

look at everyday things, try a few games to loosen up, and generally shake the envelope a bit. And who knows? By the end of this chapter you may already have had your first interspecies conversation.

Remembering

Remembering is a funny thing. To remember is to recall or to keep in mind. Take the word apart and we have *re,* meaning to restore or do again and *member,* meaning a part of the whole. When we remember, it is as if we are putting parts of ourselves back together again. We are recalling those parts of ourselves that have scattered or wandered beyond the boundaries of our conscious memory. When we speak of re-membering in larger terms, we might think of remembering ourselves with the Web of Life and all our relations—the animals, the plants, other humans, and the earth. As we re-member our essential connection with all life, we remember our oneness. We open to wholeness and begin to experience a more complete version of who we truly are.

Did you know that the ability to talk to animals is nothing new? In fact, it is very old, for almost every culture on the face of the earth has legends, myths, and stories about humans and animals conversing freely. An Eskimo song describes it like this:

We carry within us the wonders we seek without us.

SIR THOMAS BROWNE

In the very earliest time,
when both people and animals lived on Earth,
a person could become an animal if he wanted to
and an animal could become a human being.
Sometimes they were people
and sometimes animals

and there was no difference.
All spoke the same language.
That was the time when words were like magic.
The human mind had mysterious powers.
A word spoken by chance
might have strange consequences.
It would suddenly come alive
and what people wanted to happen could happen—
all you had to do was say it.
Nobody could explain this:
That's the way it was.[1]

Can you remember this time? Can you recall talking with animals as naturally as talking to your friends and family today? What would it be like to become an animal, to know the world as a whale singing the deep resounding songs that travel for miles within the ocean depths? How would it feel to know the language of all creatures? How would life be different if you could talk with songbirds and wolves, deer and butterflies? Take a moment. Nobody's watching. Close your eyes, let yourself re-member.

As you imagine what life is like from this perspective, you might see a story forming in your mind. One of the ways we come to know ourselves is through stories, be they ancient myths or our own imagined tales. There is something within these stories that is alive and powerful—something that wants itself to be known and re-membered.

When I close my eyes and open to my story, it begins something like this:

Once upon a time there was a common language shared by all. Raven and Bear, Coyote and Spider, Frog and Human: all creatures

The first peace, which is the most important, is that which comes within the souls of people when they realize their relationship, their oneness, with the universe and all its powers, and when they realize that at the center of the universe dwells the Great Spirit, and that this center is really everywhere, it is within each of us.

BLACK ELK, *THE SACRED PIPE*

felt a common bond. We were, each one of us, part of the All, and we all knew the language of the earth. We were able to communicate with rocks and plants, land and sky and water, and even beyond, stars and sun and moon. We understood each other, whether we wore the hard shell of Turtle or the delicate wings of Honeybee, the splendid pelt of Wolf or the silvery scales of Salmon. There were differences, of course—that was part of the beauty of the plan—but we were united with underlying essence of one. Everything was alive and sacred, and our little planet thrummed with the shared language of Being.

It is not exactly clear how it happened that we humans moved away from our natural ability to communicate with animals and the whole of nature—the wind, the water, the rocks, the earth. Perhaps we wanted to experience what it would be like to forget our connection to everything else. Maybe it would be like having amnesia or falling into a very long dream. Maybe we wanted to be the stars of our own story, our own enchanted fairy tale, in which each adventure would hold a clue to help us rediscover ourselves in a new way.

When we allow ourselves to sense with our body, hear with our heart, and see with our inner vision, we begin to experience the world in a different way. We begin to remember things we didn't know we ever knew. When we tap in to the mythic consciousness that is held in ancient stories, legends, folktales, and fairy tales, we connect with a deeper kind of knowing. We recall our oneness with the Web of Life.

This is why learning how to enter mythic consciousness is such a wonderful thing. By listening to the stories of old or allowing the power of a story to come through our own creations (be they stories, songs, dreams, dances, or paintings), we feed the bird of the forest; we taste the medicine that helps us recall the things we have forgotten. We come to know ourselves in new ways.

An Animal Communication Game
WHAT'S YOUR STORY?
Part One—Re-creating Once Upon a Time

This game is just for fun. It's a way of revving up creative juices, tuning in to group energy, and learning how to tap the flow of mythic consciousness. It works best with three or more players.

The rules of the game are simple. Sit in a circle and close your eyes. Choose one person to start with the opener *Once upon a time . . .* Now, invite a story to unfold. Allow your imaginations to run wild. Open yourselves to whatever images begin to play within the inner theater of your mind. What do you see when you peer into that place called Once Upon a Time? Be silly, be serious; be scary, be sensible; let the mythic troupe of characters within you act freely as the story emerges.

Let every person add a sentence or two. Take turns as your group story travels in a circular fashion, around and around, each person adding more details as the story line grows.

What is fun about this game is that while everyone in the group is partially responsible for the story, no single individual is in control and so no one knows exactly where the story will go. While a story might start out lighthearted or bizarre, quite often a deeper message emerges as you go deeper into it. The story that results is a reflection of your combined group energies.

As you play this game with different people and in different situations, notice how you feel as you add your portion to the larger story. Each time you add a sentence, notice "where" inside yourself that image or phrase comes from: Is it designed to get a laugh? Are you surprised by what you said?

Notice, too, your ability to tap in to the group energy as it moves along. Do you get a sense of the group story unfolding through you? Do you find that the story holds a personal message or meaning for you? Our stories often reveal things about us that we are surprised to learn.

Playing imaginative games gives us a safe space in which to explore our creative abilities. As we play, we get to "try on" the ideas of hearing animals, speaking to animals, even becoming animals, and what this feels like within our thoughts and feelings.

animal mythology: The myth of the musk oxen

I have always been interested in mythology, and I love to hear the "stories of ourselves" that all human cultures tell. Would you be surprised to hear that animals, too, have a mythology? I don't mean human myths about animals, or those stories that show our relationship with the animal world, but mythic stories that animals hold about themselves and their own beginnings.

As I am a new student of animal mythology, most of the myths that animals share with me are beginning myths or creation stories, ones that speak of how that animal species came into being.

For example, I once had a talk with a group of musk oxen. If you know anything about musk oxen, you may recollect that they are a short, wooly, ancient species of arctic mammal. In Alaska, the musk ox was once hunted to extinction. The group I talked to was part of a farm herd that had been brought to Alaska in an effort to recover the musk ox population.

The musk oxen told me many things about their life on the farm. I was impressed by the long-term view they held, as they spoke not just of this lifetime, but of their past and future. In fact, the musk oxen related that they are "bridgers"—animals who serve to bridge the ancient past with the present and beyond. As bridgers, musk oxen hold a certain type of ancient knowledge. They told me:

"We have lived through several periods of life on Earth in different climatic environments. We live in herds, and yet we have individual consciousness. We have traveled across many lands, across many times. We work closely with the earth. On one layer of our existence, we have our families, our own likes and dislikes, our individual areas of interest, and our specific jobs within our herd. And yet we have a conscious connec-

tion to our role as a species that spans time. That information is available to us in any moment, and it is easy for us to connect with this.

"In this sense, our history on Earth is ever present with us, and we are very much aware of it. Humans are aware of our history to some degree as well, for when people who know musk oxen speak of us, they often tell others about our place on Earth before this time.

"We have an oral tradition that is full and rich with myth and stories. We enjoy stories, especially those of our travels and of all the history Earth stores within our bones. We will share some of these stories with you should you be interested."

"I would love that," I exclaimed, for I was fascinated by all the musk oxen had to say. And so the musk oxen agreed to share a story. "We call this beginning story 'The Story of Our Becoming,'" said the musk oxen. "It is the story of how we first became aware of ourselves as what you call Musk Oxen."

We are part of the earth, and it is a part of us. This we know: all things are connected like the blood which unites one family.

CHIEF SEATTLE

THE STORY OF OUR BECOMING
The Musk Oxen ~ Dawn Brunke

In the time before time, a golden ray of sunshine once fell to the earth upon a large brown rock. The rock was a boulder shaped low in front and high in the middle. It was covered with a crawling brown lichen plant that was soft to the touch. As the sun warmed the rock, the rock yearned to move and leap about. The sun warmed the sleeping consciousness of the rock and Rock said, "I would like to move, to dance and walk around this land. I would like to be a moving, living being."

For some time, Sun and Rock warmed each other with this idea of becoming. Rock imagined four legs sprouting from where it lay upon the earth. Rock had known animals, had heard them in passing and felt their fur as they passed. Rock knew the smell of animals and longed to be one of the animals who moved with others as they thundered past his solid, stationary spot on the land.

As Rock grew legs, he imagined other parts sprouting as well: a lowered head, a large bulging back. Rock began to move, tentatively at first. Brown lichen warmed and began to grow, warming itself into the rock being's long hairs and fur. Rock was becoming Animal. And Animal began to fashion, from emerging consciousness, eyes and ears, nose and mouth. Most of this animal's being was large and solid, rocklike, to remind the new animal of Rock—of the first being—before Rock became Animal who became us, the Musk Oxen.

Musk Ox
Photo courtesy of The Musk Ox Farm

I sat amazed at this wonderful story. The musk oxen paused, giving me a chance to take it in.

"This is our story, our myth," they added after a few moments. *"We live in close concert with the earth in this way and have a special relationship with rocks and large objects. We have a special fondness for grasses and plants and lichens. We stay close to the earth, short in stature, because that is who we are. We carry our information in relation to Rock, the hard suchness of our Mother Earth. We have a very clear line into our history. We welcome you to sit with us and share in our becoming."*

An Animal Communication Game

WHAT'S YOUR STORY?
Part Two—Tapping Mythic Consciousness

This game is a deeper version of the first, and it works best with small groups of friends who have a common goal to learn more about animals, mythic consciousness, and themselves. First, decide as a group the animal species that you would like to focus upon and agree to open to a deeper energy that will tell you a story about this animal.

To help focus group energy, you may want to begin with a short visualization of your animal. You may even want to create a small altar on a table around which you are seated, using pictures, statues, or figures of the animal. Draw upon whatever you think of to help set the mood. You might lower the lights, use candles, or do a meditation together. There is no right or wrong, simply an unfolding of a shared group dynamic.

As before, sit in a circle and take turns sharing one or two sentences at a time. Begin to feel the story coming alive through you as you speak. Allow yourself to tune in to and sense the larger story being spoken *through* you. This is a surprising and playful exercise in opening to a larger voice! It is something of a jazz approach, for no one voice is totally responsible, and yet all are an important part of the rhythm, each unique voice contributing a distinctive element to the song.

Watch for the magic that happens between your thoughts and your spoken part of the myth. Watch for the magic that unfurls as the story moves from one mind to another. Allow the myth to take you into the mystery.

You may want to tape your story as it is spoken and then all can listen to it. Quite often, stories like this are significant in some way to each member of the group, though this may not be realized until the story is finished. Take time to share your thoughts and feelings afterward. The same story holds different messages for different listeners. If the story doesn't hold a personal message for you, that's fine, too. Most of all, have fun, feel the energy, and enjoy the game!

Entering Dreamtime:
When Nowhere is Now Here

As bridgers, the musk oxen hold their view of the ancient past right along with the present. Well, isn't *that* an interesting way of seeing the world? I was surprised to find that many animals who shared myths with me have similarly related the idea that the mythic world is always present. As a group of horses once told me, *"For us, myth is a continuing present. It is not held in the past, something that is old, to be dug up and regarded as a curiosity. Our experience is that myth is very much alive in every moment."*

How is this possible?

"Visualize it as the pages of a book flipping open," the horses advised. *"Every page is part of the story. If you read the text on one page you find yourself within one time frame of the story, while if you read the text on another page, you find yourself in a completely different time frame of the story. Yet, all pages and time frames are held within the same focus of the book."*

Isn't it amazing that sometimes all we need do is shift our vision ever so slightly to suddenly see things in an entirely different way? If you have read a lot of myths or ancient stories, you may have observed that many of them take place nowhere in particular. Maybe the story is set in an ancient forest or in a village or atop a mountain; but there is no clear mention of exactly where and when it took place. Now, what would happen if we shifted our focus as those horses and musk oxen do? Would we, too, discover that *nowhere* is *now here*?

By relaxing into the mythic consciousness that is always present, we open to a more expansive experience of time. We begin to naturally attune ourselves to the living flow of myth that moves within

The only reason for time is so that everything doesn't happen at once.

ALBERT EINSTEIN

and throughout our world. The native people of Australia, the Aborigines, speak of this as entering Dreamtime.

Dreamtime is not so much about dreams as we know them, but about a way of living in relationship to the earth and other beings. The Aborigines say that Dreamtime exists around the edges of time. It is always present, always here, always now. To get there, you don't travel to a different place or a different time. Rather, you shift your attention.

Some people say that all states of human consciousness exist as a wide spectrum of frequencies. You might imagine this as a radio or television receiver. Our everyday consciousness is set to one channel on the dial, while mythic consciousness is tuned in to another channel. The same is true, of course, for dream consciousness, meditative consciousness, and other altered states of awareness. Each station or frequency holds a particular way of seeing or hearing the world from a different perspective. To move from one station to another, we simply change the dial and shift our focus to another channel.

As we tap in to mythic consciousness through stories, meditations, or shifts in consciousness, we gain greater access to the mystery of what all peoples once knew. We can re-member that time when people could talk with animals, plants, and all of nature. And we can bridge that time and those abilities to the present, to our conscious selves. Just like the musk ox.

By opening frequently to the ancient wisdom and power held within mythic stories, we may find that we can more easily see right through the veils or separation between the worlds—the worlds of past and present or of mythic and ordinary awareness. We may even meet and talk to our ancestors, ancestral animals, animal guides and spirits who wish to communicate with us. We awaken that slumbering self that has forgotten this magical connection of time and space. We re-member at deeper levels and bring forth previously unknown aspects of ourselves that live within us.

The distinction between past, present, and future is only an illusion, even if a stubborn one.

ALBERT EINSTEIN

An Animal Communication Exercise
DREAMTIME MEDITATION

Find a quiet place, get comfortable, and close your eyes. Breathe deeply and relax your body. Take a few moments to center and deepen, relaxing your mind. When you feel ready, imagine yourself stepping around the edges of time, moving into Dreamtime.

Allowing your imagination to guide you, take a look around. Where are you? What does the land look like? What is your sense of this place? As your focus deepens, you may hear, smell, feel, and even taste aspects of the Dreamtime.

Take a few moments to see if an animal approaches you. If not, invite one to come and talk with you. Explain that you are interested in learning more about animals in this world. As you focus your intention with a genuine desire to learn more, you may be surprised to see who or what shows up!

If an animal appears, ask if it has a story or message to share. You might see a group of animals. What matters is not so much what happens as how you relate to what happens. Notice your feelings. Listen; look around; be receptive. Follow your curiosity. Let go and have fun.

On ending, take some time to record your experience in a notebook or journal. This is an important part of the meditation, as it both records and validates your experience in writing (or drawing, if you prefer) and is a tangible way of beginning the translation process from one mode of awareness to another. In addition, the material you experience now may be very helpful to you at a later date.

everything you can imagine . . . The Legend of the unicorn

One evening while watching *Legend*, a film that features a scene of two beautiful white unicorns, I felt an energetic buzzing in the middle of my forehead. Closing my eyes, I felt the buzzing radiate outward in a spiral—as if I, too, had a unicorn's horn. As an experiment, I imagined the "horn" on my forehead connecting to a mythic unicorn's horn. *Aha!* Through the simple act of imagining, something unlocked within me. Suddenly, I was meeting a unicorn for the very first time.

Sometimes rather than setting out to read or learn about a mythic creature, we are unexpectedly touched by mythic consciousness. It can feel startling, for it is as if the energy of the animal has come for us, out of the blue, and we haven't a clue as to why. Feeling the unicorn horn was one such time for me.

When experiences like this occur, it is wise to hold them lightly, to refrain from immediately judging them and getting lost in questions such as "Is this true?" or "Is it real?" It is easy to dismiss our feelings as being silly or strange when we question the reality of the mythic world from the viewpoint of ordinary consciousness. But by doing so, we lose an opportunity to experience the profound gift that has just come our way.

Everything you can imagine is real.

PABLO PICASSO

> *"Do you know, I always thought unicorns were fabulous monsters, too? I never saw one alive before!"*
> *"Well, now that we have seen each other," said the unicorn, "if you'll believe in me, I'll believe in you."*
>
> LEWIS CARROLL,
> *THROUGH THE LOOKING GLASS*

When an animal appears in an unexpected way, and we have the wherewithal to thank it instead of running away, we are one step closer to uncovering a mystery. By asking "What does this show me?" or "What part of myself have I forgotten that this animal comes to remind me?" we become part of the experience. We become participants instead of observers. And off we go, lucky us, on yet another journey of re-membering.

Why lucky? Because experiences like these hold great treasure indeed. You'll see!

Rather than negating unusual experiences, therefore, we are wise to suspend judgment until we have gathered additional perspectives. The first thing I did after meeting the unicorn was to write about it. As noted in the Dreamtime meditation, recording our experiences not only helps later in recalling the details of what happened, but the very act of transmitting this onto paper is a way of physically bridging worlds, of allowing us to appreciate these events in more than one way.

Second, I did a bit of research on unicorns. By familiarizing ourselves with assorted scientific facts, historical observations, symbolic traits, and visual representations of the different animals that come to us, we accumulate a much wider, richer range of views.

Did you know, for example, that from earliest times, people have viewed horns as possessing magical or medicinal properties, and that the unicorn's spiraled horn was the most treasured of all? While the oldest human description of unicorns dates to the fifth century B.C., unicorn legends exist all over the world. These fascinating creatures have been associated with love, innocence, wisdom, and a deep comprehension of nature. The unicorn was most popular during Medieval times, and the unicorn horn (known as the *alicorn*) was believed to hold such healing power that it could purify polluted

Don't be satisfied with these stories, how things have gone for others. Unfold your own myth, without complicated explanation, so everyone will understand the passage, *"We have opened you."*

RUMI

water, cure fevers and infections, and even pull one from death. The unicorn thus became a symbol of medicine. Remarkably, the unicorn was not considered mythical during these times, but quite real and important. It even became an emblem of royalty, and its image can still be found on tapestries from the Middle Ages and supporting the coat of arms of the British monarch. This is the power of mythic energy that some animals embody—to persist in our collective awareness as they deftly move through time.

While this information reveals an intriguing human perspective on unicorns, it is still only one way of understanding unicorns. We might best use it as general background information, drawing upon those details that speak to us. These might provide insight for a more personal interpretation of our experience. When working with myths and stories, it is important to realize that our own feelings are just as important—if not more so—than facts or history.

As I read my notes and recalled what the horn first felt like as I connected with the unicorn, the words that popped into my mind were: *intuition, insight,* and *imagination.* To me, the unicorn horn seemed an exaggeration of the third eye—that point in the middle of our forehead slightly above the eyebrows. From a metaphysical perspective, the third eye is the seat of psychic abilities and telepathy. On a personal level, the unicorn horn thus seemed not so much to represent healing or purity to me, as a union of intuition and imagination. And so I saw another layer of the puzzle.

A number of animals have explained it to me like this: mythic experiences, daydreams, and stories all hold sacred pieces of remembering for us. These shards of wisdom may be hidden in images, actions, or words within a story; they are kept as secrets, for they hold power. They are the ingredients of the potent medicine alive in the story. When we enter the flow of mythic consciousness in a

The myth is the public domain and the dream is the private myth. If your private myth, your dream, happens to coincide with that of the society, you are in good accord with your group. If it isn't, you've got a long adventure in the dark forest ahead of you.

JOSEPH CAMPBELL

receptive manner that can hear the deeper message of the story, the door unlocks. Our feelings and awareness vibrate in such a way that we ourselves become the key.

The door opens. Suddenly, the secret is ours to know.

> *Imagination is more important than knowledge.*
> *Knowledge is limited. Imagination encircles the world.*
> ALBERT EINSTEIN

Ask yourself: 'Did this imaginative experience happen to me?'
If the answer is yes, and it can only ever be yes, then it is real.

PATRICK JASPER LEE,
WE BORROW THE EARTH

Break down the word *imagination* to find *image* and *nation*. Indeed, we might think of the imagination as an inner nation of images that creatively represents meaningful connections, ideas, possibilities, and probabilities. Using our imagination entails seeing those images that exist beyond, below, above, around the edges, and through our normal way of seeing the world. Entering the Image Nation means relying on our inner eyes and ears, listening to our inner voice. It was this that allowed me to connect with the unicorn in the first place!

The more we play with our imagination, the more we discover surprising insights and unexpected connections. By drawing upon the vast wealth of our imagination, we begin to notice how many events in the everyday world are filled with treasure, meaningful coincidences, and invitations to adventure. This, too, is the message of the unicorn, as told to animal communicator Tera Thomas.

MESSAGE FROM THE UNICORNS
The Mythic Unicorns ~ Tera Thomas

We are all around you, the unicorns of legend and myth. You believe that we exist only in your imagination and so we are not real. There is a secret we have to tell you. The greatest, most magical power you possess is your imagination. Who says it is not real? Think of that. Do you have any proof that it is not real? We will tell you that your imagination is as real as the nose on your face.

All living beings exist on many levels. The things you can see and touch and taste in this dimension are only a small percentage of what is real. Begin to open your minds and hearts to the possibility that there is more available to you in this life than you have been led to believe.

Close your eyes and think of the unicorns. If you believe in us, a unicorn will come to you. Hop on her back and allow yourself to fly. We can show you a perspective outside of your physical reality so that you can see a bigger picture of who you are in existence. We can teach you to move through realities with fluid grace and beauty. We can show you that magic is alive and well and that life is full of miracles.

Learning to trust your perceptions and your imagination will take you far in your journey to communicate with all species. Let us be of assistance to you. You will be amazed at what you will find.

Now I will believe that there are unicorns . . .

WILLIAM SHAKESPEARE,
THE TEMPEST

Awakening to the Living Myth

Myths are like mirrors: one of the many ways we come to see and know ourselves. Good myths, legends, and stories always tell us something about who we are. As Joseph Campbell explains it, the first function of mythology is to "waken and maintain in the individual a sense of wonder and participation in the mystery of this finally inscrutable universe."[2]

When unraveling the hidden mysteries held in the stories and experiences that come to us, we must each follow our own set of clues. We must become sensitive and insightful detectives. The way we pull together the pieces of our story from different sources—scientific facts, intuitive feelings, historic observations, symbolic patterns, legendary attributes, creative imaginings—reveals a larger, more meaningful picture. We get a new vision of who we are and how we see the world.

A magic occurs when we tap in to universal wisdom and discover the patterns that play beneath the events in our lives. Artists, dancers, writers, poets, musicians, film directors, and storytellers all recognize the potent medicine alive in a good myth. It is what connects us to who we have been, who we are, and who we will become—to all the forgotten parts of ourselves.

As we become more in sync with the deep down messages that

A MEDLEY OF MYTHIC MOVIES

Legend, 1986 film with Tom Cruise, Mia Sara, and Tim Curry, directed by Ridley Scott. When a unicorn horn is broken, darkness descends on the forest and a mythical journey to the underworld begins.

The Dark Crystal, 1982 film directed by Frank Oz and Jim Henson. An elf-like Gelfling must find the missing shard of a huge dark crystal in order to restore balance to the peaceful Mystics and slobbering Skeksis.

Labyrinth, 1986 film with David Bowie, directed by Jim Henson. When goblins steal her baby brother, a young girl makes her way through a menacing, mysterious labyrinth to meet the King of the Goblins.

The Tenth Kingdom, 2000 Hallmark miniseries with Kimberly Williams, John Larroquette, and Scott Cohen. By way of a magic mirror in Central Park, Virginia and her father travel through fairy-tale kingdoms, meeting nasty trolls, enchanted birds, a prince who is a dog, a wolf who is in love, and a queen who is different from what she seems.

want to be expressed through us, we become more intimately aware of all the characters of this world—human, animal, land, wind, and star alike. We notice more clearly messages of wisdom and truth. We hear the voice of Wolf, Turtle, and Grandmother Spider; we feel the ancestral energy of ancient horse herds or musk oxen speaking through our imagination, intuition, and the telling of our stories. Details come to us—a natural flow of thoughts and ideas, experiences and feelings. As we embrace those details that clamor to be told, shaping them to a story, we become the being who gives order to the story, the one who shapes a new myth to be told to the world.

Myths are not untrue. Rather, they are the core truths of who we are. Perhaps they hold such expansive mind-shattering truths that we cannot know them all at once. And so mythic energy dances through our lives. We are touched constantly by its beauty and mystery. How we see it, feel it, and welcome it is up to us.

In connection with a deeper flow, we know that we are part of many worlds, many times. We remember that we all came from the desert, the forest, the sea, and the sky. We share in the atoms of all beings—Whale, Sea Turtle, Elephant, Butterfly. We don't have to go anywhere to learn anything. It is all here, inside ourselves.

The Bird of the Most Beautiful Song of the Forest is alive and well.

It is within you that the divine lives.

JOSEPH CAMPBELL

THE GREATEST AGE
Spirit of All Horse ~ Penelope Smith

I am the Spirit of All Horse. It's important that I speak as we are all changing so rapidly. I am watching over the children of both my species and your species. They are coming together in a new way in this age where horse and rider will be one. Throughout the ages there have been people who have experienced this oneness. Now, we are all moving to where we can experience this.

Many children, of both your species and mine, are gravitating toward each other—to express a oneness where there will no longer be any need for metal pieces in the mouth or pulling horses in ways that hurt, for confinement in small dark places that smell and make horses long for the wild. There will no longer be any need for places that hurt humans and horses alike. There will no longer be any need to cry out in anger or anguish. In this place we will all be together and fly as nature intended, in one light of life.

I am the Great White Horse of the ages, who comes to beings in their hearts. All who tune in to me see the spirit of greatness that we all are. I form as a horse because a horse represents nobility of spirit. I am carrying many beings along with me. Throughout the ages I have appeared in stories, lore, and legend.

Watch the children, and you will see how they come upon our backs in a different way and we walk together as rider and horse, interchangeably as one spirit. This is the greatest teaching I can give you. As we come together as one spirit, our forms begin to intermingle so that there is no difference among a human, a horse, an insect, a rock. Our particles intermingle in joyous union.

This is the age of unity and joy—a destiny that is not the complete dissolution of form but a combination of form and spirit that is delightful, that no longer requires excessive separation and domination and feeling of hurt. There is no time like this time. There has never been a time like this. It is very exciting for us in spirit and in form, for we are uniting our molecules in a way that has never been seen. It is delicious. This is the greatest age that has ever been seen.

2
Becoming
Doctor Dolittle

"Now listen, Doctor, and I'll tell you something. Did you know that animals can talk?"

"I knew that parrots can talk," said the Doctor.

"Oh, we parrots can talk in two languages—people's language and bird-language," said Polynesia proudly . . .

"My! You don't say so!" said the Doctor. "You never talked that way to me before."

"What would have been the good?" said Polynesia, dusting some cracker-crumbs off her left wing. "You wouldn't have understood me if I had."

"Tell me some more," said the Doctor, all excited; and he rushed over to the dresser-drawer and came back with the butcher's book and a pencil. "Now don't go too fast— and I'll write it down. This is interesting—very interesting—something quite new . . ."

So that was the way the Doctor came to know that animals had a language of their own and could talk to one another.

HUGH LOFTING,
THE STORY OF DOCTOR DOLITTLE

Hugh Lofting, the creator of Doctor Dolittle, had great fondness for animals. During World War I he was so touched by the behavior of regimental horses and mules wounded in battle that he later invented a character who could talk to animals and "do for them what was not and could not be done in real life."[1]

Lofting wrote more than a dozen books that celebrate the exchange of thoughts and ideas between a human and animals, thus inspiring countless readers to regard animals in a different way. Even today variations of his characters inspire us to think beyond the confines of convention.

There is no need to run
   outside for better seeing,
Nor to peer from a
   window. Rather abide
At the center of your
   being ...
Search your heart
   and see ...
The way to do is to be.

LAO-TZU

> You know they say the great thing about being a kid is it's
> so easy to pretend. You can have a conversation
> with your dog, or a baseball or a banana. Well, what if it
> wasn't pretend? What if you could have a conversation?
> I mean, not with a baseball or a banana, that's
> ridiculous, but with your dog . . .
>
> "LUCKY" THE DOG,
> DOCTOR DOLITTLE, 1998 FILM

Although the good doctor who did so much to help animals was fictional, there's a surprising key within his name, Dolittle. It's true: to effectively speak with animals there is little you need do. In fact, the more you scurry around trying to do this or do that, the further you remove yourself from feeling that deep down connection with all life. Animal communication is not so much about thinking as it is about sensing, not so much about doing as it is about being. One secret of becoming a real-life Doctor Dolittle is to do little and be.

DO Little and Be

While there are many ways to fine-tune our natural abilities to talk with animals, it's important to know right from the start that this form of communication is all about relationship. It's about relating to all beings (including ourselves) in an honest and authentic manner. It's about re-membering our common essence and sharing our thoughts and feelings from that connected state of awareness.

Tuli Bear, a cat speaking through animal communicator Tera Thomas, points out this awareness of connection by advising, *"Open your heart to every living thing. We are all connected to each other, a part of each other. Close your eyes, take a deep breath, and just feel it. You will know this is true. Isn't it wonderful?"*

Tuli Bear
Photo by Tera Thomas

Cease listening with the mind and listen with the vital spirit.

CHUANG TZU

As we open to the energy that flows through all life, we open ourselves to instant relationship. We *know* that we share a common awareness, for we feel it flowing through us, connecting us with every other living being. Our ancestors tapped in to this connection and communicated fluently with the natural world. We also carry this ability. Although we may not constantly hold the awareness in our everyday lives, it's simply a matter of shifting perspective, deepening, and tuning our consciousness to recall this connection whenever we choose.

different ways to sense the world

Llama, dolphin, eagle, cat; human, salmon, whale, and rat: underneath our physical bodies—our fur or feathers, skin or scales—we are all composed of the same universal essence, or energy. Still, obviously, we are different. Among the 1.5 million species on Earth that we humans have classified, each has a totally unique vibration in form. Each species' perceptions of the world are unique as well, because they are based on sensing mechanisms (be they fingers, whiskers, trunks, or antennae) and the particular ways we use those sensing mechanisms to know the world.

Most animals perceive the world much differently than we do. Many animals can see energies, for example; they can "read" our thoughtforms and emotions, knowing instantly if we are afraid even though we may be sitting still or showing no visible signs of fear.

Some animals have completely different sensing mechanisms from ours. Consider the bat's ability to echolocate, the squid's undulating propulsion system that powers it through water, the snail's intimate sensing of the world through the length of its body. Consider how the jellyfish, with no brain, heart, blood, or gills, is able to move, sense, and taste its world. Can you imagine life as a jellyfish?

Part of the adventure of communicating with other beings is learning how to open our senses, to take in (as well as send) feelings, thoughts, ideas, and sensations in ways that can be mutually understood. In *The Story of Doctor Dolittle,* that was one of the lessons the good doctor needed to learn as he mastered his ability to talk with the animals.

> At tea-time, when the dog, Jip, came in, the parrot said to the Doctor, "See, he's talking to you."

We always have a choice: we can limit our perception so that we close off vastness, or we can allow vastness to touch us.

CHOGYAM TRUNGPA,
SHAMBHALA: *THE SACRED PATH
OF THE WARRIOR*

"Looks to me as though he were scratching his ear," said the Doctor.

"But animals don't always speak with their mouths," said the parrot in a high voice, raising her eyebrows. "They talk with their ears, with their feet, with their tails—with everything . . ."

After a while, with the parrot's help, the Doctor got to learn the language of the animals so well that he could talk to them himself and understand everything they said.[2]

SO HOW DOES IT WORK?

As we relax and deepen into a quieter, more tranquil state of being, our logical mind slows down. Our habitual ways of seeing the world begin to shake loose, and we become more receptive to perceiving in different ways. As rigid thoughts of how reality "should be" release their hold, we shift to a more intuitive state of being, one that is quite naturally capable of telepathy.

Telepathy really isn't so unusual. Most likely, you have had many experiences of "just knowing" what someone was thinking or going to say. Perhaps you have been so in tune with a person that you felt a heart-melding, mind-to-mind connection in which there was no need for words. When we label this *telepathy* and decide it is weird or scary, or become judgmental about whether it is possible, we move away from the reality of something that is very natural to us all. Some day, conventional science may find a model to explain exactly how this works (and many in the quantum physics field have proposed theories). But for now we might just as easily think of it as engaging the "universal language," for that, too, is what it is.

The intuitive mind is a sacred gift and the rational mind is a faithful servant. We have created a society that honors the servant and has forgotten the gift.

ALBERT EINSTEIN

Be brave enough to let your sensitive side show.

RAINBOW (LLAMA) ~ TERA THOMAS

Rainbow
Photo by Tera Thomas

Telepathy is instantaneous—it is direct perception, immediate sensing. The word *telepathy* comes from *tele,* meaning "distant or far away," and *pathy,* meaning "feeling or perception." Telepathy is feeling from a distance, or perceiving from far away. It transcends the way we normally understand time and space, for with the help of telepathy we can expand and deepen our awareness to connect on inner levels with any other being—be it the cat sitting by our side or a cheetah speeding across the African savannah. With telepathy, we rediscover our fluency in the universal language.

When we telepathically connect with a cat or cheetah or any other animal, we naturally draw upon our own way of understanding the world—our own sensory mechanisms—to make sense of that other being's thoughts. That is, we instinctively make use of our brain's unique "software"—the programs or sensory ways in which we see, feel, hear, taste, smell, and generally make sense of the world—in order to interpret the perceptions, feelings, thoughts, and observations of others.

Telepathically, we receive information from animals in many different ways—visual images, inner feelings, intuitive flashes. We then "translate" these inner impressions in ways that we can understand. When communicating with animals, here are the most common ways that humans send and receive information:

- **Inner seeing** makes use of pictures, like slide shows or movies within the inner theater of the mind. These images may be something an animal is actually seeing, or they may be visual representations of thoughts or feelings—a tail-wagging, jumping dog representing play; a curled-up, purring cat denoting pleasure.

- **Inner hearing** can be in the form of sounds, thoughts, or even words and sentences. You might actually hear what an animal is hearing. Or, you might sense an animal's thoughts within your mind. It can be surprising to receive thoughts that are different from your own, for many animals have a unique way of using words, and some even speak with an accent.

- **Inner feeling** can include physical feelings, such as the sensation of an ache or pain in your body that corresponds to the animal's body, as well as emotional feelings,

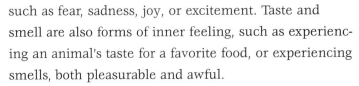

such as fear, sadness, joy, or excitement. Taste and smell are also forms of inner feeling, such as experiencing an animal's taste for a favorite food, or experiencing smells, both pleasurable and awful.

- **Inner knowing** is a form of intuition and immediate insight. Often, you "just know" something about an animal. You may sense it as a gut feeling or a hunch; other times you simply suddenly understand the whole experience.

While there is no set rule on how we receive and send information, many people discover that they have a preference for one mode over another. This can be true for animals as well. Animals that are extremely visual (birds of prey, for example) may be more likely to send pictures or images, because that is their dominant sense, whereas an earthworm may send feeling-oriented information.

In the beginning, you may find one mode easier than others. If you are very visual and artistic, for instance, you might get a lot of pictures or inner movies, and you may want to practice sending images in return. If you like to talk and share ideas, you might sense an inner translation of words and sentences that allows your connection to resemble a dialogue. If your expertise is in feeling, you may want to focus on sending emotions. We draw to ourselves the forms of communication with which we are most comfortable. Over time and with practice, however, we may find we have a talent for other methods or that we enjoy communicating in a variety of ways.

TO FIND MORE MEANING
Maya (cat) ~ Gretchen Kunz

I am deaf, so I don't see or hear things like you do. Plus, I'm a cat, which means I see in different ways, especially with motion and lights and

I would like young people to know that the world does not revolve around what you see and taste and touch. Too many times you look out with eyes that cannot see the world as it truly is. Only with your "inner eyes" can you truly know what is going on.

BEAU (DOG)
MORGINE JURDAN

shadows. But, most important, I'm an individual, and each individual sees things in different ways.

Every one of us can use these different ways to find more meaning in everything we do or see. It's all valid, you know. And I think if you knew what everyone else sees, how differently, you would be amazed.

That is one exciting thing about being incorporated in a physical body! You get these senses, and they work in many different ways, and no two individuals—from person to animal to tree—are exactly alike. So enjoy yourself! And who knows what your next lifetime will bring . . . what you will see then?

You cannot teach a man anything; you can only help him discover it in himself.

GALILEO

The Basics

You may be astonished to learn that some teachers insist nobody *really* teaches anyone to communicate with animals. They say that instead it's really about helping students remember what they already know. As teacher, author, and communicator Tera Thomas notes, "There isn't a 'how to.' You can't teach anyone to communicate with animals—but you can help them to uncover their abilities and plug themselves in to their connection with all of life. That's the only 'how to' there really is."

The basics of effective animal communication are not that much different from basic communication skills between people. You share an interesting thought or observation and then you await a response. The response may excite you to share something else and listen eagerly as a reply again comes your way. And so it goes, back and forth, an exchange of information, ideas, thoughts, feelings, laughter, sadness, joy, and delight. What could be more natural?

A STUDENT'S VIEW

The first workshop I went to was a complete bust. My skeptical friend who went with me was successful, but I got a big fat nothing. At the second workshop I attended, I was able to connect and communicate with several animals. I don't know exactly how it happened, but it did.

I told an animal communicator at a later workshop that it had taken me more than two years to learn how to do this and that I still felt like a baby beginner. She laughed and said, "You could always do this! It just took you two years to get yourself to the place where you realized that you could."

MAGGIE BAILEY, STUDENT OF ANIMAL COMMUNICATION

Remembering How to communicate with Animals—four easy steps

1. Attuning: Attuning is about moving deeper in relationship, feeling the intimacy between you and your animal friend. If you intend to talk with your dog or cat, you might want to play first. This has the triple benefit of dispersing any nervous energy you might have, diffusing any wound-up energy your animal may have, and getting the two of you more quickly in tune.

Then, to begin your communication, find a quiet room or somewhere peaceful in nature. Make yourself comfortable and settle down. You might sit near your animal and stroke its fur, enjoying your closeness and sensing your kinship. You might spend some time in meditation, closing your eyes, quieting your mind, appreciating a loving connection to your animal. Don't force the situation; rather, let it unfold. Allow the center of your being—your heart, your mind, your soul—to connect with your animal. Feel your animal connecting to you. Sense the flow between the two of you. Breathe deep. Remember, it's all about relationship. Smile; make it easy. Your only goal is to quiet yourself and welcome the adventure.

2. Stating Your Intention: When you sense a connection with your animal, you are ready to send a message. Address your animal directly, just as you would a good friend. It sometimes helps to explain yourself and express what you intend to do. You can use words ("I'd like to talk to you") or images (picture yourself conversing back and forth) or feelings (feel your desire to share with your animal). You can even use all three (say it, picture it, sense it). Use whatever mode feels best to you. In truth, it doesn't matter so much what you do or how you do it, because you already know that this isn't about doing, but about being. Allow yourself to *be* in that place that genuinely desires to connect. It may help to express your feelings—"I'm feeling nervous about this, but I'd really like to talk to you." Or, "I'm feeling excited and I can't wait to hear what you have to say." Make it short—either visualize or feel or say or think to your animal your desire to communicate. If this is your first attempt, that might be enough. Or, you might ask a question: "Is there anything I can do for you (more walks, different food)? What's it like to be you (a dog, a cat, a horse)? Do you have a message for me?"

Nature has given us two ears, two eyes but only one tongue—with the goal to make us see and listen more than we should speak.

SOCRATES

3. Receiving: You can call it listening, sensing, feeling the open being. Here's where you let go of everything. Here's where you recall that quiet space within yourself and open wide for the answer to come. Let go of all your thoughts about what could happen or what might happen or what you hope will happen. Sshhh—how can you hear what an animal is saying when you are listening to your

Whether you feel communication from an animal or not, it's important to thank the animal. By giving thanks, it shows us that you honor and respect animals as fellow beings who deserve kindness and respect.

KC (DOG) ~
CATHY MALKIN

own doubts or thinking what you're going to ask next? Be open to the experience itself. You are relaxed and receptive. You're on the other end of the telepathic phone line waiting for your friend to tell you something wonderful. Be patient. Go with the flow. Welcome any and all feelings, sensations, images, words, smells, tastes, or combinations thereof. Don't judge what you get or wonder if it is "right." It is what it is! Allow the full message to come to you before you send a second message. In the beginning, just one round of sending and receiving may be enough. Then again, if you receive a clear message on your first try and want to send more, go for it!

4. Closing with Gratitude: As my wise old dog Barney used to say, *"Good manners never go out of style."* Offer warm feelings and thanks as you end your conversation. Send a mental handshake or hug. By thanking your animal, you acknowledge your appreciation and make this first contact something you can build upon. Remember to thank yourself, too! Thank your intuition, your inner self, and your desire to connect with life in a deep and meaningful way. Give thanks to your excitement and your magnificently creative imagination, which aids in your ability to sense in new ways. Even if you don't get anything the first try, remember to thank your animal and yourself for a very good start. Really mean it, too, because although it may seem that what you are doing is little, what you are *being* is deep and expansive and very great indeed.

> *I want to thank you for making the effort to get to know us and talk to us. You should be congratulated, because even trying is a very evolved thing to do. I think everybody should do it, but then, I have very high expectations! So, good show! I am proud of you, and you should be proud of yourselves!*
>
> MAYA (CAT) ~ GRETCHEN KUNZ

sharing the mystery

Every time you sit down with your dog or cat, tune in to a whale or dolphin, or trade thoughts with a goldfish or ladybug, you are relating to another being. You are sharing yourself in a way that is unique to you, and that dog or whale or fish or bug is sharing in a way unique to him or her. Every conversation, just like every relationship, is a little bit about sharing our own inimitable take on the mystery of life.

KC, a cat speaking to animal communicator Morgine Jurdan, puts it this way: *"There are many ways to communicate with animals. Each person and each animal being unique leads to unlimited variations. Don't get stuck trying to force yourself into just one way, or judging your abilities by someone else's standards. Part of your journey is about discovering who you are. The more you learn about yourself, the clearer a channel you will become to understanding animals, plants, nature, other human animals, and all of life."*

There is no "one way" for everyone. There is no "right way" either. We each need to find what works for us. We humans are sometimes so hard on ourselves. We confuse ourselves by comparing ourselves to others or doubting our own experiences. We write books on how to do things like this, when really it's the most natural thing— just to be!

As you continue to tune in to your animals, your friends' animals, and animals you meet in the wild, remember that the universal language is one we already know, one that we share with all life. Because it has been awhile since humans have used this language in a conscious way, we are a little out of practice. So be kind to yourself. And celebrate yourself, for in learning how to remember, you are helping the entire world to remember, too.

Never a day passes but that I do myself the honor to commune with some of nature's varied forms.

GEORGE WASHINGTON CARVER

The world is evolving quickly, much more quickly than many know. It is a confusing time and a wondrous time because you are in the midst of a dramatic evolutional stage. Be part of the evolution! Whatever you choose to do in this life, do it the very best you can, and with love. It will serve you well, more so than you can ever measure.

EMILY (DWARF HAMSTER) ~ KAT BERARD

Princess
Photo by Mary Kay Wolfshohl

This is a great planet! Know that you are important to this world, to its evolution, and that your contribution of self—your unique self, your talents and skills and personal touch—is needed and very important. Do not underrate yourself in any way. If you find yourself in such a place, climb right back out and keep going. We—the collective We of human and nonhuman beings—need you. Truly.

PRINCESS (DWARF HAMSTER) ~ KAT BERARD

As you enjoy the adventure, remember to take time. Nothing deep and awesome and revealing to your soul can be rushed. So take it easy. And take heart—all you need to be is you.

Tips, clues, Reminders, Games

The following tips and exercises from a variety of two-legged and four-legged perspectives may be helpful reminders as you follow the clues you find, uncover the subtle mysteries of your path, and discover your own unique, brilliant ways of tuning in to the animal world. Happy trails!

Become a student

The best teachers of animal communication are most often animals themselves. If you are not used to seeing animals as remarkable instructors and fine observers of life, then you may be surprised to find that a horse has much wisdom, a fox deep insights, a mosquito keen wit, and that all life has something special and precious to share. If you are willing to let go of the idea that humans are "better" or "smarter" or "more sophisticated" than animals, then you may be ready for the tremendous experience of having an animal for a teacher. If that happens, consider yourself lucky indeed.

My best teachers have been the animals. I tell my students that, too—trust the animals and let them be your teachers. I'm pretty much here to cheerlead and help you remember your abilities.

TERA THOMAS, ANIMAL COMMUNICATION TEACHER

START NOW
Buddy (horse) ~ Carole Devereux

You don't need to wait to grow up to talk to animals. You can do what you want with animals right now, while you are young. There is no waiting required. My advice is to start now. Today!

Go outside right now and talk to the first animal you see, whether it's a bird or an insect or a squirrel. Ask what it's like to be that animal. If it's a bird, ask, how does it feel to fly? Let yourself go; let yourself feel what the bird feels. Does she like living in your town? Is there anything she knows that is fun to do, like rolling and twirling in the wind?

Don't limit yourself to animals. Stand under a tree with your arms open wide. Look up into its branches, its open arms, and talk to the tree. Smell the pine needles under your feet or the rotting leaves in the rain. Earth is communicating with us all the time. We know what clouds say when they are dark and heavy—this is an ancient, primal communication. Use it today. Remember it now. Learn it again.

If you love it enough, anything will talk with you.
GEORGE WASHINGTON
CARVER

Buddy and Carole
Photo by Jim Steinbacher

Engage your Imagination

If you are having difficulty with the idea of "sending" or "receiving," then consider putting your imagination on double duty. Try visualizing your message as a small package of images, thoughts, and feelings. Wrap it up neatly in your mind and let it float through the air, special delivery, to your animal. You might imagine a little door that opens in your forehead or heart to send the present on its way. Your tiny packet sails across the distance between the two of you, entering the "door of perception" in your animal's forehead or "the door of feeling" in your animal's heart. To receive, imagine the process in reverse. Another method is to "beam" your message to your animal friend like a laser beam or gentle ray of light. Get creative; allow your imagination to devise the perfect method for you.

Think "As If"

You can also use your imagination as a jump-start to communication. Many teachers advise imagining animal responses to your questions. As donkey talker Karen Morrison says,

> If I have any advice to give, it's this: In the beginning, think to yourself "as if" you're communicating. Imagine what an animal would say to you if you could hear its thoughts; and then pretty soon you will be hearing its thoughts. It's really that simple.
>
> Sometimes I get thoughts back from my donkeys faster than I can make up any reply in my mind. That, I think, is the key. The answers to my questions come almost before I'm through asking them the questions. What the donkeys say is always surprising to me, and sometimes funny, and their replies are something I don't seem to make up myself. It's very intangible; a reply is close to what I might imagine but yet it isn't quite what I'd say myself.

When I'm playful I use the meridians of longitude and parallels of latitude for a seine, and drag the Atlantic Ocean for whales. I scratch my head with the lightning and purr myself to sleep with the thunder.

MARK TWAIN

With practice, you, too, will deepen and begin to receive responses that are not quite what you would have imagined. Hey, you're communicating!

mean what you say

Sometimes we place much too much emphasis on our words, as if by saying something it is true. We can fool ourselves this way, making it a habit to say one thing and mean another, declare one thing and

---

An Animal Communication Exercise
SEE FROM YOUR ANIMAL'S VIEW

One way to start "seeing" and communicating with your animal companion is to view the world through his or her eyes. Begin by meditating or getting very quiet. See if you can feel your animal's energy and presence, whether he or she is physically near you or not.

Now, physically put yourself on your animal's level—that means lying down on the ground (for small friends such as hamsters, turtles, and snakes), sitting on the floor (for short friends such as dogs and cats), or standing on a chair (for tall friends such as horses, cows, and llamas). Position yourself where your eyes are at the same level as your animal's eyes. See what they see (look closely); smell what they smell (breathe deeply); imagine how the wind would feel ruffling your coat (mmm . . .); imagine what their paws or hooves or belly feel while touching the ground (warmth? vibrations? dampness?).

If you've never done anything like this, it may seem silly. But it will change the way you view your animal's world. Cats, dogs, and other animals who are "vertically challenged" do not see at your eye level, so their view of the world is completely different. This exercise will give you new insight on what it's like for your animal friends to live in this world.

KAT BERARD, ANIMAL COMMUNICATOR

feel another. In other words, we can be emotionally incongruent. If you allow this to happen, you may appear strangely out of sync and even dangerous to some animals. It is important to keep your feelings, images, and thoughts in harmony when communicating with an animal. If you are nervous or fearful, then say so. Share who you are in the moment. Not only will you send a clearer message, but you will be clearer within yourself.

Listen carefully

Just like humans, some animals are shy and need time to warm up to you. Others simply don't care to talk very much. Every animal has his or her own individual rhythm and way of communicating. Some take time to form their responses while others blast you with multi-layered answers and questions of their own. If you don't understand something an animal is showing you, ask for clarification. Also, don't presume an animal immediately understands your point of view. Take time to listen attentively, just as you would like to be listened to yourself.

And don't rush it. KC the cat reminded Morgine Jurdan that a companionable silence can be part of any conversation. *"Animals need time to think sometimes. Be patient when listening for a response. Do not assume an animal is not willing to talk just because it takes a few moments to respond."*

Let Go

If things aren't going how you think they should or how you thought they might, then it's high time to let go of expectations. Every conversation will be different anyway—so what's to expect? When we let go, we surrender ourselves to the wonder of experience. Thoughts fall from our head effortlessly, and every part of us becomes more

By letting it go it all gets done
The world is won by those who let it go.
But when you try and try
The world is then beyond the winning.

TAO TE CHING

sensitive and receptive. By letting go of projections of what should be or could be, we are freed to find out what is. We become an open door, free to experience this moment—right here, right now. So make it easy on yourself: let go.

> *Bend with the wind, dance with the breeze, let life flow*
> *through you like a laughing brook. All life is precious*
> *and filled with wonder. We are all so fortunate to*
> *be here. Embrace each other, welcome all species,*
> *we don't have a moment to waste.*
>
> INKA (LLAMA) ~ TERA THOMAS

place a long distance call

Perhaps you would like to talk with your dog sleeping in another room, or a horse grazing in a pasture. Contacting animals at a distance is a natural extension of your communication abilities. Just as if your friend were sitting beside you, attune yourself to that animal. You know what he or she feels like. *See* the animal in your inner mind. *Feel* the connection. Now, talk just as you would in any other communication. One of the great things about telepathy is that it transcends space and time. With enough centering and depth, you can talk to any being, any place, any time.

FEEL THE LOVE

Relax and be in the love. Just feel the love of all creatures—for you and you for all of life. Bask in the sunshine and feel the love permeating everywhere. That's all that telepathy is about anyway—it's feeling the love that we have for each other. It's on the carrier wave of love that we receive our understanding and our messages.

SHERMAN (CAT) ~
PENELOPE SMITH

Be patient

Delphine Denommé learned the lesson of patience while consulting her animal friend for help. As she explains,

> I was trying to consciously communicate with Myrtille, my young cat. I have come to regard her as a teacher or guide. Lying in bed, close to her, I was trying (maybe too hard) to get a message. Her face was close to mine, and she was looking at me. I kept getting

Delphine and Myrtille
Photo by Alexandre Denommé

My advice is to take a deep breath when something comes at you that you are not expecting. See if you can respond with love; open your heart and your "inner eyes" to a deeper level of understanding.

BEAU (DOG)
MORGINE JURDAN

nothing. I was thinking, "Please, you've got to help me in this. Teach me the subtleties of animal communication, please."

After several minutes of lying silent and motionless, just staring at me, she put her paw on my nose, very gently and slowly. It was awesome because she had never done that before. The gesture was so kind and gentle, the gesture of a parent to her impatient child.

I got: *"Be patient, don't try so hard. You'll get there; don't worry."* I felt like a child comforted by a very ancient being. I was—how do you say it in English?—lightning-struck! I felt very moved.

An Animal Communication Project
CREATE AN ANIMAL COMMUNICATION JOURNAL

Recording your conversations with animals is invaluable, especially as a beginner. Many times you will get messages or impressions that cannot be immediately verified. By writing down your talks with animals, not only are you confirming that your conversations are important but you are creating a record to which you can refer back at a later date.

Write down all of your attempts to communicate: what you said or did, what you got back. Recording even bits of dialogue, partial images, feelings, and thoughts will provide something you can build upon. It can be extremely helpful and validating to reread a journal and see how these pieces really did make sense. So, grab a journal and dedicate it to your animal talks. You will not regret it!

This lasted only a few seconds, but it had great meaning for me, and for once I will not allow any self-doubt into this interpretation. It really was a magical moment.

Meet failure: a wonderful teacher

Anyone who has never made a mistake
has never tried anything new.

ALBERT EINSTEIN

While learning anything new, we're likely to encounter a few obstacles. Talking with animals can feel awkward in the beginning. Maybe our technique seems stupid, or we don't sense anything, or we can't stop thinking of what we want for lunch. The mindful thing to do when this happens is to acknowledge our feelings—"It's all wrong! It doesn't feel right! I'm not getting it!" Great! By expressing your frustrations, you move closer to living your truth.

When we try to make things right or insist that we are getting something when we know we aren't, we remove ourselves from the truth of our experience. We lose connection—not only with animals but with ourselves. Whereas, by acknowledging our feelings, we stay true to ourselves. Most animals will respect us for that.

We need to respect ourselves, too. Deepening our abilities to communicate with animals naturally leads to deepening our abilities to communicate with ourselves. The more we know ourselves, the more we sense when we are in the flow of connection and when we are not. This is why communicating with animals is so important—not only do we learn from animals but we are moved to discover our true selves.

practice and trust

Like almost everything in life, the more we practice the better we become. So, practice talking with your dog; make it your habit to greet the birds on the trees; say hello to all creatures you meet. Have faith in the process.

As KC the cat (through Morgine Jurdan) says, *"Always trust that with the proper intentions things will eventually become evident. Make the intention to communicate clearly and respectfully with all animals, and you will receive assistance from your own guides, helpers, and animals as well. Simply trusting the process and having fun with it will eventually lead to success."*

If you don't get anything in a communication, try again later. There is no need to worry or berate yourself, no need to compare yourself with others. You are you, and your adventure is unfolding in its own perfect way. Believe it!

We can have all the knowledge in the universe, and it comes down to one thing: practice. It comes down to going home and step-by-step implementing what we know.

CLARISSA PINKOLA ESTES,
WOMEN WHO RUN
WITH WOLVES

Fall seven times, stand up eight.

JAPANESE PROVERB

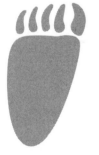

Get over Yourself

Maya, a cat who lives with communicator Gretchen Kunz, shared by personal example some advice for all: *"My person is a professional communicator, and sometimes she will get so stressed out or unsure of herself that she gets blocked and can't communicate, even though it's one of her favorite things to do! I tell her, 'Get over yourself. It's gonna be okay. You can do it. Stop worrying about it and it will work out!' Sometimes she listens to me, and sometimes she doesn't. But, eventually, she has to get over her doubt and stress and fears and* relax, *and then she'll do it. It works every time."*

Maya and Gretchen
Photo by Marci McLendon

consider everything

Funny as it seems, sometimes the odd thoughts, perplexing images, and confusing messages that you think are "wrong" may actually be "right." Did you hear the phrase of a song or suddenly remember an animal you once knew while communicating? Did a curious image flicker through your mind's eye? Some messages come as important clues embedded in your thoughts and feelings. Other messages that seem weird or highly unlikely may turn out to be exactly true. Similarly, some answers may be very different from what you expect or may contradict what you've been told about an animal. This does not mean that they are wrong. Some questions have many answers, and a lot of different perspectives are valid. Consider everything and learn to accept what you get without judgment.

"Lots of people talk to animals," said Pooh. "Maybe, but…" "Not very many listen, though," he said. "That's the problem…"

BENJAMIN HOFF, *THE TAO OF POOH*

REMEMBER THREE THINGS
Delphi (dog) ~ Patricia Jepsen

The first thing is Be Quiet. Someone has something to say. How are you going to hear that person (could be a mouse, you know!) if you are busy talking? Listening is powerful.

The second thing is Respect. That's when you are humble enough and quiet enough to know that every person—could be four-legged, could be two-legged, might even be a bird in the air or a worm on the ground—deserves your respect. That business of one person being more important than another has got to stop. There is no species more important than another.

The third thing is Love. When you say you want to understand what another person is saying or when you want them to understand you, the best way is through the heart. When you love someone—despite the differences you might have—you make a friend of that person. And if you love with your heart, you will have friends all over the earth. You will be able to understand them when they speak. World peace is made this way.[2]

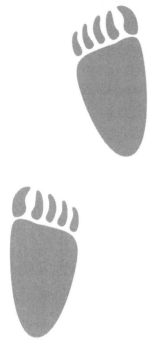

Jenny
Photo by Carole Devereux

see with your heart

Don't worry if you get it wrong. It's all right.
We dogs know what's in your heart. So don't be
discouraged. You have to keep on trying. Never ever give
up. Wait, then return and try again.
See with your heart, hear with your eyes, and feel with
your ears. Mix it all up. Be different. Dogs love
it when you play games with them. Make this a fun
game and don't be so serious; have fun.

JENNY (DOG) ~ CAROLE DEVEREUX

HɑVE FUN

Although it's great to have a plan—to sit down quietly and have a nice heart-to-heart—it's also great just to lose yourself in the joy of the moment. Many animals are experts at fun. Some conversations will be sprinkled with humor, jokes, puns, and gentle jibes of glee. Other animals may purposely bring humor in as a healing aid. As my dog Zak is fond of reminding me, the vibration of laughter is an opening; it allows us to laugh at ourselves and shake loose our own self-imposed limits. *"Never underestimate the power of humor,"* says Zak. So, don't be afraid to let yourself laugh. Wisdom isn't always serious.

When Tera Thomas asked a collective of wild squirrels for some pointers, they responded merrily. *"What do we say to young people? Don't listen to adults! Ha! Ha! Bet that could get you in trouble, right? We all have to let the elders guide us, but sometimes we youngsters know and feel things that adults don't understand. And that is okay; it doesn't mean that you are wrong. Play and have fun with your communication skills. You can't have doubts when you're laughing."*

Why not be oneself? That is the whole secret of a successful appearance. If one is a Greyhound why try to look like a Pekinese?

EDITH SITWELL, BRITISH POET

BE YOUR BEAUTIFUL, FABULOUS SELF

Three smart cats are in total agreement on the topic of being yourself.

One of my philosophies in life is to always love yourself. If you think you're fabulous, others will, too. It's always worked for me! Practice saying it with me: "I . . . Am . . . Fabulous!" Try it again. Now think about how pretty and smart you are. See if that doesn't bring a smile to your face, and make people respect you and look at you more often!

MAYA (CAT) ~ GRETCHEN KUNZ

Maia
Photo by Tera Thomas

Love yourself. Look in the mirror and tell
yourself how beautiful you are. When you
embrace your own unique self you are telling the world
how grateful you are to be here. And that makes all
species want to share their own beautiful selves with you.
We are all beautiful. Remember that.

MAIA (CAT) ~ TERA THOMAS

You are each beautiful, a one of a kind original, just like a painting or a great work of art.
So, stop trying to be like everyone else and be who you really are. When you love
yourself and appreciate what makes you unique, you begin to appreciate the
uniqueness in everyone else, too. You understand that there are many
points of view. There will be less arguing and more acceptance. You can celebrate your
differences and have more fun! Look into the mirror every day and say "I love you"
and the world will really change, and so will you.

KC (CAT) ~ MORGINE JURDAN

enjoy the voice of variety

Messages from animals range from insightful to hilarious, serious to affectionate. The more animals you talk with, the more you'll get a sense of how every animal has a distinctive view. As you continue to talk with a variety of animals, you may encounter group, herd, or collective voices, and also species voice. Some animals will engage a more expansive spiritual voice or speak from the perspective of the "higher self." Although some humans like to distinguish these voices, many animals will quite naturally flow from a personality base to a spiritual perspective to a larger group voice and back again all in a single conversation. Sometimes it is not so important "who" is talking as what's being said and how open you are to the relationship.

Listen to this, and hear the mystery inside . . .

RUMI

An Animal Joke

A dog went to a telegram office, took out a blank form, and wrote: "Woof, woof woof woof. Woof woof woof, woof woof."

The clerk looked at the paper and politely told the dog: "There are only nine words here. You could send another 'Woof' for the same price."

"Thanks," the dog replied, "but that wouldn't make any sense at all!"

SWIMMING FOR JOY
Goldfish ~ Dawn Brunke

Greetings! We are goldfish and we sparkle and dance around the world with splashes of color and grace and light in all types of bowls and aquariums. We are small and colorful and shiny, and so appeal to children of all ages. We don't require much care. In fact, we are perfectly happy to live in the wild, in ponds and lakes. But those of us who formed the domesticated goldfish tribe have, as a group, come into your homes in gentle and beautiful ways.

We offer our services to humans as a calming influence of beauty and grace. Many people are inspired to buy goldfish—perhaps for distraction or looks or even as a pet. But we do much more, as do so many of the animals who come to live in and around your home.

As for communication skills, fish are very easy to talk to! We goldfish are most often joyful creatures and are very aware of your attention. We may not seem as if we are "listening" to you, but we are actually superb listeners. Part of our service is to instill the qualities of deepening and calming within your homes, which includes the ability to listen well. If you want to learn how to listen and hear animals talk, come sit with a goldfish! Come meditate beside our tank. Watch us with your eyes and allow us to soothe your thoughts. Close your eyes and see us swimming, dancing upon the screen of your mind's eye. Our swimming is a dance of meditation, a peaceful spiral of movement not unlike music, with soothing splashes of color and bubbles and flickering tails.

We are, all of us, connected in so many ways. By virtue of this, it is possible for you to tune in to any animal being you choose. If you have a sincere desire, you can hear the voice of any being.

We offer you guidance and reassurance simply by our presence. Ours is a different way of relating in the world; because you are often not accustomed to this way, you may not recognize it. And yet this is part of our beauty as well. We bring to you the pleasure and beauty of the mundane—that which sparkles in ways you might never imagine until you open your eyes, open your ears. We are all here, listening, dancing, swimming for joy.

3
Magical Meetings

This being human is a guest house.
Every morning a new arrival. . . .

RUMI, "THE GUEST HOUSE"

ne day, while listening to a young woman relate her dream, the intrepid explorer of human consciousness Carl Jung experienced something extraordinary. Just as the woman was describing the golden scarab she received in the dream, Jung heard a gentle tapping on the closed window behind him. Turning around, he noticed a flying insect knocking against the windowpane. Jung opened the window and caught the creature as it flew in. Looking more closely, he was astonished to find that it was a beetle—in fact, a member of the scarab beetle family—behaving very contrary to its usual habits in tapping against the windowpane as if wanting to enter the room.[1]

Jung used the term *synchronicity* to describe these types of meaningful events—things that happen unexpectedly, seemingly out of the blue, but are highly significant and undeniably powerful for the individuals involved.

The unlikely arrival of the beetle just as the woman was speaking of the golden scarab in her dream brought a profound transformation to both Jung and the woman. The woman improved dramatically in her treatment, and Jung intensified his exploration of the mysterious connections between the conscious and unconscious worlds.

And the beetle? Jung wrote about this meeting more than fifty years ago. Now, you are reading about it. Such is the power of one small creature appearing at just the right time.

The power of magical meetings

The crux of a magical meeting is, of course, that it's magical. I use the term not in the sense of occult powers but to describe an overpowering quality of awe and wonder. The more we question how and why these meetings occur, the more magical they may seem. Who, for example, was responsible for the synchronous arrival of the beetle: Jung? The woman with the dream? The beetle? Or perhaps the energy of beetle wisdom expressed through the living beetle?

Look for the magic that is around you in nature, flowers, and all the animals that share this planet with us.

ROY, OF SIEGFRIED AND ROY,
ILLUSIONISTS

And why a beetle? Why did the woman receive the gift of a golden scarab in her dream? Why not a hummingbird or a golden rabbit? If we did a bit of research on beetles, especially the symbolic significance of what beetles represent, we might be astounded to learn that there are more than 280,000 kinds of beetles. In ancient Egypt the scarab beetle in particular had great significance and was associated with new life. Because beetles go through a dramatic metamorphosis (from grub to winged), they are also linked with resurrection and change.[2]

So, you see, there are many threads connected to such a magical meeting. Was the dream so compelling that the woman's spoken words of the golden scarab called forth a living representation to appear? Did the beetle (the dream beetle or the living beetle) signify the imminence of the woman's dramatic change, or did it cause the change? Was Jung so intent on observing symbolic connections between the conscious and unconscious worlds that he was drawn to notice the beetle on the window just as a patient was speaking of the same insect? Or was a deeper force at play—an energetic alliance between dreamer and patient, dream image and living being—which somehow opened all parties to a larger perception of reality?

At a certain point, we are moved to the sensation of experience—no longer deciphering the world only by thought or questions, but *feeling* our place within this grand web of life that so elegantly supports the interdependence of all things. In feeling our connection to everything, we may sense the flow of synchronicities in a way we have never before considered. We come to see, in fact, that it is not a matter of synchronicity happening to us, but, rather, that synchronicity is ever present. To our thought processes, this may seem a subtle shift; to experience it, however, is profound.

Every time you don't follow your inner guidance, you feel a loss of energy, loss of power, a sense of spiritual deadness.

SHAKTI GAWAIN,
DEVELOPING INTUITION

In sync with synchronicity

It was one of those days, when it was a minute away from snowing, and there's this electricity in the air, you can almost hear it. And this bag was just dancing with me, like a little kid begging me to play with it. That's the day I realized that there was this entire life behind things, and this incredibly benevolent force that wanted me to know that there was no reason to be afraid, ever. I need to remember. Sometimes there's so much beauty in the world, it's like I can't take it, and my heart is just going to cave in.

AMERICAN BEAUTY, *1999 FILM*

Real magic happens when we are transported to a different frame of mind, seeing the world and meeting ourselves in a completely different way, if only for a moment. Part of what is magical about

An Animal Communications Project
RECORD MAGICAL MEETINGS IN YOUR JOURNAL

Last night, walking through the desert foothills, I heard a sound. It was loud and clear—a call from an animal. The night was so cold and dark and quiet that the sound was piercing. Turning toward it, I wondered what animal could possibly make this sound, and it was then I saw the flashing streak of a shooting star—a bright white arc racing from one side of the black night sky to the other. I felt a rush of wonder, a deep appreciation for all things. My heart soared, suddenly in tune and connected with everything—the desert, the mountains, the night sky, the shooting star, the call of the unknown animal, and the earth herself, this incredible planet where we all live.

JOURNAL ENTRY, WHILE ON VACATION IN ARIZONA

Recording unusual encounters with animals in your Animal Communication Journal is a wonderful way to remind yourself of the magic that is all around you. You might designate a section of your journal for Magical Meetings, or you might enter them as they come, along with your other animal communication talks and experiences. Either way, your journal is a great place to record these meetings as well as any events related to animals that don't quite make sense. Sometimes, meetings with animals can foreshadow experiences yet to come. Other times, these meetings are confirmations of things we have already learned, or reminders of what we may have forgotten. They serve as verification that we are on the right track.

In addition to the encounter, you might write your feelings, emotions, or thoughts about the event. You might sketch the animal or meeting place as a reminder. You might also write of future meetings with animals that you'd like to have. An Animal Communication Journal welcomes creativity. Like a patchwork quilt, it holds a unique collection of pieces of your life and offers a reflective view of your relationship with the animal world.

synchronicity is that the elements of such meaningful events are always present. As the street magician David Blaine puts it, "The signs are everywhere, always." It is simply a matter of listening, hearing, seeing, sensing what is around us all the time.

When we are in sync with the flow of the universe, we are open and aware, centered in the here and now. Because we are not expecting any one thing, we are naturally focused on being rather than doing (though we may be doing things as well—walking in the desert, waiting for a train, standing outside watching the sun rise). In such moments, we shift from living our lives to experiencing the flow of life living through us.

This is when messages come to us effortlessly, like magic. It is no longer an exhausting process—something to search for, somewhere to go, something to discover, something to figure out. It is all here now, and we are "getting it" in the unique way that is perfect for us.

One early morning, standing on the porch of a cabin in Arizona, gazing into the morning sunrise, I was struck with a compelling insight. Whereas the night before my thoughts were confused and chaotic, now, quite suddenly, everything was intensely clear. The clarity was so sudden, in fact, that it was physically jolting and for a moment I gasped in shock, wondering how this could possibly be real. At precisely that moment, Smokey, the large gray dog who lived on the premises, raced up the porch. Paws pounding the stairs, he ran toward me and pushed his soft muzzle into my hand. Backing up, he looked up at me, wagged his tail, and barked—once, twice, three times—then raced away just as quickly as he had come.

I broke into laughter. For several minutes I could do nothing but shake my head in astonishment and laugh out loud. Because of Smokey's actions, I could no longer deny my experience. Although at the time I hadn't yet opened to animal communication, I knew

'Tis the gift to be simple, 'tis the gift to be free.
'Tis the gift to come down where we ought to be.
And when we find ourselves in the place just right,
'Twill be in the valley of love and delight.

SHAKER SONG

An Animal Communication Exercise
INVOKE A MAGICAL MEETING

To invoke a magical meeting, you open yourself to the wonder of synchronicity. As with many of these exercises, the key is not so much in taking action, but in letting go and trusting.

Find a quiet place and spend a few moments centering. Breathe deep and focus on a specific question, problem, or area of concern. As with all things, the clarity with which you express yourself is often equal to the quality of what you receive back.

State your concern out loud. Then ask for a sign or encounter in which an animal will show you something that will help you with your concern.

Now let go. Release your request and go about your daily business. Quite often the "answer" to your question comes when you are not expecting it. It may be accompanied by a feeling of surprise or an internal *"Aha!"*

While some magical meetings involve real animals, others may feature the image of an animal in a book, on television, or in a daydream. Your magical meeting may involve animal sounds or tracks, animal bones, or perhaps even a pile of scat. In any case, you will know inside when your answer has arrived.

Enjoy the experience and note your feelings before you try to comprehend meaning. Sometimes there is no meaning other than delighting in the experience itself. Other times, deeper connotations will unfold naturally.

As with other animal experiences, you may wish to record your questions and the answers you receive. Sometimes several answers will show up, and sometimes the same animal will reveal itself in different ways or forms over a period of time.

through every atom of my body what Smokey was saying: *"Yes! Believe in yourself! What you feel now is realer than real."*

While we are not always in sync with synchronicity, the good news is that there are ways to slide in, feel the wave of oneness and ride it. The trick (this is magic, after all) is to do it in an indirect sort of way. It helps to understand our own framework for seeing the world. We need to know how it *feels* when we tap in to deeper communion with an animal. We need to sense that vibration, that frequency, in order to come to know it. Then we can use it, tune in to it, be fluent in changing our channels of awareness and flowing to those deeper states of connection.

If you have a particular focus or question, for example, you might offer that to the universe and trust that an answer will return. You may even call out, with no expectation, simply for the joy of communicating. And then, magic happens.

This morning I was waiting for my train at the station in the middle of the fields in a small village. There is a cat whose domain is around these fields, and he seems to entertain people as they wait for their trains, which are often delayed. He doesn't let himself be approached and touched. People freak out when he comes too close to the rails, but, obviously, he is the one who decides how he shall live.

This morning, I saw him in the fields, in the distance, playing. I tried a quick mental "Hello! You're so beautiful!" And guess who came running through the fields to rub against my legs? He came right to me, among the fifty or more people on the platform! This put a huge smile on my face and I completely forgot that damn train with its thirty-minute delay. The smile is still here, now, two hours later.

DELPHINE DENOMMÉ

The really valuable thing is the intuition. The intellect has little to do on the road to discovery. There comes a leap in consciousness, call it intuition or what you will, and the solution comes to you and you don't know how or why.

ALBERT EINSTEIN

step by step

By invoking a magical meeting, we are asking the universe to respond to our request. It is a simple three-step process: we ask; the universe responds; we receive.

Usually, the asking is easy. In the case of animal communication, we express a desire to converse and relate in deeper ways to animals. As long as we let go of trying to control the situation, the second step is also easy. The universe always responds as we allow our request to float out to all creation. Do little and be. For every question we put out, an answer becomes available.

This brings us to the third step, the one many people find hard to accept: we receive our answer. We actually take it in. It sounds simple enough, but all too often we get in our own way, blocking the door to the most magnificent gifts that stand before us.

Some magical meetings happen so quickly that we aren't even aware of having asked a question. The beetle taps on the window; the dog races up the porch; the cat runs directly to us. We can feel the power of such events.

The trouble comes when we don't like the answer that comes our way. Animals can do amazing things right before our eyes, and yet because they are not what we expect or hope or desire, we refuse to believe they are our answer. Here we meet a different face of the magical meeting.

Sometimes beloved animals show up in our lives as messengers, guides, or advocates. But other animals can also show up, to reflect things we might not initially be thrilled to see. Maybe we were hoping for a wonderful light-filled message from a playful dolphin, only to find that a housefly has shown up as our personal messenger. Maybe we figure that if we wait or pretend not to notice that we will see a "better" animal soon.

... treat each guest honorably. He may be clearing you out for some new delight.

RUMI, "THE GUEST HOUSE"

An Animal Communication Project

CREATURES I LOVE TO FEAR AND LOATHE

Do you squirm at the sight of a snake? Shudder at the thought of a bat? If you'd like to learn something interesting about yourself, make a list of all the animals you most dislike or fear. As you note each animal, write down what frightens or annoys you most. What is your greatest fear about meeting this animal? Invite all your feelings to come out; don't censor or hold back. This list is just for you.

Now ask yourself: why do you fear what you fear? (Why do some people fear sharks or snakes and others cockroaches?) We often fear things that we don't know much about. Could it be that the animals you fear show you something hidden about yourself?

As you learn more about a particular animal—through reading, observing, or talking with that animal—you may be surprised to find your feelings of fear or annoyance shifting to wonder and intrigue.

Letting go of old beliefs and preconceptions about an animal, we begin to see with new eyes. Moving past our prejudices, we may be astounded to discover how fascinating this animal truly is. How could we have not seen this before? It is only as we begin to know animals as they really are—unblinded by our beliefs about them—that we open to genuine relationship.

What is needed, rather than running away or controlling or suppressing or any other resistance, is understanding fear; that means, watch it, learn about it, come directly into contact with it. We are to learn about fear, not how to escape from it.

KRISHNAMURTI

The key here is trust. While at first glance, a fly may seem more of a nuisance than a perfect answer, this is often because we haven't yet explored the wisdom that may be hiding within the fly. We have yet to appreciate the real value of the gift that is buzzing right in front of us.

A feeling for flies

Everything that lives, even a common domestic housefly, has something of value to share with you—whenever you are ready for the experience.

J. ALLEN BOONE,
ADVENTURES IN KINSHIP WITH ALL LIFE

Everything that irritates us about others can lead us to an understanding of ourselves.

CARL JUNG

A number of people have written to me of their unusual experiences with animals. And the one creature I have heard about most in connection with unexpected magical meetings is . . . drum roll . . . the fly. How is it, you might ask, that something so little can have such a huge impression on people?

For example, Patti Henningsen reported the following.

After I finished your book, I had my first conversation with a wild animal, which happened to be—a fly! I was trying to appreciate the flies outside. As I asked to get a closer look at them, they began flying in front of my face. One showed me his beautiful stripes and I got from him, "I'm a race car!" His stripes did indeed look like a NASCAR. Then his buddy showed me his stripes, which were totally different. The two flies then flew around in an oval, just like the shape of a racetrack! That was awesome!

Most people do not have a good feeling for flies. This is because we usually think about flies in a certain way. As young children, we learned to label the world—good, bad; nice, yucky—and most likely, we accepted very early on what other humans told us: that flies are of the bad and yucky class. If we never bother to examine this belief, we are doomed to accept the commonly projected view of our culture that flies are dirty nuisances or spreaders of disease.[3] This projection dramatically colors our feelings about flies. We don't appreciate the colors that dance on a fly's wing or hear the beauty in their buzz. Rather, we see the fly and automatically feel bothered. Fearing

"TO LIVE IN JOY"

One afternoon, while reading your book, I was thinking about all of God's creatures and not just my beloved dogs. A little fly landed on my arm and then jumped down onto the open pages of the book. Instead of swatting at it as I would usually do, I stared at it and mentally said, "Do you really have consciousness?" For a moment, the fly didn't move. Then it lifted its two front legs into the air like a prizefighter. Lifting its middle two legs, it then started acting like a court jester. Finally, it moved its lower legs into the air, as if standing on its head. This entire experience lasted two or three minutes. At last, the little fly turned its head and stared up at me with its huge "bug" eyes. I mentally heard, *The Creator wants us all to live in joy.* The little fly then flew off, and I looked down at the chapter of the book I was preparing to read. It was on pests, such as flies, and how joyously they live their lives. I burst out laughing and went on with my reading....And yes, it's true!

SANDI METZER

contamination, we wave our hand, annoyed at this pest—"Kill it, it's only a fly"—*squash!*

And so we deprive ourselves of relationship. We forget that every creature in the world is unique, every meeting an opportunity to deepen in connection—not only with another living being but with our own feelings.

Would you be surprised to know that the small fly has not always been hated? In many cultures, flies were once regarded as impressive beings, worthy of respect. The North American Blackfoot tribe tried to imitate the fly's cunning ability to harass the enemy without being captured. Egyptians associated flies with the human spirit and often made jewelry in the likeness of flies. Both African and South American tribes viewed flies as soul creatures possessing supernatural powers. In the Navajo tradition, Big Fly was believed to mediate between people and the spirit world and advise tribal members by sitting near their ears.[4]

In his book, *Kinship with All Life,* J. Allen Boone writes of a remarkable relationship he formed with a housefly named Freddie. Before he learned much about Freddie's fine qualities, Boone had seen all flies as disagreeable pests. As he assumed flies to be unfriendly, they were. As he believed they would bother him, they did. Just like an echo, everything Boone expected about flies came back to him in outward experience.

One of the first things Boone did to relate to Freddie as a fellow being was to erase all judgments he had against flies. In leaving his prejudices behind, Boone resolved to "learn the secret of right relations" and meet Freddie as a tutor, companion, and fellow adventurer in life. What he found was nothing short of amazing:

> The more I was able to see beyond the physical form of Freddie the Fly, the easier it became to recognize him as a fellow expression of the Mind of the Universe. I could then listen with him as

The question is not how to connect with a fly— we are already connected. The question is how to translate that connection into appropriate behavior. Cultivating a genuine feeling for flies can help.

JOANNE LAUCK,
THE VOICE OF THE INFINITE IN THE SMALL

well as to him. And again I realized that all living things are individual instruments through which the Mind of the Universe thinks, speaks, and acts. We are all interrelated in a common accord, a common purpose, and a common good. We are members of a vast cosmic orchestra, in which each living instrument is essential to the complementary and harmonious playing of the whole.[5]

As we move to a state of being that welcomes encounters with all variety of animals—all our relations, all our fellow members in this vast cosmic orchestra—we may find wonder, knowledge, insight, and delight in the magical meetings that occur. In sharing ourselves with all beings, no matter their form, we may be surprised by just how much fun this can be.

No one is to be called an enemy, all are your benefactors, and no one does you harm. You have no enemy except yourselves.

SAINT FRANCIS OF ASSISI

To Know the Living Being

When J. Allen Boone wanted to learn more about animals—to really know the living being beneath the fur or feathers—he asked his friend Strongheart, a German shepherd, to help.

Boone wrote, "All that Strongheart had to do as instructor was to be himself. My part was carefully to watch everything he did and search for character qualities in him. My book of synonyms aided me to find the names of qualities, and the dictionary gave me a more thorough meaning of the qualities. Then I would list these qualities in my notebook and study just what he did with them in his moment-by-moment living."[6]

Boone did not look for "good-dog qualities" as listed by dog trainers or dog show judges. Instead, he searched for qualities that we all respect and wish to have within ourselves, such as loyalty, compassion,

"I'VE GOT IT MADE!"

I was heading home on the New York subway reading *Animal Voices*, when a fly landed on the book. "Okay," I thought to myself, "maybe this is a sign, and I'm supposed to talk to this fly."

"Hello," I said.

"Hello, hello!" said the fly, in a peppy, young male voice.

I took a moment to really look at him and admire him.

"You're fascinating and lovely to look at," I told him.

"Yeah, yeah I am! Aren't I neat? Did ya look at my wings and all?"

"Beautiful! You're not cleaning yourself like other flies I've seen do."

"Well, I'm not dirty! Heh heh! Plus, I'm trying to cling to this book! Take a good look, while you can."

"Amazing! Say, I wouldn't think a subway car would be a very good place for a fly to live. What about all the people? Where's the food you need?"

"Oh, you'd be amazed at all the food you could find here. Plus, the people here are usually so dazed and crammed in—if I land on one, they just twitch. They never swat at me, like in other places. I've got it made!"

"What's it like, being a fly?"

"It's so cool! I love it! I can fly! I can stick to things! And did you see my eyes?"

"Wow! When you see through them, is it like in the movies when the camera looks through 'bug eyes' and you see hundreds of little images?"

"Kind of like that. But a MILLION times better!"

"Whoah! So, is there anything you want to tell me?"

"Yeah! I love you! I love humans! Life is good!"

"Well, great—thank you! Anything else?"

"Yeah!" And here, I kid you not, he began to scat sing! *"Za-ba-dup-dwee-da-dee-da-dwee-daaahh!"*

And with that he said, *"Good-byyyyye...!"* and flew away.

The kicker of the story is that when I looked back at the book and turned the page, there was an interview with a fly who said he loved life and humans, too!

Now, how's that for confirmation?!

GRETCHEN KUNZ

perceptiveness, and humor. Boone so enjoyed this method that he applied it to other animals—ants, snakes, even a little fly named Freddie.

Boone's method is an excellent way to see beyond what we think we know about animals. In addition to noting the unique abilities and gifts each animal brings to the world, it is an opportunity to observe qualities of spirit that are expressed through all beings.

Quite often the animals we most fear or hate are the ones that offer the greatest lessons for our own personal growth. As we remember our connection with all beings, we begin to realize that everything we see in an animal—lion, turtle, whale, or fly—offers a mirror to our own deeper being.

[Pray] that we may apprehend and rejoice in that everlasting truth in which the highest angel and the fly and the soul are equal.

MEISTER ECKHART

An Animal Communication Project

OBSERVING ANIMAL QUALITIES

Use J. Allen Boone's method to learn more about the animal of your choice. You might observe your cat, dog, or goldfish at home, or go "into the field" to watch a wild animal's behavior.

To begin is easy; all you need is a notebook, a pen, and an animal (or group of animals) you can comfortably observe. Like Boone, you might also consult a dictionary and thesaurus to help refine your insights about various qualities.

If you do this over time, with a variety of animals, you may notice your perspective of life changing dramatically. You may become enchanted with the incredibly diverse ways that so many creatures who share our planet express qualities that unite us all. Indeed, you may be surprised to find that you really do have more in common with a dog, a bird, or a beetle than you ever imagined.

magical meetings
of the creative kind

. . . meet them at the door laughing,
And invite them in.

RUMI, *"THE GUEST HOUSE"*

Magical meetings occur for many different reasons. Animals may come to us as messengers of deeper connections or unpredicted possibilities. They may appear as signs, to emphasize a particular truth, to nudge us to see things in a different way, or to lead us to some insight.

Magical meetings may also occur spontaneously when we are playing or being creative. Most animals groove on creativity. When we are in a creative state of being, we are in sync, in "right relations" with ourselves and the world. At times, our heightened creativity calls out to others, as if inviting them to share the joy. As we open to playful, creative states of being, we may find that animals naturally come to explore with us. They may even join in our play, adding their own insights to form a larger creative vision. Consider the following experience that Karen Morrison had one fine evening with one of her donkeys, Truffles.

Valentine, Truffles, and Señor were inside the Donkey House eating a bale of hay. It was such a beautiful night that I'd carried my little gray five-gallon pail outside and was sitting on it, up-ended, about fifteen feet from the door. I could see the clear sky all around me. I'm always surprised at how much light Grandmother Moon gives when she is only a slice of herself up there in the dark.

I sometimes like to take off my glasses and look at the stars. They turn into enormous sequins, the kind that beautiful princesses in fairy stories have on their ball gowns. The sequins flash and sparkle in the heavens, and I imagine that Mother Earth has dressed herself up for a royal evening at the theater, a command performance by the Queen of Heaven Herself. Having strewn her skirts with diamonds, pearls, and crystal beads in honor of Our Lady the Queen's presence, Mother Earth looked lovely with all her starry ornaments arrayed upon her dress and entwined in her hair.

Mother Earth's gown isn't black tonight, I noticed. It's that darkest shade of blue that's one atom off from black. The trees to the North are black, though. They're Mother Earth's escorts, dressed in fine tuxedos, and I can't see their white shirtfronts because they're not facing me. They've turned instead to watch the Queen of Heaven descend the galaxy's grand staircase, clothed in the Milky Way's own glittering splendor. This is what I'm thinking.

Truffles came out of the Donkey House to see what I was doing. "I'm watching a play," I whispered. "And I'm pretending the Queen of Heaven is here and is going to watch, too."

Truffles said, *"Oh, you don't have to pretend that. Our Lady is here. She's always here. And She watches every performance."*

"Do you suppose Saint Francis of the animals is in the audience with her? Way up in the exclusive seats, with all the angels and saints?"

"The nice thing about this theater," Truffles said with Unshakeable Donkey Certainty, *"is that there are no exclusive seats. Every seat in every row is in the best section of the house. The Great Architect designed it that way on purpose."*

The most beautiful thing we can experience is the mysterious. It is the source of all true art and all science. He to whom this emotion is a stranger, who can no longer pause to wonder and stand rapt in awe, is as good as dead: his eyes are closed.

ALBERT EINSTEIN

This is love:
to fly toward a secret sky,
to cause a hundred veils
to fall each moment.
First to let go of life.
Finally, to take a step
without feet.

RUMI

Truffles stood behind me as I sat there on the best little gray seat in the house, and she gave me a few minutes to consider the august company I was in. Then she reached down and put her dark chocolate head on my shoulder and sighed happily.

I said to her, "Look at our dear Grandmother Moon up there in the Southwest." Truffles turned her head to look. "Grandmother has been chasing Evening Star, trying to catch her, and she's never going to, you know."

"I know," said Truffles. *"I've seen this play before. I've watched Grandmother Moon chase Evening Star every night for the past week, and every night Evening Star runs just ahead of Grandmother and jumps down and hides behind the Rockies to the West; and Grandmother can't find the brightest star again until the next night."* Truffles looked at me. *"Why doesn't Grandmother Moon just stay still and wait for Evening Star to come around again tomorrow and run right into her arms?"*

"I don't know," I said. "I wonder if it's because Evening Star thinks that if she were caught by Grandmother Moon, she would have to shift shape through all the months of the year the way Grandmother does, instead of remaining the brightest star in the sky. I think Evening Star likes playing the constant one on stage. I think she likes being the first and most striking star and doesn't want to change with every night's performance."

Truffles thought this over. *"You may be right,"* she said. *"I feel the same way about myself."*

After a while Truffles went back inside the Donkey House and I sat in the theater a little longer. I still had my glasses off, enjoying the giant blurry jewels in Orion's belt low in the East, when all of a sudden there was a sharp flash to the south. Oh,

the one time something out of the ordinary happened in the sky, I'd made myself too blind to see it! I put on my glasses and checked to see if the plot had changed, if Grandmother Moon had caught Evening Star for once, and that's what had made the flash. Nope. The chase was still on.

Perhaps the flash was just Mother Earth rearranging her dark dress, and one of her diamonds had fallen to her feet. Or maybe it was Evening Star's conniving and ambitious understudy, who, waiting hungrily in the wings, had signaled that she could be caught if Grandmother Moon wished it so.

"Or possibly," Truffles said softly from the doorway, *"The Queen of Heaven looked down from her balcony and flashed a smile at Saint Francis of the animals."*

I liked that ending the best.[7]

Karen, Valentine, Truffles and Señor
Photo courtesy of Karen Morrison

when the time is right . . .

Magical meetings can happen at any time. We might meet an animal messenger unexpectedly—a scarab beetle knocking on our windowpane or a dog running up to bark at us. Or we might open ourselves to the energy of synchronicity and move with an animal into a deeper appreciation of life—be that animal a fly in a subway or a donkey friend enjoying a glorious night sky.

Magical meetings aren't just for humans, however, for such events occur for animals as well. Sometimes we are the messengers of wisdom, or the ones to offer guidance and assistance. Sometimes we are called upon to be there for our animals at just the right time, for just the right reason.

Connections occur in many different ways. Never underestimate the power of our intimate connections in ways both seen and unseen—in manners both logical and full of sense, purpose and meaning, and in ways magical, strange, or coincidental.

GOLDFISH ~ DAWN BRUNKE

Max is a big black Labrador retriever who showed up one evening on our back porch in the middle of a winter windstorm. He was traveling with another large, dark dog. As it was quite cold and neither dog had a collar or identification, we let the travelers spend the night in the laundry room. This was not well received by Barney and Zak, our two dogs who felt the house was theirs.

After many days of no luck finding the dogs' people, my husband and I considered keeping the dogs. Having four dogs in our small house would be difficult, though, and Barney and Zak were not keen to share their space. I kept saying, "Maybe if it was just one dog. Surely if there was just one, we could manage to keep it." Be careful of what you say, for you may find your words coming back to test you.

The next day, the larger dog took off. He did not show up that evening, or the next, and soon it looked as if Max would stay. He became a part of our family and happily assumed the role of a big, friendly dog.

After I learned to communicate with animals, I asked Max several times whether he had been abandoned or was lost. What had happened? With his jovial good humor, Max always managed to sidestep the question, and eventually I realized he didn't want to talk about it.

One day many years later, I was sitting at the computer when Max came over and gently placed his muzzle on my knee. This was unusual behavior. As I looked into his kind, brown eyes, Max gazed at me and said he had a story to share.

Sometimes we are humming in just the right vibrational key. Sometimes our hearts are open and we are the ones being asked to listen, to bear witness to a sadness or a moment of vulnerability, to be there for our animal friends in a deep, meaningful way. So, we open to a magical meeting of the heartfelt kind.

MAX'S STORY

Once upon a time when I was a wee black Lab, I lived in a yard with my mother and brothers and sisters. It was cold and rainy. That is how I remember it. There were some doghouses we shared with other dogs, but it never seemed warm enough and we didn't get a lot to eat. My mother was chained up and we puppies were sometimes shut away in a box or in the doghouse, but sometimes we crawled out and ran around. We wanted to be close to our mother. There was one boy who came and held us, but sometimes when his friends came, they would drop us from high up and that was not fun. One of my sisters hurt her shoulder that way and was damaged.

Then there were dark times that I don't remember well. I don't know if we were in a dark place or if I just don't remember, but it makes me feel dark and lonely and cold. This is part of the reason I don't like the cold and wet. It remembers me on unhappy times, even though I loved my

While with an eye made
quiet by the power
Of harmony, and the deeper
power of joy,
We see into the life
of things.
WILLIAM WORDSWORTH

mother and brothers and sisters. There were some bad things happening, not just with us Lab puppies but with other dogs. And that is how it came to be that the idea to get away from there was in my mind, and in the minds of many of us.

My mother had the memory of a good home, of being in a kitchen with good smells, lying on a little rug, and a woman making things called "soup" and giving some to my mother. When we asked our mother why we were here and not with the woman who made soups, she said it was bad timing and chance and accident, meaning things happened and went wrong and that is how she came to be caught by this man and living here. She wished for us a home with the warm soup smells and happy times. She wished for us to play with her, like she had known other mother dogs playing with their pups. This made her very sad and sick.

Then one day she was gone. That day was when another dog and I broke away and we ran and ran and ran, looking for the warm smells. That is how we came to your kitchen. You gave us some food, not soup, but still you were nice and your house was warm and light. There were other dogs and we hoped they would say we could stay. They said no, not enough room here, and wanted us to move on. But they also heard your wishes to maybe have one of us stay, and my friend, knowing I was tired and sad, left me to find another home. I hope he found one; I think he did. And now I am here.

I am so happy to be living here and loving all of you. And I am happy to tell you my story, too.

I want to tell other people to love dogs and treat us well because we are so happy to help you and be with you. Ask us to do whatever you want and we will try, because we—black Labs especially—love to make you happy. That is what we love to do . . . to make you happy with us and then we are happy with us, too. We love you!

Black Labs Forever!

Max
Photo by Dawn Brunke

The greatness of a nation
can be judged by the way
its animals are treated.
MOHANDAS GANDHI

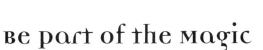

Be part of the magic

Like every other experience noted in this book, magical meetings are about relationships. Whether we ask for an animal to come to us or "just happen" to find ourselves in a meaningful encounter with a fly, a beetle, or a beloved black Lab, we are part of the magic and mystery of such meetings.

As we become more consciously aware of the power of magical meetings—as we honor the exchange of knowledge, wisdom, and love that is present in such encounters—we celebrate the deeper connection of all creation.

Some magical meetings are so full of inspiration that we may feel inclined to leave an offering or tribute—a bit of food, a flower, a small rock altar, a prayer of thanks. Perhaps our magical meeting changes the way we feel about a particular animal, moving us to treat all animals of that species in a new, respectful manner. Or maybe we feel compelled to share our message with others—to write about it or weave the details into a story, painting, song or dance, or poem. What will you do with the magical meetings that come your way?

> *Be grateful for whoever comes,*
> *because each guest has been sent*
> *as a guide from beyond.*
>
> RUMI, "THE GUEST HOUSE"

 ## TWO THINGS YOU NEED TO KNOW
Willie (cockatiel) ~ Morgine Jurdan

There are two things young adults need to know. One is how to fly and the other is how to land. Of course, you would expect this kind of comment from a bird! You might wonder how this applies to humans.

Flying requires a lot of tenacity. It requires that my wings go up and down a certain amount of times and that my body and head are aimed in a certain direction and that I know where I am going and can find a good place to land. Flying requires all my attention. When I fly, I am in the here and now, like young people need to be.

I think being present and aware is a great gift. You learn a lot when you look in front of you and see what is really there. When you glide around from moment to moment, always aware of how you are feeling and what is really going on, it becomes effortless.

You also need to be aware so that you will know where you are going to land. What are the consequences of your actions? Where are they going to take you? Will you be happy with your landing?

Flying is not what it seems to be. Sometimes it is easy and there are few obstacles, and other times it requires a lot of skill. Isn't that true with life?

Open your eyes and pay attention to what is right in front of you in the moment. Remember that flying takes practice and a lot of attention. If you remember that and practice this in your daily life, things can change. Trust me; I know. I am a very smart and wise bird, and beautiful as well.

Willie
Photo by Morgine Jurdan

PART TWO

seeking
animal wisdom

4
power animals, spirit animals— ambassadors of awareness

In the beginning of all things, wisdom and knowledge were with the animals; for Tirawa, the One Above, did not speak directly to man. He sent certain animals to tell man that he showed himself through the beasts, and that from them, and from the stars and the sun and the moon, man should learn. Tirawa spoke to man through his works.

CHIEF LETAKOTS-LESA

Since ancient times, humans have sensed a link between animals, nature, and the spiritual world. As Chief Letakots-Lesa of the Pawnee tribe told his people, the Great Spirit is often revealed to us through animals.[1] How is this so?

Having a distinctive awareness of the world and specialized abilities that humans do not have (such as flying or breathing underwater), each animal group carries its own gift—its unique medicine or teaching that it expresses and exemplifies in the Web of Life. This is why in most cultures through the ages, animals have been—and still are—regarded as messengers of spirit, ambassadors of wisdom, and guides to other states of consciousness. As vehicles of connection to the sacred, animals—be they living animals, dream animals, spirit animals, animal guides or teachers, power animals or totems—help us open to the deeper mysteries of life.

Throughout history, humans have engaged a variety of ways to call upon special animal spirits or to awaken the animal energy within ourselves. We might wear animal masks or skins, or adorn our clothing with animal claws, teeth, bones, or fur. We might mimic animal movements or behavior, or the calls, sounds, or songs of special animals. Some of us might observe and write about the qualities of animals, or draw their images on our caves or tombs; some might adorn our doors or walls with paintings, tapestries, or other artistic representations of their likeness. We might sing praise or dance honor to the animals we admire, or fear.

To call upon an animal's power is to request relationship with the spiritual energy of that animal. We might implore an animal to be our guide as we visit different worlds or states of consciousness. We might even blend our energy with an animal, merging in feeling and consciousness to such a point that the deeper energy of that animal moves through us as well.

We should understand well that all things are the work of the Great Spirit.

We should know that He is within all things: the trees, the grasses, the rivers, the mountains, all the four legged animals, and the winged peoples.

BLACK ELK

Nothing but Emu

While visiting Australia, author Jean Houston observed an Aboriginal woman of the Emu totem enter "into the body, mind, and spirit of the great bird so totally that for an instant her human form disappeared into the bird form. There was no emu present for her to imitate, but she had so closely identified with her totem that every movement and feature had become emu and nothing but emu. And whereas, previously, this woman had been silent and withdrawn, for a time afterward she became vocal and expressive and taught us much. When I asked her how this had happened, she told me, 'I caught my Dreaming—I was my ancestor.' She had become her totem."[2]

In the Aboriginal view, to "catch your Dreaming" is to connect with the animal spirit that links you to your family and land. Within the Dreamtime, ancestral spirits often assume animal forms that have deep-rooted connections to the shape and energy of the land. To say you have Kangaroo Dreaming or Honey Ant Dreaming or Emu Dreaming is to say you are connected to the energy of the animal spirit that comes from a particular area of land, from which you and your family come as well. To become your totem, then, is to feel the energy of that animal spirit move through you so completely that you, too, for a while, become that animal, sharing its movements and thoughts, its wisdom and abilities.

It's a different kind of world to grow up in when you're out in the forest with the little chipmunks and the great owls. All these things are around you as presences, representing forces and powers and magical possibilities of life that are not yours and yet are all part of life, and that opens it out to you. Then you find it echoing in yourself, because you are nature.

JOSEPH CAMPBELL,
THE POWER OF THE MYTH

Animal Altar
Photo by Dawn Brunke

An Animal Communication Activity
CREATE AN ANIMAL ALTAR

Want to engage some animal wisdom or deepen your appreciation of a power animal? Consider creating an animal altar.

An altar is a special space designed to focus attention. It can be a focal point for meditation or visualization, a place to remember animals of our past, or a space to engage an animal energy we hope to learn from. An altar can even be a bridge to our personal Dreamtime.

On my desk is an informal animal altar. Gathered around me as I work are a Zuni bear fetish carved of malachite; a small blue-glazed clay bear cub; a silver mosquito sent to me by a friend; a turquoise newt; small photos of my dogs; a pink plastic frog and purple lizard my daughter gave me; and a long orange tail feather shaken free from a rowdy parrot who once befriended me. While none of these things has great monetary value, each is important, as it holds a particular energy that touches me. And that is all that matters.

Creating an altar can be simple or ornate, casual or elegant. For a base, use a shelf, nightstand, dresser top, or desk space. Collect animal figurines, pictures, carvings, or even parts of animals (found feathers, fur, teeth, or claws) that are important to you, and arrange them in a way that is pleasing. By doing this, you create part of your own reality, one that reveals your personal relationship to the animal world.

Use your altar in combination with other experiences you have. If you dream of an animal, you might add a figurine or drawing of that animal to your altar. Write a question you have of an animal and leave it on your altar as a request to engage this energy at deeper levels. Let your feelings, intuition, and imagination guide you.

Part of the fun of having an altar is that it can easily be changed as we change in relationship. Animal altars are mirrors that reflect our personal connection with animals, as well as windows that reveal how we view our role within the great Web of Life. In either case, they are a way to reconnect with animals—and ourselves—in deep and meaningful ways.

When we refer to a power or spirit animal, a totem, or an animal Dreaming, we are speaking of the larger energy of what that animal both holds and represents—its power, its medicine. For example, to call upon Cat energy is not just to call a single cat but to invoke the power of all cats. Why? Because the spiritual essence of Cat is found at the core of cats as a species. The archetype of Great Cat resides in all cats—those who are living now and those who are not yet born, those who are in the spirit world and those who share their wisdom as ancestral cats. The voice of Great Cat is eternal—it is the energetic signature of what makes all cats Cat.

Thou art the Great Cat, the avenger of the gods, and the judge of words, and the president of the sovereign chiefs and the governor of the holy Circle; thou art indeed . . . the Great Cat.

INSCRIPTION ON THE ROYAL TOMBS IN THEBES

Totems of Today

The origin of the word *totem* is linked to the idea of family or tribe. A totem is an animal that serves as a uniting symbol of a family, clan, group, or tribe. The totem is a universal concept, as most people of all cultures and times have aligned themselves with animal powers.

Many Native American clans identify with totem animals—Bear, Eagle, Wolf. There are national totems (the American bald eagle), state totems (in Alaska, the ptarmigan), and group totems—the Elks, the Loyal Order of Moose, the Lions Club. Even sports teams have totems—the Miami Dolphins, the Seattle Seahawks. If you start looking, you will see animal totems used everywhere: in television and film (the NBC peacock, the MGM lion), as car names (Jaguar, Mustang, Beetle), on sports equipment (Arctic Cat, Puma).

We recognize totemic qualities in others when we say someone is clever as a fox, strong as an ox, eagle-eyed, or busy as a bee. Although we may not consciously realize it, such animal symbols reflect our yearning to experience deeper powers and engage specialized abilities.

An Animal Communication Activity
TUNE IN TO YOUR TOTEM—FIND YOUR FETISH

Bear Fetish
Photo by Dawn Brunke

A fetish is a small representation of an animal designed to hold its "medicine." To use a fetish is to consciously call upon that animal's power for help or guidance. The fetish represents a desire to link with our totem or power animal in order to recall our own deeper powers.

Humans have used fetishes for thousands of years. Early fetishes were stones naturally formed into animal shapes. To find such a stone was an invitation to learn the wisdom of that animal. Modern fetishes are carved of wood or stone; some are fashioned with fur, feathers, shell beads, or other natural decorations that highlight the unique abilities of the animal.

Some fetish makers pray over their carvings or imbue their creations with energy. You can also do this as you find, buy, or make your own. You can use any small animal figure as a fetish, and you can personalize it by adding beads, feathers, or something important to you.

Use a fetish for contemplation and meditation, as a reminder of an animal's medicine or teaching, as a physical reservoir of power and guidance, or as an inspiration to deepen in appreciation and connection with all life.

Animal wonders are everywhere. Every animal is a wonder that helps remind us of our own wonderfulness. When we see one aspect of the world with new eyes, we begin to see ourselves with new eyes as well. All of Nature is our totem. . . . Every time we see the uniqueness of one animal or plant, we also discover something new and unique about ourselves.

TED ANDREWS,
ANIMAL-SPEAK

Totems celebrate the speed, nobility, cunning, and other admirable qualities of animals. By observing an animal and its unique traits, we can better appreciate that animal's power or medicine. The more we genuinely open to the teaching of an animal, the more we align ourselves with the spiritual energy that moves through that animal—and the more we see the qualities of that animal within ourselves.

While group totems symbolize shared energies, the personal totem—our own individual power animal—is more often a protective spirit or guide. In some cultures, a baby is given a power animal at birth, for it is believed a child cannot survive without one. Even if we do not often use the term *totem* or *power animal,* our culture has not lost connection with this belief, for we customarily surround babies and small children with teddy bears, plush dogs, hippos, elephants, and other soft and furry animal toys. These are our early totems, for many of us our first connection to the animal world.

For children of all ages, our culture also celebrates Disney totems and other well-loved fictional animals—Bambi, Winnie the Pooh, Dumbo, and Lassie. Though it may seem silly at first, it is important to remember that each moment and every meeting offers us the opportunity to recognize the energetic significance that flows beneath appearances. The question is: will we allow ourselves to see deeper than the surface? Are we willing to peer beyond the mask?

Jean Houston writes of a conversation she had with a man who wore the Mickey Mouse costume at Disneyland. The man related that a special thing happened as he gazed into the eyes of small children who beheld wonder as they saw him, for "he felt that he was the great mouse and that he also was the essence of the heart and spirit and knowledge of all animals."[3] In those moments, the man aligned himself with the larger energy of Mouse and, deeper still, allowed the essence of that animal power to radiate through his being.

power animals

It is often said that we do not choose our animal totem. Instead, our power animal chooses us, appearing when we are ready for its teaching. It's a good arrangement, because it prevents us from selecting animals based on outward show, our own desires, or what we think we need. Power animals are about *power*—about the energy that moves beneath ego, appearances, and superficial wishes. When a power animal comes to us, we are presented with a clearer reflection of who we really are and what we really need.

Some power animals don't show themselves immediately. It is as if they are testing us or waiting for us to come to a certain level of consciousness before they make themselves known. Sometimes, we will not understand why an animal has chosen us. "What wisdom can a snake have?" "Why do I keep seeing rabbits?" "What could I possibly need to know from an ant?" "I am small and cute; how can a big, hairy buffalo be my power animal?"

A power animal may fascinate us—or it may frighten us. Although the reason why that animal has shown itself to us may not be immediately apparent, the more we explore the relationship, the more we see how our link to that animal is undeniably appropriate.

Power animals may look like animals we know or they may appear much differently, with certain features exaggerated. Small power animals such as mice or moles might appear huge, as if to emphasize the strength and magnitude of their power. Large animals might appear small, perhaps to accentuate a delicacy or the subtleness of their teaching. Power animals may be living or extinct, legendary or mythological.

Some power animals come as lifelong teachers. Others come for a shorter time, maybe to deliver a special teaching or guide us through

Spirit Animals are urgently calling out: "Do you see us? Do you hear us? Look for us, listen for us, reach for us—we are here! We are waiting for you to remember our ancient bonds of community, to honor us, your relatives, with care for the Earth and the well being of us all. We are waiting for you to remember yourselves and to cherish one another. We are waiting and we are watching. Please—look for us—and remember."

VICTORIA COVELL,
SPIRIT ANIMALS

An Animal Communication Exercise
POWER ANIMAL MEDITATION

Find a quiet place and get comfortable sitting or lying on the ground. Breathe a few good, deep breaths, and relax. Close your eyes.

Gently, easily, travel inside yourself, down, down to a place that seems to call you. Maybe it is a meadow or a river; maybe there is a hidden cave or a small blue lake. It is some place in nature that speaks to you, for it has already been selected by you and your power animal.

Relax. You do not have to visualize anything. All that you need will come to you. Enjoy the place where you find yourself. Imagine yourself more fully present; feel the earth beneath you, the air on your face. What do you hear? What do you see?

When you are ready, request your power animal to come. Some animals appear of their own accord, walking up to meet you or running past. Some animals appear very large or small, perhaps in a different color or shape than you know them in waking life.

Allow the vision to unfold. Watch what happens; notice as much as you can. Look. Listen. Take your time. Does your animal engage you in some way? Does your animal have a message for you? It may be a visual sign or a feeling. It may be a telepathic communication or a symbol. Allow the message to fill your being, knowing that you will remember all you need to know.

When you feel the meditation is over, remember to thank your animal. Take time to record your experience. Note your thoughts and feelings about this animal. Were you surprised by the animal that appeared? Have you ever met that animal in real life? In your dreams? What part of you was most touched by your meditation experience? How does the message fit within your life?

a difficult period. We can also call upon the power of a particular animal totem to help us with specific tasks. It is possible to have more than one power animal and even work with several at the same time. Different power animals help us with different teachings. They may appeal to different parts of our being. There are no rigid rules here, only creative possibilities.

A personal power animal often reveals both our strengths and our weaknesses; it may mirror urgent needs or hidden abilities. By finding our animal totem, we reconnect with a deeper part of our self. Maybe we reclaim it; maybe we run away. In either case, our power animal offers us an opportunity not only to learn more about animals, nature, and the world, but about ourselves.

How do you know if you've met your power animal? Many times you'll see a pattern emerging as your consciousness begins to wake up to the relationship. For example, maybe a turtle shows up in your meditation but you are unsure this means anything. Later that day, while flipping through television channels, you see a documentary on turtles. That night, your best friend describes a turtle dream. A day later, while shopping, you notice some T-shirts with colorful

All animals can be your totems—as many as you can concentrate on at once! Also, you can have different ones over time. The key is to look into the inherent qualities of the totem and see what they mean to you, how to adapt them to yourself. You can really do this at any time with any animal. Even animals have animal totems! Mine is often a big, white bird. I was once one, you know. It reminds me of the spirit of flying, of seeing far, and the spirit of the hunt. These are important to me. What is important about your totem/spirit animals?

MAYA (CAT) ~
GRETCHEN KUNZ

Turtles
Photo by Dona Woodward

turtle designs and observe a woman wearing a silver turtle pin. Could Turtle be trying to tell you something?

Most of the time, deep down we know our power animal when it appears. In truth, it does not matter so much what we call it (power animal, animal guide, totem animal) as that we honor the message or teaching that every animal offers. The sharper we become in noticing the animals around us, the greater the assistance, guidance, and enjoyment that comes our way.

Meeting a power animal is only the beginning of what may become a remarkable learning process. But it is up to us to engage the relationship. We must ask questions and observe to discover which aspect of this animal's medicine is most appropriate for us.

Teachers open the door, but you must enter by yourself.
CHINESE PROVERB

Learning More: Embrace the Eclectic

Let a man decide upon his favorite animal and make a study of it. Let him learn to understand its sounds and motions. The animals want to communicate with man. But the Great Spirit does not intend that they should do so directly. Man must do the greater part in securing an understanding.
BRAVE BUFFALO, TETON SIOUX MEDICINE MAN

The following ideas are different ways you might explore your relationship with the power animals that cross your path. Take what fits. It is a wonderfully self-affirming act to ponder a wide range of thoughts—neither accepting nor refuting but simply trying on an assortment of ideas, testing them out, and listening to what speaks most powerfully to your heart, mind, and soul.

question, contemplate, gather clues

One of the best ways to learn more about yourself and your animal is to be a detective. Question everything. Gather clues. Make lists of the animals you see: living animals, dream animals; animal images on television, in magazines, on clothing, jewelry, and billboards. Do animals figure in your reading material or in phrases you hear? Do you notice any recurring patterns? Contemplate deeper meanings; consider alternative explanations. Have you ever been bitten, cut, or attacked by an animal? Some shamans believe that such animal encounters are a test of one's ability to handle an animal's medicine, or may be an initiation into an animal's power.

Research, write, Reflect

Research your animal through books, articles, documentaries, and the Internet. (See the resources section in the back of this book.) The more resources you consult, the more varied material you have to draw upon. Make note of your animal's unusual abilities and areas of expertise. Does it have any magical attributes? How is it portrayed in myth or legend? What are its teachings and totemic qualities? Many animals hold several brands of "medicine" and spiritual gifts. Which one is most meaningful and fitting for you?

observe, study, scrutinize

Observing animals in the wild or through nature films may help you move past fears and misconceptions. To see past our bias is not always easy; sometimes we are not even aware of our prejudices. So it may help to note any strong emotional feelings you have about an animal up front. Record all feelings—good, bad, ugly, magnificent—that you associate with this animal. Go wild and give yourself permission to explore this honestly. What disgusts you? What fascinates

You must understand the whole of life, not just one little part of it. That is why you must read, that is why you must look at the skies, that is why you must sing and dance, and write poems, and suffer, and understand, for all that is life.

KRISHNAMURTI

you? Now, let go of all preconceptions. Take up your observation post. Pretend you are an anthropologist studying a being from a different culture. Allow the animal's actions, movements, and activities to teach you. How does this animal express its skill and wisdom? Do your emotions accurately reflect the animal you are observing, or do they reflect hidden parts of yourself? What is the deeper message of your animal, beneath your likes and dislikes?

Display, Dream, Dance

Displaying posters or drawings of your power animal is an energetic call to connection. Place small statues of your animal in your room, make an altar, or collect fetishes to keep or share with others. Make and wear jewelry that incorporates your animal's likeness. Dreaming or daydreaming about your animal may also intensify your connection. If you are so inclined, develop some dance steps or movements that awaken animal powers within your body. Mimic your animal's gestures, song, or sounds. Draw on any inspiration to better hear, see, and feel the animal that is speaking to you.

Select, Consult, Engage

One of my friends has a large bowl on her dresser containing animal figures made of stone, wood, and glass that she has collected over the years. Each morning she chooses one and slips it into her pocket or bag to accompany her for the day. If she needs a bit of strength, it may be Tiger who comes along. If she hasn't laughed much recently, it might be Coyote, to remind her of the importance of humor. Although this approach requires that you have some basic familiarity with animal teachings, it is an excellent way of learning more. Going through some heavy changes? Ask Butterfly to share her knowledge of transformations. Need a lesson in loyalty? Consult

Dog! With this method, you make a conscious decision to approach an animal and engage its teaching for a specific reason.

What if you aren't sure what animal medicine you need? Another approach involves using animal cards to discover a suitable teacher. Buy a deck or make your own with animal photos or drawings on cardboard. Turn the deck face down, state your question or concern, and intuitively select a card to find your answer in the guidance of the animal image that appears.

Trust, Talk, and Listen

By now you know that working with power animals is about opening to relationship. As you learn more about your animal, you can't help but deepen in knowledge, understanding, and relationship to yourself as well. In this relationship, honesty is always required. We can only go as deep with another as we are willing to go with ourselves. One of the best ways you can learn more from your animal is to talk and listen. Don't be afraid to question and converse about anything that concerns you. At times, your power animal may ask questions of you as well. What wisdom do you have to share? This, too, is part of relationship.

Absolutely everything you are experiencing at this moment in time is able to talk to you, wherever you are, whoever you are with!

PATRICK JASPER LEE, *WE BORROW THE EARTH*

finding voice

There are so many ways to talk with animals. And so many animals and animal groups with whom to talk! There are also numerous levels of communication that are possible. We might speak to an individual living animal or an animal in spirit form. We may contact a communal species voice or tune in to the tone of an animal totem.

Just as each animal species holds a particular teaching, there are

also groups of animals that work together with a specific focus. These may be smaller groupings within a species, or members of different species that band together with a common teaching goal.

How does this sound, and how do you know what "voice" you are hearing? The more you talk with a variety of animals and animal groups, the more you will have a sense of the level you are engaging. Also keep in mind that the voice you tune in to corresponds to the voice you need to hear. It is the vibrational tone that most closely responds to your energetic request for knowledge. The message may tell you much about the animal, of course, but also something about yourself.

For example, when I began noticing rabbits in my life, I did some research. I found that the main teachings of Rabbit may include paradox, fear, fertility, quickmindedness, and the ability to hide, turn quickly, and shift in position. That's quite a range! In order to learn more, I tuned in to some rabbit beings who offered their insights:

THE RABBITS' SECRET
The Rabbits ~ Dawn Brunke

There is much about rabbits that is magical—much power that we hold but hide from first view. Why do you think a magician pulls a rabbit out of the hat? Why not a mouse or a small terrier or a Siamese cat? Why not an opossum? Rabbits hold a secret. We hold magic.

One facet of rabbits is reproduction—and humans have observed that rabbits multiply easily, quickly. This, too, is a magic of sorts—the magic of creation!

Rabbits are very fast creatures. Often we seem not to be, especially when we sit still for long periods of time, and then dash off. Rabbits are about silence, of deeper meanings, of holding in the secrets of creation and smiling about that knowledge. Rabbits move with a cunning air.

Rabbits pop up in unexpected places. We are small; no one suspects us. That is our cover.

Rabbits also relate to love, and we do use our gentle nature to help humans overcome deep-seated fears of rejection and insecurity. But rabbits are so much more. The rabbits you see on Earth now are such a small perception of who we Rabbit Beings truly are.

If you explore the nature of rabbits, you may glean a bit more about who we really are. Study rabbits. Have a few rabbit dreams. Ponder our deeper nature.

Call on us and one of our rabbits will help. You are always welcome to "hop along" with us for a period of time to get to know us better. There is more to our rabbit story and we will be pleased to share with you.

As the rabbit beings pointed out, to truly know an animal and deepen in relationship to its teaching requires some time, patience, and a variety of views. That is why—especially when initially opening to animals—it is so helpful to gather many different facets. Observe your animal, learn its habits, talk with it, and dream about it. Allow yourself to follow the intriguing variety of ways in which that animal speaks to you. Listen to what resonates most powerfully within you.

You can also play with the order of how you do these things. At times you may prefer to consult reference books first and then tune in to your animal. At other times you might want to plunge in and talk with your animal first. Afterward, you can compare the message you got to what others have learned.

And here's another twist. Instead of asking to speak with a specific animal group, you might just toss out a question and see who responds. This is a fascinating way of not only learning how to deepen your connection with animals but how to hear from a wide variety of animals. As an example, for this book I put out the call to "speak with an animal or animal group caring to share observations,

Ideas are like rabbits. You get a couple and learn how to handle them, and pretty soon you have a dozen.

JOHN STEINBECK

insights, and words of wisdom to the young people of this world who want to connect with nature, animals, the planet, and themselves in a more profound manner."

I was surprised—and delighted—to get my answer from a group of animals living in a large crater in Africa I once visited. Although I hadn't connected with any of them then, the fact that these animals responded revealed to me how deeply we are touched by animals even if we are not fully aware of it at the time. Here is what they said:

We are the animals of the African landscape. We come to you as a group of animals who have gathered together to live in a particular habitat with one another. We provide food for one another; we provide balance to one another. We gather together many different outlooks on life. We reveal a larger, more beautiful pattern, because of our coexistence on the same small parcel of land.

We have changed this land by our relationship with her. We each contribute an essential part to our little world here, and that is the wisdom we wish to pass on to other children of the planet, just as we pass this information on to our children, not so much with words as we are doing now but by example. We are a living example of a group of beings living in a greater harmony.

This is our wisdom not only for young humans but for all humans on the planet at this time. We each have our own grouping—zebra, hippo, rhino, lion, ostrich, and more—some of us come and some of us go. We move in relation to this parcel of land, and yet we are all committed to our role here, to our piece of the pattern that brings a balance and beauty to the whole living landscape.

We encourage our young to explore and see the greater pattern, the force of the life living through us all, and how this "energy" flows through many different species to create an ongoing creative experience for all. We

Waterbuck of Ngorogoro Crater
Photo by Dawn Brunke

Patience is the companion of wisdom.

SAINT AUGUSTINE

speak to respecting diversity yet feeling, living, and enjoying our connection to all. We encourage all humans to feel this deeper thread of connection.

Our wish for humans is not to act too quickly but to observe the patterns of what IS before moving to change or direct things based on small ideas of what is "right" or "wrong". We see this, though in a different way, with our young. Youth would always like to change the system; sometimes this is a positive force. But we also carry an older energy and so we—all older generations—hold a wisdom, and our advice is to see deeply before you act.

Energy shifts of her own accord. To move with that natural shift is to move with a deeper appreciation of life. Our wish is to feel deeply the life living through you before you begin to act on changing life yourself. This is an older and deeper wisdom. It is our gift to you.

Thank you for asking us—the Animal People of the Ngorogoro Crater—our opinions.

celebrating variety

It's wise to keep in mind that it is the *human* view that differentiates between speaking with a living animal, an animal spirit, a power animal, or a species voice. Clearly, there are different flavors to each type of communication, yet many animals do not differentiate between voices such as we do. Many animals shift easily from one mode to another and back again. If you are speaking with an individual animal about a particular type of wisdom, you may find your conversation opening quite naturally to a deeper group voice.

As Penelope Smith notes, "All telepathic communication is the same. Some people separate animals into parts, saying they're communicating to the higher self or this or that. How the animals do it is that we're a whole being: ego, higher self, body—everything is all one. Now, there are different kinds of communication. For example, one time while at a zoo I made contact with a buffalo, though it was the universal consciousness of All Buffalo—what might be called an oversoul—that came in and communicated to me. It was obvious it was not this individual in the zoo talking about his particular thing. It was All Buffalo. You can tell the difference in the communication: the universal wisdom of All Buffalo is communicating, but it's also coming through this individual."

The more you tap in to communicating with different animals, the more likely you are to experience a variety of voices—even in conversations with a single animal. Some talks will naturally move from connection at the individual level to more spirit-based or species-based connections. When you think about this, it really isn't so strange. Most everyone has experienced talking with a friend about an emotional issue when the conversation naturally deepens. Sometimes, we bring great wisdom to others in just this way.

"I just communicate," Penelope told me. "Animals are tapped in to the universal. They don't go all freaky about this like humans do. When we tap in to the human oversoul, we get all of human history, all of human wisdom that's there. Do we have to freak out about it? No, it's there within us. It's part of all of us. All soul wisdom is part of everybody. It isn't any harder to communicate to a whale compared to a tree compared to a spirit. It's all the same!"

It is true that humans love to explain things, isn't it? An effect of our language and thinking processes is that we love to compartmentalize, to separate this from that, tree from wolf, human from animal. We go to great lengths to deliberate and explain, to describe how this is different from that. We believe that if we can explain it then maybe we can know it.

To experientially know something, however, is to feel it throughout our being. This requires a shift in our thinking, a change in how we see the world, a movement to deeper being.

More and more as we come closer and closer in touch with nature and its teachings are we able to see the Divine and are therefore fitted to interpret correctly the various languages spoken by all forms of nature about us.

GEORGE WASHINGTON
CARVER

εxceptional Beings

Isn't it funny how the simplest things are often the most profound? When opening to animals, all we really need remember is simply to be—to meet and talk and laugh and learn from the wide diversity of animals who share our planet. Every animal, every being, every group consciousness holds a different piece of the whole. There is Elephant wisdom and Whale wisdom, Rabbit wisdom and Human Being wisdom. Although we are all part of the same oneness, each of us has a different view, a different gift and teaching to share. Why not embrace them all? Enjoy the varieties that come your way! Even when you don't expect it, a passing animal may have just the message you need to hear.

One day, while conversing with me on the telephone for this book, Penelope Smith said that a bumblebee came buzzing right past her nose. Although we hadn't expected to talk with bumblebees, the bumblebee told Penelope he had something to share:

I represent bumblebees. We are different from other bees. We are not hive bees. We are not group bees. I zoom all over the world, I and my kind. We are one being, so I do not differentiate this body in this place from my body in another place because we zoom everywhere.

Bumblebees do not live very long. Our bodies decay very rapidly. To you, it looks like we live a short time. To us, we live infinitely. We live in all our forms at once. So, as one piece falls back to the earth we continue. We are both individuals and One Bee, and all of us recognize that. Bumblebees are exceptional . . .

("Ha! There isn't a species who doesn't think that!" exclaimed Penelope.)

Bumblebees are exceptional, continued the bumblebee. *We have a unique way of going around the earth. As bumblebees, we respect both the younger or newer forms as well as the older forms. It all is a continuum of life and we are all a part of each other. When you have the awareness that bumblebees have, you will realize that you are not separate from anything, and that everything is a continuum of cellular transformation.*

It's very important in this time to not get distracted by thoughts of separation. We bumblebees do not resist anything, even if we are smashed or cut up; we simply feel all as part of the next transformation. We are so united with all the young and all the old—all the bumblebees—that we do not suffer as you do. The only reason you suffer is because of your feelings of separation, your thoughts of separation.

I recommend that you no longer regard yourself as young or old, but that you regard yourself as a continuum of human life. If you regard

Last night, as I was sleeping, I dreamt—marvelous error!—that I had a beehive here inside my heart. And the golden bees were making white combs and sweet honey from my old failures.

ANTONIO MACHADO
(TRANSLATED BY ROBERT BLY)

yourself as a continuum, you will feel the deliciousness of being young and the deliciousness of being old.

You will no longer feel that you are something different from everybody else. You will simply feel the movement of life and experience all joy, all pain, all feeling as a continuum. This is the essence of Bumblebee wisdom.

As we embrace the wisdom that is available to all, we share in a deeper sense of unity. We feel the underlying oneness that pervades all creation, as well as the uniquely distinctive ways this oneness is expressed in our world. And so we know in our heads and in our hearts, in our bones and in our souls, that we are all—each and every one of us—exceptional beings.

TO THINE OWN SELF
The Cat Council ~ Gretchen Kunz

Greetings. We are Cat. We are part of every cat's consciousness and soul. We are unifiers. We are spirits, and we are one.

We are glad about this book. People need to know and respect the different consciousnesses of animals because all creatures and beings are alike. While we are a group of individual cat spirits, we are also Cat—that energy that shapes the frequency of Cat. We are the unique things that represent Cat and that Cat represents. For example, we are alertness and balanced energy; we are love with the realism of chase and survival. We are domesticated and in that way tied to humans, but of our own choice. We bridge the wild and domestic worlds in a way that is unique to ourselves.

Because we cats are domesticated and live with you, we learn from you and you learn from us. We use energy to touch your hearts and heal you, as we heal the worldwide web of energy. We also balance energies and heal wounds in the universe. We are concerned with this Earth, as we love its forms, and our job is to bridge the gap between nature and human societies, between the solid and the spirit, the universe and Earth. But mostly, we deal with the energies on Earth, for we are of its flesh.

Now, here is a lesson for human youths, for all people, whom we love. Watch our natures. Cats are singular. We have respect for our own selves. The vibration of Catness is unique. In being Cat, our consciousness is shaped by this way of being. Most cats will tell you they enjoy being Cat. The uniqueness of being Cat suits them. It feels right for their purposes.

In being Human, you have a frequency, too. The choice to be in a human body affects you. We are all part of the same energy, but our parts of energies vibrate in different ways, and our bodies are the shapes of our frequencies. Part of why we take a certain shape—Human, Plant, or Cat—has to do with what we have to learn from being that way.

Being Human is quite a choice. You can learn much. It has advantages and disadvantages. One of the human ways is to quest for information. This can lead to great things, such as physical treatments for diseases. But there is so much to learn in the physical realm, with machines and information communicated through human language and pictures that can distract you from your soul. Remember— how you live in the physical realm is affected by your energies of spirit, so it is important to stay in touch with and believe in your true self.

Cats can help. We can balance your energies and be examples for you. Cats are uniquely themselves. Each cat is Cat, and thus accepts the role of Cat in the world. Moreover, cats are generally proud of being cats. A cat may not like all other individual cats, and some may be more enlightened than others, but we all recognize each other as cats, part of the Cat state of being. You need to recognize each other as similar in the same way, as Human, as part of the same state of being.

But our bigger lesson is this: we respect ourselves, our wishes, who we are at the core. You cannot get a cat to do what it does not want to do without duress. We rarely feel guilty. Study cat society and you will see we respect ourselves. Our relationships are fluid, but we always try, as your poet says "to thine own self be true."

Remember, you are always you. It can be fun to play with being different ways, and it is good to try new things, but you must always respect yourself. There is a soul within you, shining bright. Cats can help show you this. See how we meditate—try it. Be silent and still and feel the inner you of yourself. Know that wherever you travel and whomever you meet, your soul is still there. You may change your view on things, but you are still uniquely you. And just as the cat is splendid in itself both as Cat and Individual, so you are. Knowing that will assuage your fear, and you will take more kindly to other people, animals, plants, spirits, and things. Do you understand?

Feel free to ask us questions and we will answer you! We love humans, and look forward to the coming exchanges, where we will all be one in energy and love, respect and knowing our self, ourselves.

Peace, Love, and Deep Knowingness to you, from the One, the Many who are Cat.

5
animal guides and teachers

Come forth into the light of things.
Let Nature be your teacher.

WILLIAM WORDSWORTH,
"THE TABLES TURNED"

There are all kinds of teachers. Some are clever and some are funny; some are unconventional and some favor rules and order. It is not so different with animals. If you observe several mother dogs or cats with their pups or kits, you'll see a wide range of teaching styles. Some moms are task oriented and won't tolerate dissension, while others are easygoing. Still others have no seeming interest in teaching whatsoever.

Animal guides and teachers are those animals that come into our lives with lessons to share. Sometimes we hold lessons for them, too. Some animals teach other animals—not only their young but fellow creatures, no matter the species. Some teach individuals and some teach large groups. Conversely, you may be taught by an individual animal or by a team of animals. There are also spirit-based teachers who work with both humans and animals from a different realm.

Within the grand plan, we are all teachers in some way for one another. And so, of course, we are all students, too. We may seek out our teachers or they may find us. We may know when we are being taught or we might not suspect it until much later. Sometimes we may think we are teaching someone else, when we are really the ones gaining the lesson. The flow of the teacher-student relationship bounces back and forth like a cosmic game of table tennis. And sometimes—when that little white Ping-Pong ball is poised just above the net—we find ourselves teaching and learning at the very same time.

A Teaching partnership

Author, communicator, and teacher Tera Thomas teaches her classes in animal communication with a group of animals who live with her at Hummingbird Farm. While some animals are permanent residents, others (such as deer and squirrels) come and go. When Tera asked the animals to share their thoughts with readers, they answered as a group.

We are the Hummingbird Farm animals, come to speak to you on our role as teachers. We begin this discourse as a collective because we often work as such. Each of us came here with purpose, answering Tera's call for teachers to assist her in her own life and in teaching others.

People often ask if we know we are teachers. We assume they are wondering whether we consciously participate as teachers or whether we are just there in the form of llama, cat, deer, squirrel, and so on, and the teaching happens by default. The answer is a resounding Yes! We are conscious of our role. With great purpose, we each answered the call and came to partner with Tera and with each other. It is blessed and fulfilling work for us.

We work with students as individuals. We tune in to each student and find where he or she needs support and advice. Most often we are very gentle with people, but occasionally we have to cut through a great deal

It is absurd for men to vaunt their superiority over the animals when, in matters of great importance, it is they who are our teachers: the spider for weaving and mending; the swallow for architecture; the swan and nightingale for singing.

DEMOCRITUS

of resistance, and we can be razor sharp. We do not mince words, and we always tell the truth even when it is painful. Because we tell the truth with no judgment or malice, it can be received and understood on a very deep level. We came into our physical forms (as various species) with the express purpose of working with humans. Nonhuman animals have a unique ability to take human animals beyond their perceived limitations. It is with great reverence that we offer our services to the people who come to Hummingbird Farm to open their hearts and learn.

This is not a unique situation. Animals all over the planet are part-nering with humans to teach others. Some of these partnerships are con-scious and purposeful, while others are not so conscious. Rather, they are partnerships formed by a human who has an open heart with animals, and the animals come to work with that person in more subtle ways— as therapy animals, assistance animals, sometimes as a silent partner with a human health care provider, or even as neighborhood dogs and cats that have a special relationship with their person. There are many animal/human partnerships on the earth at this time and they are all powerful components at work to bring the awareness that we are all related, that we are not separate.

It is through these partnerships that our basic message is spread—we are one. Give this message a space in your heart and open yourself to your powerful connection with all of life. We call you to claim your birthright. When you commit yourself to partnership with other species and the earth, a world of incredible love and beauty awaits you.

Nature is trying very hard to make us succeed, but nature does not depend on us. We are not the only experiment.

R. BUCKMINSTER FULLER

The Life of an Animal Teacher

Many animal communicators request and enjoy their animals' assis-tance with classes. Just as the animals of Hummingbird Farm came in response to Tera's call, Penelope Smith feels the animals living

with her also came specifically to be teachers. "That's what we do here," said Penelope. "They don't come to me otherwise. And, then, they expand in their mission. As they get more experience with the body, they expand on what their mission is and everything else."

So, what does it entail to be an animal instructor, assisting humans in the stirring ways of animal connection? Yohinta, a fifteen-year-old tortoiseshell cat living with Penelope, agreed to share her experiences in helping teach humans to deepen, heal, and communicate. Through Penelope, this is Yohinta's story.

Yohinta
Photo by Michele Bustamante

DOING WHAT I'M MEANT TO DO
Yohinta (cat) ~ Penelope Smith

When I first started out as a kitten with Penelope, people were lots of fun. Then I realized they had all kinds of emotions that hurt them. I focused on the people who had the most emotion and I would comfort them. They would cry all over me and get my fur wet. That's when I was a kitten.

Then people would come and they had other things—heavy, dark masses of energy. Sometimes I didn't like it because they weren't so interested in becoming lighter as they were on blaming other people than

themselves. I got tired of those kinds of people. Fortunately, there were only a few.

But mostly, I've had a lot of fun with people. I choose the ones who have a lot of emotion that they don't know what to do with, and I act as a sponge. They put it into me and they get relief. First I soak it up and then I eat it, like a fire eater. It feels good—being fulfilled and doing what you're meant to do. When people feel better, I feel great. I'm able to handle a lot of their stuff by burning it up. They want me to do that because they are oftentimes younger souls who don't know how to handle emotion like I do. So, I've helped many people that way. I've sat on their laps and told them to cry it all out and scream it out, and I would burn it up.

As I got older, I could no longer take so much emotion. And people who were coming didn't do the same things with emotions as they did before. They didn't seem to need quite as much work, which was fortunate because I wasn't as available to them as my body got weaker. I couldn't handle their energy and so I got frightened and kept to myself.

Then, as people got lighter, I was able to come among them and give them comfort. I no longer have the capacity to burn up emotion as I did when I was a young cat. I can no longer handle that kind of energy. So, now I just comfort them, and they comfort me, too.

teaching by carrier wave

Another animal educator who lives with Penelope is Sherman, an orange cat quite popular with students. As an aware teacher, Sherman works in his own unique way with the people who come to Penelope's retreats.

"Sherman says there are so many good, young people," Penelope told me when I asked if Sherman had any advice for readers of this book. "There are still problems and abuse, but Sherman focuses on all that are coming forward and already carrying love and unity. He says to those who are still troubled, *'Relax, feel the sunshine'*—like a cat, of course! But he wants them to know that that is how they feel the love—by relaxing, by feeling. And he wants them to know that he is there for them. He says that from his place here, he contacts all those who are coming into awareness of connection, and he is quite willing to help. He is not so much a teacher as people used to think of teachers, as a carrier wave.

Nature is an unlimited broadcasting station, through which God speaks to us every hour, if we only will tune in.

GEORGE WASHINGTON
CARVER

Sherman
Photo courtesy of Penelope Smith

"Sherman shows me an image of how he sits here and makes connections. When people get on a certain wavelength or vibration, they automatically hook in. He is showing me very clearly that he holds this vibration and as people come up to him—whump!—they get it! He says that all his wisdom, all his knowledge, all his love is available on that vibration—as is everyone else's."

"It's a tuning, isn't it?" I asked.

"Yes," said Penelope. "You just lift your head out of the muck of illusion, out of the daily news of what's bad in the world—just lift up, breathe, get some tea, get out in nature, listen to some good music, or whatever it takes. Then you're on that vibration and then you've got it. Then everything is available, all of these dear, wonderful animals, and the rocks and the plants—they're all there; they are all vibrating their love."

Once the spring thunder
bursts,
myriad beings on the earth
are awakened.

CHINESE PROVERB

Animals in the classroom

Some animals teach while alive and then continue to teach after their physical body is gone. Consider Kite Chaser, also known as KC, once a Keeshond dog, who has passed on to the spirit world. For many years, KC worked with his communicator friend Cathy Malkin as a humane education volunteer, visiting classrooms to help students deepen in appreciation toward animals. KC is also one of the few animals to ever receive an honorary Masters degree (as a Conscious Canine) for his work.

Here's KC's story, through Cathy, along with some advice for readers.

PLANTING SEEDS OF KINDNESS
KC (dog) ~ Cathy Malkin

When I was in my Keeshond body, my work was multifaceted. When Cathy and I first met, she was quite ill. So, my first goal was to help Cathy heal and gain self-confidence so that we could set off on our life's work together teaching kindness to children.

My work as a humane educator came about because I'm called as a spiritual being to help people connect with their humane-ness. By

TUNING IN TO THE UNIVERSE
MAYA (CAT) ~ GRETCHEN KUNZ

I am attuned to the energies of all kinds of spirits and thoughts around me. There is a group of cat spirits (some of whom still have bodies and some of whom don't) that I connect with to talk about what's going on in the world. We share information, so if I want to know something that's happening on the other side of the world, one of the other cats will have some contact with the energies there and hook me into them.

Can humans do this? Of course! The more you practice, the more you can tune in to the feelings and energies of all the beings and things around you, even if you can't see them. Is it easy? Well, I think humans are more easily distracted than we are, and not as used to it.

How to practice? I'd say, meditate. First meditate on little things, like clearing your mind and relaxing. Then, get to know what you and some of the energies around you feel like. This is especially good to do if you have animals near you who will do it with you and respond to your energies with theirs.

Keep expanding your feelings until you feel—or imagine you feel (sometimes you have to pretend before it works and you believe it!) more space and energies around you, over a wider range. This may sound hard to believe, but anyone—and I mean anyone—can tune in to the wider energies that encircle the earth and our universe and connect to any other being.

If you want to know more and experience this, spend time learning from people and animals and things without words. Like staring at the stars, or meditating with people who do it a lot, or just lying with your favorite cat, listening to her purr.

The more you relax into it, the more you can feel that vibration behind everything. In doing nothing, you can feel the something behind it. Once you tune in, you will start seeing forms in the something, and then the fun really begins!

humane-ness I mean that it's important for people to connect with the part of themselves that feels love and compassion for their inner selves and also for the preservation of this Earth and her multitudes of creatures.

I prefer working with children and young people to help strengthen the animal-human bond, because their awareness of who they are as spiritual beings hasn't been socialized out. It's hard for some people because they are stuck between knowing their true selves as spirit and living up to society's expectation that they become human "doings" not human "beings."

I love reaching into children's hearts planting "seeds of kindness," as Cathy would say. By helping kids to feel the love and compassion that radiates from my heart to theirs, I help them understand that we are truly the same, even though we live as different species. There is common thread that unites us all—love.

It is important that kids know they are deeply loved and adored by other living beings. It is a shame that love is not so freely given in the human species. That's why the love of an animal is precious—it is given freely and unconditionally.

I found working with students to be so satisfying. I would enter a classroom and quickly sniff out every desk and backpack (sometimes I would get lucky with a morsel of food). When possible, Cathy would have the students sit on the floor with me so we could be close to one another. I liked that the kids could see the world from my point of view. While Cathy taught the kids about responsible animal care or how to protect wildlife, I would scan their hearts and minds telepathically. Then, when I felt their hearts open, I would send them love and joy, both energetically and by physically touching them.

It gave me great joy to see a child who was sad shift into the moment and be present with me. Once they did that, the love and joy was contagious. A smile would appear and laughter soon followed. Once they are feeling love and joy, I know I have reached their hearts and, at least for a short while, each kid in the classroom would feel good about his- or herself.

Inch by inch, row by row,
Please bless these seeds
    I sow.
Please keep them
    safe below
Till the rain comes
    tumbling down . . .
ARLO GUTHRIE

My goal in working with young people has always been to connect with their hearts and help them to feel the pure love and joy that is universally known across all species of life. I want them to know that they are not alone, but surrounded by many beings who love and care about them.

The main thing I would like to share with young adults is to feel their connection and understand that we are all one—we are all interconnected and interrelated. It starts with each individual as one empowers oneself to create a world of love and harmony. It's like a stone thrown into a smooth lake and the ripples start moving outward in a circle from the center.

My spirit exudes love. For in the end that is all there is. It is important that humans see themselves as spirit first, human second. I know this is why Dog is here and chooses to live so close to humans. This is why I came.

Love all God's creatures, the animals, the plants. Love everything to perceive the divine mystery in all.

FYODOR DOSTOEVSKY,
THE BROTHERS KARAMAZOV

KC and Cathy
Photo courtesy of Cathy Malkin

teachings of the sled Dogs

Teaching is an ongoing process. Sometimes we need to learn; other times we are called upon to help guide and teach others. Back and forth the roles of teacher and student shift, changing as our needs and circumstances change. Sometimes the teacher leads the student to yet another teacher or level of awareness. Sometimes teacher and student merge and a blending of energies occurs.

Because I live in Alaska, the Iditarod sled dog race is a big event in our family. Although we do not have sled dogs, we live in Knik, sled dog country, home to Iditarod headquarters, official start of the race, and general neighborhood of some of the most famous mushers and sled dogs in Iditarod history. Every March we join many others on the sidelines of the Iditarod trail to cheer on the dogs and mushers as they glide past us on their long (nearly twelve hundred miles long!) journey to Nome.

To those who are unfamiliar with sled dog racing, this race is sometimes misunderstood or believed to be cruel and abusive to the dogs. Although my experience has shown me that most sled dogs not only want to run but want to run as a team more than anything else in the world, it is always wise to go to the source. When I asked a sled dog named Queenie to share her perspective of racing and what it means to be a member of a race team, she responded true to form by a fast-paced answer that soon led me to unexpected terrain.

OUR HEARTS BEAT TOGETHER
Queenie (dog) ~ Dawn Brunke

I love to run, to be a part of the flow of movement. Our hearts beat together. When we are racing smoothly, we are a group, like one being. We can see all perspectives, as if from each other's eyes. We join our thoughts, our

sights, our feelings. Our hearts beat together, we breathe together; we are all part of one being, one team. Sometimes our musher feels this also, though it is harder for him to be part of our team in the same way. Still, he tries.

We can feel when there is a break from this flow—when there are troubles or worry. We don't like to climb as much as we like to run, so sometimes we feel scattered when doing things like that, and the flow is disturbed. It need not be, but that is our learning. It is easier for us to feel part of the team and flow when we run, flying fast as the wind, a part of the wind. We are not separate but a part of the movement.

We love to be part of the one team, but at times there are fights and disagreements. Our energy becomes pitched when we run. When it is harnessed and we pull together, we can win a race! But at rest or in the yard, we often fall back into another mode of being.

Iditarod Sled Dog Runners
Photo by Dawn Brunke

It is as if we are of two ways of being. We are individual dogs with our own needs and wants, but we are also a team, and that, too, is part of our learning and part of our love. There is a flow about that, a way of

being in which we feel a part of something larger than ourselves. We work together for the team. Our relationship with our musher is part of this.

The downside of this bliss is our separation from the oneness of running with the team—for we do not race or run every day. Some days are needed for rest, but as a rule most of us, on this team, would like to run more.

We have our own likes and dislikes among the group. I am close to two other dogs. I am the "runner up" dog in this team, meaning position number three or four. I have led at times, though I prefer to be in this position. It is my place and it is where I feel most fine. If you want to know more about us as a group, you should talk to the spirit of sled dogs.

spirit of sled Dogs: The Teacher's Teacher

Spirit of sled dogs? Although at the time I didn't know there was such a thing, with Queenie's help, I was able to tune into the "spirit of sled dogs" through her. This sometimes happens when talking with animals—as if you are transferred to another line in order to speak with a manager or supervisor. In this case, I connected with a being who seemed to be a group leader or energetic guide to the sled dogs.

The conversation led me to discover another aspect of the teaching relationship—in effect, the answer to: who teaches the teacher? By connecting to teaching spirit guides, animal (and human) teachers can refine their skills. These spiritual beings also serve as directors and mentors to teachers. I have since spoken with several such spirit guides who take an active role in holding the vibration of a larger teaching for various animals to attune with and so impart a living example of this teaching for others.

At the time I spoke with the sled dog spirit, however, I knew none of this. Here is what I learned.

THIS ONENESS IS A HEALING

I am the spirit of sled dogs in this area. There are several of us working together here. We work with dogs and humans in an attempt to harness the flow that this dog, Queenie, spoke of.

When a musher is in tune with his or her dogs, there is an openness that occurs, a real exchange between animal and human. This exchange is about sharing information in a common way, to feel as one, to move as one, to see from the point of view of every member of the team.

There is then an opening with the land herself. Many of my dogs are aware of the feel of the land as it meets their paws, or as their bellies pass over it as they run, walk, or race. When a human also opens to the land in this way, or shares the feeling through the team dogs, there is then a deeper triangulation of movement—a group oneness of human, dogs, and land. This oneness is a healing. At this time, this is our aim, a movement toward healing. You might remember the origins of this race: it also was a race for healing to occur.*

There are many ways in which healing can occur, and becoming in tune with other animals and the land is one such opening, one such deepening. Our race, the Iditarod, is about movement through land, space, and time by the joined forces of animals and humans. It is, in fact, a celebration. There is much about this race that has yet to fully blossom into human consciousness. Many people still see it as something to be won or lost. But that is not how we see it.

---

*The Iditarod commemorates the 1925 race in which twenty teams of sled dogs and mushers worked together over a course of five days, inhospitable terrain, and fierce weather to relay serum to a far northern Alaskan village that was threatened by diphtheria.

Within a few miles I was locked into a mystical dance with the sweeps ...I was complete, and part of that completeness was that we, the team and I, were in some way doing what we were meant to do—heading north into the sweeps.

GARY PAULSEN,
*WINTERDANCE:
THE FINE MADNESS OF
RUNNING THE IDITAROD*

Most of my dogs see it as a joy, a flowing movement. They feel the worries, concerns, and dreams of their musher. They work with the musher, and you can see the results in the interaction between human and dogs. The real point of the race, from our perspective, is to engage humans in an opening process both with dogs and the land. For those who watch, it is also about an opening of spirit, an extension of the human will to meet with other species and pull with them through adversity and odds.

The sled dogs are unique. Among other racers, such as racehorses and greyhounds, the focus is elsewhere. Our focus is much more about working with humans, helping them to enjoy the freedom and bliss of opening to something larger and—for a time—being held within the oneness of movement and flight.

As for accidents, injuries, and deaths, most sled dogs are aware of their purpose. Most come to this incarnation for a specific reason—to engage in this activity. Those who die on the trail know this life was about running. There is rarely regret; certainly there's no regret from this side of the perspective, and rarely regret even when that dog is physically dying.

The reason humans have so many projections on this race is that it stretches beyond your normal viewpoints. For those who feel the race is abusive and exploitative, there is often a sense of deep injustice operating within them.

Remember, we all choose our incarnation. There are many, many beings who desire to become sled dogs. This is not an area where I need to look to recruit souls! There are some deaths among the young, and it is a practice of some breeders to terminate the lives of pups who are not considered fit to run. Some souls willingly enter into the sled dog body even with this chance. It is their choice.

There are too many dogs being bred at this time, and in the sense of "now a word from our sponsor" it would be best for human breeders not

THE SUBTLE, SILENT WAY
INKA (LLAMA) ~ TERA THOMAS

Whether our guides and teachers are living animals or spirit animals, individuals or groups, our lessons are uniquely suited for our particular needs. Some teachings may not make sense to us at first. Or, we think we understand, but then we find we haven't opened to the fullness of the lesson until much later. In addition, many of us—students and teachers alike—are not fully aware of the energetic lessons we hold simply by being who we are.

Inka, a llama who resides with Tera Thomas at Hummingbird Farm, notes that the way we understand our lessons corresponds to our own unique way of perceiving the world. For example, if we think in terms of subtle energy fields, we may understand an animal's teaching in those terms; whereas if our worldview does not include such things, we may simply note that we feel better being around a particular animal.

Many llamas are teachers, some in very quiet and subtle ways, and others in quite specific ways like me. All llamas carry the wisdom from the stars and balance it with the earth. We offer that gift of balance and knowledge to all who are open to receive it.

We work with the subtle energy fields of the earth and of specific physical bodies. For example, when we work with the humans that come to our home, we view their energy as a map of colors. If one color is missing or if there is too much of a color in a person's field, we assist that person to correct their balance. This is usually done without the person's conscious awareness, but often we will mention in the workshop that a specific color would be beneficial for that person. Also, we assist others to bring the energy of spirit through their bodies and to connect it and manifest it on the earth.

For people who don't want to think about energy fields or manifesting spirit, I would say, we just make others feel good. Many people who live with llamas could not tell you specifically what the llamas do, but they say that when they spend time with llamas the people feel more relaxed, their stress level decreases, and they just feel good. Who needs to know why? That's what some people think and that is okay with us. We are very pleased to do our work in that subtle, silent way.

Everything in this world has a hidden meaning . . . men, animals, trees, stars, they are all hieroglyphics. . . . When you see them, you do not understand them. You think they are really men, animals, trees, stars. It is only years later . . . that you understand.

NIKOS KAZANTZAKIS

to focus on income so much as quality of life and finding good homes for all animals who come to them. Our intolerance runs more toward breeders who work with calculations to see how many offspring their dogs might fetch in terms of dollar signs. This is far more exploitative than dogs running in a race and having purpose.

This is not easy information for some humans to hear. We feel it is the human perspective that is skewed on many of these animal issues. Rather than project on animals with a purpose, look to humans without a purpose. Or humans with a questionable purpose. Sled dogs love to race and to be part of a team spirit. If more humans tried this, perhaps you would find your own aggressive tendencies lessening.

~ IN LOVE, SLED DOG SPIRIT

A conversation with christina

Christina is a cow. Some might say she is no ordinary cow, though if you really listen to what Christina teaches, you soon realize that there is no such thing as an ordinary cow—or ordinary anyone, for that matter.

Christina lives with her writer friend Rita Reynolds, who also provides a hospice sanctuary for animals in Virginia. The following conversation between Christina and Rita reveals another facet of the student/teacher relationship—friendship. For when we peer beyond the fur, feathers, scales, or skin, we recognize in spirit our friends, family, teachers, cohorts, fellow voyagers in this incredible world. When we meet each other at these deeper levels and recognize who this being underneath truly is, we may be astounded. Who would have guessed your best old friend would be wearing a cow suit this time around?

"Christina, I know you are a cow, but since you came into my life, I have always felt there is so much more to you than, well, 'cow.' What do I sense?"

"My friend—and that about says it all. I came into your life not only as a very old friend and companion but also to help you see certain things more clearly. A partnership is what we share, because even though you are unaware of it on your conscious level, you asked for me to come to help you in your understanding. I could have come in any form, but chose that of cow because it is one I have experienced before and am particularly fond of. Of course, timing was important. I might have come a year or so sooner, but it would have not worked out."

"What do you mean?"

"You would not have been ready in your development to receive the words and wisdom I offer you. You have been writing them down for some time now—your therapy you call it! In fact, it is your soul's schooling."

"Yes, often when I sit down to write one of our conversations, what I originally thought I would write about changes the minute my fingers hit the keyboard! And what ends up on paper is something I need to understand or explore. And this is one such time, so may I ask you some questions?"

"Of course. I am in no hurry."

"Is life as precious as I believe it is? There are so many terrible things that happen, especially regarding war and hunger and disease. Why is life so great?"

"The answer to your question is simply, Yes. Life is even more precious than you think it is, because when you are thinking, you are using only your brain. If you allow yourself to be still for a moment and simply be in the present moment with your expectations absent and your senses wide open, you would be overwhelmed by the beauty and perfection of life.

When we learn to say
a deep passionate yes
to the things that really
matter . . .
then peace begins to
settle onto our lives
like golden sunlight
sifting to a forest floor.

THOMAS KINKADE

Life—living—alive—words can never express the true levels and layers and dimensions of life. It is so much more than what you think it is.

"For example, how many human beings think something is living only if that 'thing' has a skeletal frame, blood flowing through veins and arteries, eyes to see, ears to hear, a voice? I assure you that there is not one single thing in physical form, or in nonphysical form, that is not alive—not the barn, nor the chair nor the ocean nor the stone nor the sky nor the clouds—you get the drift?"

"Yes. But I have always believed that."

"But now you have to take it another step—and everyone needs to do so in order to properly function in life on this planet—and that step is knowing that everything that exists is created, is light manifested—and, therefore, worthy of respect always and in all ways. And that, dear heart, most definitely includes yourself."

"How can a person learn to live this way? There are some people and situations that are awfully hard to love and respect."

"You learn to live with respect for everything by, first of all, being humble—realizing that you are a being of light and wisdom that knows no bounds, and so is absolutely everything and everyone else. A blade of grass, a flea, a tick—the man who cuts you off in traffic—these are no different from you: light-soul manifested into form for a period of time in order to work on individual and group evolution. Everything that is manifested into form has knowledge, wisdom, emotion; every being makes choices, feels pain and joy, and has the capacity to love, because love is the interconnecting fabric of all beings.

"I know what you are wondering, How does a cow get to know all this stuff? Right? Well, cows are actually very expanded beings. Don't be fooled by our appearance and by the fact that usually we end up as shoes or steaks. None of that matters. What matters is that we cows are an enormous force—because of our numbers and size—for balancing the

energy flow on the planet. And it is our greater understanding of life that we bring to you, to all of humanity.

"Walk in a sacred manner. You've heard that Native American expression before; it is found with many people living close to the earth because they listen to all the beings and what they have to teach them. That's what you can do to learn to appreciate all of life. And I guarantee that you will live so much more joyfully, really overwhelmed for all the life-energy around you. Want to know how to start?"

"Yes!"

"Go sit under a tree, talk to it—ask all the questions you want, then be quiet and listen, listen, listen. Listen in complete appreciation, open to all possibilities. You may get words or pictures or colors or a tone in your head—whatever it is, accept it as true, and continue. That is all it takes!"

Christina and Rita
Photo by Michael Reynolds

wisdom through the ages

While I was sitting at the computer, finishing up this chapter and wondering if there were any other animal teachers appropriate to include, the puppy we recently adopted from our local shelter raced down the stairs and jumped up with her two dainty paws on my lap. Gazing into her small brown eyes, I saw she had that look about her—like maybe her wise self was sneaking around.

"Riza!" I exclaimed. "Do you have something to share?" As I told her about the book, she ducked beneath the desk and curled up at my feet—the very same position my other dogs use when they want to have a conversation. I realized, then, that a final note to this chapter must emphasize that teachers come to us in all shapes and sizes. Wisdom can be found all around us, all the time, even through a tail-wagging, black and white, Chow Chow–German Shepherd puppy.

OLD SOULS, YOUNG SELVES
Riza (puppy) ~ Dawn Brunke

My name is Riza. Even though I am a small puppy and have lots of wild energy, I bring a teaching to you.

My teaching is about having fun. Many pups and kittens bring this message if they live with humans—and some of us come to live with humans to have fun ourselves! Having fun is a universal message from many young animals—to have fun, to run with wild abandon, to explore everything because it is all so new, to sometimes get into trouble (that is often how we learn), to cuddle up beside you, to be here for you to take care of and love, and to be someone who loves you back.

Another lesson from puppies and kitties is that we grow up. How will your care and love for us survive as we become older and not quite as cute? Will you grow with us? Will our growth show you how you also

It is the supreme art of the teacher to awaken joy in creative expression and knowledge.

ALBERT EINSTEIN

Riza
Photo by Dawn Brunke

grow, from a baby to a toddler to a youngster and teenager and beyond? Will you accept each stage of life with the teaching it brings?

I am speaking from my older self now, the part of me who is more spiritual and knowledgeable. As a puppy, I can feel this guiding self, like a teacher. Sometimes when I sleep I renew myself with this energy—it comes from my teaching self, which is a part of me, and from my guides who help me in many ways—they helped me find you!

All animals come into your life for a reason. Sometimes we come for many reasons. I, for example, also heard the call of your dog Max, who said, "Every puppy needs a home," when you asked if he would mind sharing his home with a new puppy. I bring him the fun and games of being a puppy, but I also annoy him at times, and so I bring him that teaching. He offers me the teaching of learning the rules of the house and what it means to be part of a group of dogs in your home.

Thank you for asking my opinion. I am small and cute but I have an old soul inside me, too. So do all of you—we all have guides and teachers, old souls and young selves within ourselves. When you learn how to tune in—just as you are listening to me, and as others read what I am saying—you also learn how to tune in and listen to yourself. This is a very useful thing to know, so my advice is to use it whenever you can!

A LONGING TO CONNECT
Mother Energy ~ Tera Thomas

We represent the Mother energy of the planet. The Mother breathed her own breath into your lungs to give you life. This is the Mother we speak of—not your personal mother—The Mother. The Mother is an energy that is present and available in your own life. It is the energy of creation, the energy of protection, the energy of love and of trust. We come to you now to open in you a channel to the Mother energy to support you and assist you to grow.

Think of us, the mothers on your planet. Picture a cow with a suckling calf, a horse with her foal a deer with her fawn, a kitten, a puppy. A chimpanzee, a gorilla, an elephant . . . It does not matter which animal you relate to. If you look at a picture of that animal with a baby, something is moved in you, something so deep. If you have a very loving mother, perhaps the feelings that come up in you when you think about "mother" are joyful, loving, soft, warm, and fuzzy. But, no matter what your relationship to your birth mother is, the images of a mother bear, a mother seal, a mother of any other species can create in you a longing, an ache to be known and touched to the core of your being. It is a feeling so deep, so primal, visceral, this longing to connect.

Allow yourself to deeply feel your own longing to connect and open your heart to receive the Mother. You will be embraced and held so deeply it is indescribable. It is this feeling of connection that will heal the earth. Open your heart to receive this energy. You are part of us. We are one.

6
Animal Dreams

Once upon a time, I dreamed I was a butterfly,
fluttering over flowers, doing exactly as I pleased. I was
conscious only of being a butterfly. Suddenly, I awoke and
there I was, myself again. Now I do not know: Am I
a man who dreamed he was a butterfly, or am I a
butterfly dreaming I am a man?

CHUANG TZU

A long time before I ever heard of animal communication, I dreamed of an orange cat sitting on a table covered by a beautiful cloth tapestry. Moving closer, I noticed the cat was wearing a small fez atop her head. (A fez is a felt hat shaped like a shortened cone, usually red with a black tassel.) This was not an ordinary fez, but one made from a material that looked like copper. The hat had an ornate design intricately worked into the metal, and the tassel ended in a feather. Silent and still, the cat stared at me with an air of great inner confidence. And then I knew—this cat was *wise.*

That was the whole of the dream. When I awoke, I was very excited. I didn't know why, but I *knew* that the cat's presence was important for me. After recording the dream in my journal, I drew a sketch of the mysterious cat with the hat. I was sure she held a clue—not just to the dream, but to something larger, something that would eventually unfold.

Many years later, as I began working with animal communication, I had another dream in which the same orange cat appeared. As

Journal sketch of Dream Cat
by Dawn Brunke

The eye sees a thing more
clearly in dreams than the
imagination awake.

LEONARDO DA VINCI

before, the cat sat silent, staring at me, this time from high up on a
wooden shelf in a small room. Looking up at her, I suddenly realized
within the dream that I had seen this cat before! In fact, I recalled
not just the previous dream but many other dreams in which the
same remarkable orange cat had appeared.

This realization caused me to become lucid—to know within the
dream that I was dreaming. I remembered that there was always a
moment within the other dreams (most often just before waking) in
which I would know that I was going to forget the cat. To know that
you will forget—how frustrating! Still within the dream, I marveled
how it was possible that I could forget this strange, silent yet powerful cat. She was so extraordinary! Would I really forget her again?

On waking this time, I did not forget but immediately wrote
down the dream, along with my awareness of having dreamed this
cat many times before. I paged through old dream journals to find
the dream with the sketch of the cat and her fez. I wondered what
kind of message my dream cat wanted to share. I sensed the dream
presented an ongoing process. Indeed, it would take more time
before I was ready to meet the cat on deeper levels and begin a more
conscious form of communication.

An Animal Communication Project
CREATE A DREAM JOURNAL

One of the best ways to remember your dreams—and encourage future recall—is to record them as soon as possible. Keep a special notebook and pen by your bed to make it a habit. Over time this simple act will establish a bridge between your dreaming and waking worlds. Not only will you more easily recall your dreams, but your dream self will recognize that you find its stories worthy of notation and may reward you with deeper, richer, more powerful dreams. And you will have a permanent record of all your dreams to refer back to as needed. Title your dreams for easy reference. Or include small sketches to remind you of dream characters or places. No matter how you set it up, you will not regret it—a dream journal is invaluable!

Dream Animals

Some say that animals are the greatest teachers of the dream world. Why? By simply appearing in our dreams, an animal can convey a huge amount of multilayered information to our waking self. Say you dream of a deer in a forest. Is there a part of you needing comfort from her gentle, watchful nature? Perhaps she is encouraging you to find a more graceful way of moving in the world? Or, as an animal possessing acute vision and hearing, does Deer bring you the gift of heightened senses? What does your dream deer mean to you?

Dreams speak to us on many levels simultaneously. On the large, general levels, dream animals hold mythological meaning and archetypal truths. Deer may bring to mind the tales of King Arthur, for example, or other mythic stories of individuals lured into the woods to face new adventures. Dream animals also reveal totemic qualities—Deer's symbolic traits of innocence, humility, and gentleness, for instance. Animals are often the dreaming self's shorthand, used to convey rich textures of cultural and collective meaning to our waking mind.

But dream animals represent personal qualities as well. That is why my dream deer holds a message different from your dream deer. As messengers from our unconscious, dream animals reveal the secrets, riddles, and puzzles that are unique to our own understanding and development. Some dream animals support and encourage us by sharing their talents: a seagull showing us how to ride wind currents or a mouse revealing secret hiding spaces. In waking life this

DOLPHIN DREAM

I am driving on a bridge surrounded by ocean. I see ocean in front of me and on all sides. I am excited because I am on my way to see dolphins and whales. Suddenly, dolphins appear to my left, leaping and frolicking. I watch them with joy. "Where are the whales?" I wonder. "I really want to be with the whales," I think, feeling a little disappointed. I realize I have just moved out of the joy and the moment of seeing the dolphins by *thinking*. Focusing again, I see the dolphins reappear. I greet them and thank them. Looking straight ahead, I see there is no car and there is no bridge. I am consciousness joyously skimming over the surface of the ocean. Yes!

POLLY LAZARON

may mean that we need to meet new challenges by sensing the flow and rising to new perspectives, or we need to seek out safe places or positions that cannot be easily discovered.

Dream animals may come to teach, heal, or offer us their species' wisdom. For some humans this is a wonderful introduction to meeting a power animal. Dream animals may also awaken dormant energy, stimulating strengths and skills that we may not even know we possess. Some come as answers to our questions, offering new views and insights to those areas that confuse or trouble us. Animal dreams also offer a metaphoric mirror of how our inner self sees our outward self. What we do in a dream often reveals our relationship to our own personal evolution.

Sometimes animal dreams represent real events. In these cases a dream animal may be connected to a living animal. Some dream animals are animals we know from our past or present, while others show us future relationships. Illusionists Siegfried and Roy note that their involvement with the preservation of white tigers was hinted at many years before through a recurring dream. "We didn't know there was such a thing as white tigers," Siegfried explains. "Roy had a dream about tigers who were white, no stripes, no color. I told him 'I guess you're dreaming in black and white.'"[1] Roy was not dreaming in black and white, however, and the insistence of the dream led the two to learn more about white tigers, meet them, and eventually establish a tiger preserve.

Departed animals may also appear in our dreams, reassuring us that they have found safe passage to the spirit world. Some spirit animals use the dream state as a handy method of relaying news or advice. Sometimes, if a deceased animal cannot make contact directly, he or she may "call" another dreamer to relay a message.

Because we are often less judgmental and more open to creative

In dreams begins responsibility.
WILLIAM BUTLER YEATS

DREAM MESSAGE

One day, when my friend Karen was elsewhere, her Border collie, Tivy, was killed by a car. Karen was devastated. Although I did not know Tivy well, two weeks later in a dream a dog's face appeared in front of me. The dog grabbed my face with her paws and said, "I am Tivy. I belong to Karen."

She then insisted I tell Karen the following: "I am very happy I was with you. You made me happy. I came from a cold, dark, wet place to a warm, dry place with you. June 27th was a special day and you will always remember it. I am sorry I was hit by the car. I didn't mean to get hit, but there was something interesting and I went to check it out." Tivy also showed me how she was hit by a white fender of a truck. She was in the road and it happened quickly. I saw this happen through her eyes, her head turning as the white fender hit her—then spinning—then darkness.

After waking, I called Karen and told her my dream. We both cried and Karen told me that Tivy came from Wales, where it was rainy and cold. Karen had moved from Washington (also rainy and cold) to eastern Oregon, where it was hot and dry. June 27th was the last day Karen saw Tivy alive. Karen said that she had sat with Tivy that morning and told her she loved her. Although Tivy never knew me well, I felt honored that she chose to tell me these things to pass on to Karen.

DIANE PAGEL

possibilities while dreaming, some animal guides make first contact within our dreams. They may use the dream state as a means of teaching us, or as a prelude to meeting us in our waking world. Calling us to attention within our dreams, they invite us deeper into lessons that unfold beneath our conscious awareness.

The challenge, then, is to link dream consciousness with waking life. Part of our own discovery rests with how we hold, handle, and relate to our personal dream images on waking.

The Dream Does Not Forget

When the time is ripe, the memories awaken.

DREAM CAT

Once I was able to remember my mysterious dream cat in waking life, I noticed that she began working with me in a more attentive way. I dreamed of her more often. Though she would rarely speak to me in those dreams, she would look *into* me. A feeling would move between us, linking us so completely that I understood her beyond words. Upon realizing that this cat was one of my animal guides, I found I was able to communicate with her while awake as well as within my dreams.

Although the dream cat told me her name, I had an overwhelming sense not to speak this name to others. When I asked why this was so, she replied that certain names have power, most especially the sacred names that are whispered to us in our dreams or that unfold in special ways inside our consciousness.

"How do you know if a name is sacred?" I asked her once, and she looked at me long and hard, her dark eyes peering deep into mine. *"You'll know,"* she said. *"You'll know inside."* There was no denying that the Cat of Little Words spoke the truth.

"The reason I appear to you in dreams at different times is a means of measuring your readiness for my teachings," the cat told me one day. She went on to explain that because I have an affinity for dreams, her encounters with me work well that way. Further, my own pattern of forgetting our encounters and then remembering at a later

There is the dream journey and the actual life. The two seem to touch now and then, and perhaps when men lived less complicated and distracted lives the two were not separate at all, but continually one thing. I have read somewhere that this was once true for Yuma Indians who lived along the Colorado River. They dreamed at will, and moved without effort from waking into dreaming life; life and dream were bound together. And in this must be a kind of radiance, a very old and deep assurance that life has continuity and meaning, that things are somehow in place. It is the journey resolved into one endless present.

JOHN HAINES,
MOMENTS AND JOURNEYS

TIPS FOR DREAM RECALL

Let yourself linger. On waking, keep your eyes closed for a few moments to fully appreciate and recall any fleeting dream images. Enjoy the blurred boundary between sleeping and waking as you review your dream. Important details can often be recalled in this in-between state of consciousness.

Finesse the fragments. Sometimes all we remember is a fragment: a single image, word, or feeling. Although you may be tempted to dismiss it, treat one of these precious bits just as you would any dream—record it, sketch it, or speak it aloud. When given a little inquisitive attention, even the smallest fragment can become a key to unlock an entire dream.

Sleep on it. People of some cultures believe that what we sleep on can influence our dreams. Dream pillows (filled with memory-inducing herbs such as lavender, rosemary, and catnip) may stimulate your sense of smell to encourage memories. Another method involves placing a gemstone or crystal beneath your pillow as an aid to remembering. Or try using a small animal fetish, photograph, or even the word *remember* written on a piece of paper. It is the act of placing the object under your pillow with the intention of remembering that aids recall.

Ask for help. Before going to sleep, state out loud your desire to remember fully and effortlessly all of your dreams. Request assistance from your dream animal, dreaming self, or animal guide. The more energy you focus on recalling your dreams, the greater the rewards.

date is not uncommon when working with an animal guide, especially within the dream world.

"Some animals make use of the dream state because the mind is relatively quiet then, more sensitive to creative impressions and the blurring and merging of boundaries," she explained. *"Those of us working in the spiritual realm have some influence over images and patterns, and it may be easier to insert ourselves into your dreams than by other means."*

My dream cat went on to say that in her role as a guide she required a certain level of respect, and that this is often the case for other animal teachers and guides. *"The level of respect you show toward your guide is the level of respect you have for yourself."* She pointed out that having respect—a genuine, sincere approach—shows how a person attunes to guidance, and also reflects the quality of wisdom that might be offered in return.

"Most often we teach respect by being respectful," said my cat in the hat, showing me the many times she appeared in my dreams, always quietly watching, waiting for me to notice her. I understood, then, that her presence within my dreams was a teaching in itself, her quiet approach allowing me the respect of unfolding at my own rate.

I asked the cat if she had any suggestions for readers. She replied, *"If you wish to learn more about yourself and your world, my advice is to develop a respectful attitude and relationship with your dreaming self and with your dream guides, of whom you have many. Pay attention to the animals and all the figures that come to you in your dreams. Much more wisdom is offered through dreams than you would ever suspect!"*

The truth dazzles gradually, or else the world would be blind.

EMILY DICKINSON

Embracing our Dreams

Part of the enchantment of dreams is that we never know what they will bring. They simply appear: messages, inspirations, and encouragements artistically presented in vivid dramas, symbolic images, and meaningful events. We not only observe our dreams but participate, with starring roles. Because our dream self has choices, we are cocreators. And, on waking, we are reporters, spectators, witnesses to one of the most powerful and elegant forms of communication.

Working with dreams at deeper levels requires some effort to find and embrace a wide range of possible meanings. Like detectives, we apply keen observations skills as we search for hidden clues. Like artists, we appreciate the subtle symbols and graceful connections that weave between the dreaming and waking worlds. Like animal communicators, we learn to become skillful translators who can shift from one mode of language (be it animal talk or dream code) to our everyday awareness.

CARESSING THE DREAM

Though full of insight and power, dreams are also fragile—easily forgotten, easily neglected, easily pushed aside as we spring into wakefulness. Be gentle and patient with your dreams. Resist the temptation to instantly decide, "This is what my dream means" (though sometimes, of course, you will know instantly). Some dreams need a day, a week, even a year to fully blossom. Play with multiple meanings. Consider that some messages may change or become more significant as you grow in awareness. Seek out the hidden "dream within a dream." Some dreams are like time-released potions; they'll bring you a key insight or synchronous support just when you need it most.

A dream was presented to me just as I was on the verge of proposing this book to my publisher. In fact, I had been planning a different book when the idea for this one occurred quite suddenly. A nearly complete outline formed in my mind, and for several days it would not let go. Although at first I did not want to pursue this project, I felt something nudging me to consider the task. And then I had this dream.

The Frog Dream

In the dream I walk through the side entrance of a shopping mall. There, tucked in the corner wall to my right, is a lovely stone fishpond with a waterfall. I especially like that it is located away from the busy center of the mall. As I move closer to the pond, I remember that I have a frog in my pocket. He might really like this pond, I think, so I take him from my pocket and plop him in the water.

I walk to the center of the mall, but then—in that fast-forward way of dreams—I am back again at the pond. As I look into the water to check on the frog, I see that there are now many frogs and they are all huge—most the size of dinner plates. I am amazed by the immensity of the frogs!

I then notice one incredibly enormous frog, nearly the size of a man. He starts to crawl from the pond, not like a frog jumping, but like a person crawling out, first with one leg and then the other. As I back away, he moves toward me, not fast, but with determination. Panicking at the sight of this huge frog, I turn to run away, though after a short distance, I stop and laugh. "How silly is it to be running away from a frog?" I ask myself.

As my fear fades I wonder what the frog might want. Turning back I stand still and watch the frog as he moves closer, closer, until his dark green face is only inches from my own. He opens his mouth

I learned that there were two ways I could live my life: following my dreams or doing something else. Dreams aren't a matter of chance, but a matter of choice. When I dream, I believe I am rehearsing my future.

DAVID COPPERFIELD,
ILLUSIONIST

very wide, and I lean forward to hear him. As I do so, I feel a surprising fondness for the frog; somehow I know him. I smile and he says out loud, very gently, *"Thank you."*

what does it mean?

A dream which is not interpreted is like a letter
which is not read.

THE TALMUD

Some cultures distinguish between ordinary dreams and "big dreams." Big dreams are those that have a special significance for us. They are the dreams that sparkle and burn inside of us, urging us onward, inspiring, transforming, shifting us to ever more expansive states of consciousness.

What we do with our dreams on waking is often just as important as the dream itself. How we hold our dreams and relate to the clues we get often determines the amount of power, meaning, or significance available to us. In many ways dream interpretation is like seeking buried treasure. It requires a bit of searching and digging to uncover the gold.

Carl Jung wrote, "The art of interpreting dreams cannot be learned from books. Methods and rules are good only when we can get along without them."[2] Exactly so. As in most everything, techniques may offer a useful framework or point of beginning, but true learning comes from experience. When working with your dreams, follow your own intuition and inner guidance. Allow yourself to experiment, explore, combine methods, or create your own. You'll soon discover what works best for you.

six ideas for working deeper

1. Note feelings, ideas, and first impressions. Use your dream journal to jot down gut feelings and immediate insights about your dream. Consider similar animals you have recently met or associations that occur to you. Be candid, no matter how silly or strange your thoughts may seem. First impressions often give excellent clues and create worthwhile questions to pursue.

Example: After recording my dream, I noted how even little actions (plopping a frog in a pond) can have huge consequences (later meeting a huge, grown version of that little frog). I also noted recent events—my daughter putting a plastic frog on my desk, downloading a "smiling frog" screensaver from the Internet, and acquiring two dwarf frogs. Was "frog medicine" appearing in my life for a reason?

2. Take inventory of what you know. List facts about your animal in the wild: Where does it live? What are its special abilities? Is there anything unusual or remarkable about it? How does this relate to your dream?

Example: Fact 1—Frogs are amphibians, at home both in water and on land. The connection of water and land was hinted at in my dream as the frog moved from swimming in the pond to walking on land. This could be about fluid, unformed (or unconsciously based) ideas developing a firmer, ground-based (or more conscious) life of their own.

Fact 2—Frogs go through many changes very quickly, growing from eggs to tadpoles to froglets to mature frogs. This quick development was shown both in the dreamtime fast-forward and as the frog became huge very quickly. Did this reflect something about the sudden way in which my book outline was formed?

3. Research your animal. Use books, nature films, and the Internet to learn more about your animal. Be innovative; allow inspiration to

That which the dream shows is the shadow of such wisdom as exists in man, even if during his waking state he may know nothing about it. We do not know it because we are fooling away our time with outward and perishing things, and are asleep in regard to that which is real within ourselves.

PHILIPUS AUREOLUS
PARACELSUS

guide you in drawing from a wide range of sources—biological facts, wildlife observations, totemic qualities, mythic and symbolic connections. Take notes. Some aspects may not be immediately meaningful but will make sense later.

Example: Of all my research on frogs (most of which I did after speaking to the frogs), this passage about frog medicine spoke to me most powerfully:

> Frog knows that what seems strange today may very well be a comfortable reality tomorrow. Frog spirit calls out to shift your perception of your experience and not fear that which is different. It patiently embraces a spacious awareness of unmanifested potential. . . . If Frog has chosen to appear to you, it is asking you to encourage that part of yourself that is not only open to change but understands its benefits.[3]

4. Shift your perspective. Try retelling the dream by shifting your point of view. By seeing through the eyes of another dream character, you may discover fresh insights not only about the dream but about the dreaming "you" within your dream. Use your imagination to discover what other characters think and feel. You might also step out of all character viewpoints and tell the dream from the third person (objective) point of view, like a reporter. Pay attention to fresh details or emotions. Dream shifting can be a powerful way to uncover hidden material, bounce around ideas, conjure up questions, and appreciate your dream from new angles.

Example: Imagining myself as the small frog plopped into the pond, I felt happy and excited to explore my new environment. I met other frogs, played, and grew bigger. Being the large frog climbing out of the pond, I felt I had a mission to accomplish. I was cautious as I

stepped onto the hard floor, but I knew I had something important to do and must move forward.

5. Pull things together. Are you finding new clues to your dream? Are patterns emerging? Are your feelings about your animal or dream changing? Notice your fears, areas of uncertainty, or any area of big emotion—most often, that is your untapped gold mine.

Example: The dream felt good to me—its message strong and reassuring. The more I explored the dream, the more I felt it was about this book. I recalled the initial resistance I felt about this project as well as the magical way in which the outline seemed to write itself. What began as a small thing (a frog in my pocket—the idea of the book) was now taking on huge proportions and implications. Perhaps the "thank you" from the frog indicated that at a deep level I had already agreed to write this book, though my rational mind had not immediately caught on.

6. Consult your dream animal. Using communication skills, ask your dream animal to share its reason for appearing in your dream. You might contact the group spirit of your dream animal or an animal guide. Or you might ask to speak with your inner "dream writer" to discuss the dream.

A Talk with the frog people

To learn more about my dream as well as frogs in general, I was anxious to go directly to the source. One morning I had the idea to tune in to the "Frog People." Who were the Frog People? I wasn't sure, but I imagined them as a group of frogs holding the wisdom that lives within all frogs. Closing my eyes, centering my energy, I put out a general call to the Frog People.

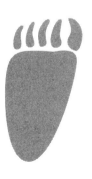

"Would you comment on this dream?" I asked. "I am interested in the significance of my dream frog. Also, do you have a message for young people reading this book, especially those who would like some advice on working with dream animals? Or perhaps some insights to the mystery of frogs," I added.

The Frog People replied that I was asking a lot of questions. They showed me this with an image of several small jumping frogs—a scaled down or "before" version of the many large frogs in my dream pond. The small frogs represented my questions, thoughts, and ideas jumping wildly with excitement, while the large frogs were the answers to the questions as they matured. The pond, they commented, was a dreamlike way of looking at a container of thoughts.

"Do you mean the pond is my brain?" I asked. The Frog People said no, not exactly, "*more like the shape of how you hold your thoughts.*" They continued, "*Your thoughts want to grow larger than your brain, and that is one of the personal interpretations we give you regarding this dream. You think a little thought and plop that idea in your brain, the holder of your thoughts. There, it interacts with other ideas and so grows in size, complexity, ambition, and desire. Soon, all of your ideas are larger. And then one gets big enough to have the courage and sensibility to crawl out of your container, which by now is simply too small for the frog creation, which is to say the idea of your book.*

"*It crawls out on its own and so becomes a different thing, a new way of being in the world. At first you are frightened of it—this big thing that has grown so much you can hardly recognize it—and so it comes after you. You are frightened, but why? Even you are not sure, except that this thing is no longer familiar. It has grown and changed. It frightens you because it is so different that you can barely recognize it as still being a part of you.*

"*This is a teaching of the Frog People, we who begin life as small sacs and become swimming heads with tails (tadpoles as you call them), then growing appendages with distinct, webbed phalanges, and so on. For humans, 'frogs' are an interesting group in that there are so many varieties of us. That is another of our teachings—our immense diversity. We exist in ponds and rivers and lakes; some of us live on land; some of us even bury ourselves and some of us live in cold conditions. We are able to surprise and delight you with our many variations."*

The frogs then reminded me of the two dwarf frogs who now swam in a large glass bowl in our living room. One night, soon after they arrived, I heard some high-pitched electric sounds and was certain it was the television going bad. The sounds came and went, and it took a good deal of convincing from my husband to prove to me that the noise was coming from the frogs.

"See? We are masters of surprise and intrigue. We slip between boundaries, and so we are about changing states of consciousness, changing your views. When you dream of frogs as you have dreamed of frogs, you find we speak about larger ways of seeing the world. We speak to diversity and enjoying the results that come from small things growing large, even if these things are not what you expect!

"Frog People are like earth People near the water. We are about fecundity and rich ideas simmering in the origins of evolution. Why do you think your storytellers chose a frog to be the magical vehicle into which a prince develops? Do you know?"

I told the Frog People I did not know. They gave me the assignment, then, to look at human stories and ponder why witches turned people into frogs and why princesses must kiss frogs to turn them back into princes. (This was a mythic connection I had not yet considered!) They told me this, too, was a teaching of the Frog People, who do not just give people answers, but make them work a little to deepen in understanding.

The myth of the frog prince relates to Frog's ability to perceive the true soul, the highest potential of everyone, which usually happens through the transformative power of love.

NICKI SCULLY,
POWER ANIMAL MEDITATIONS

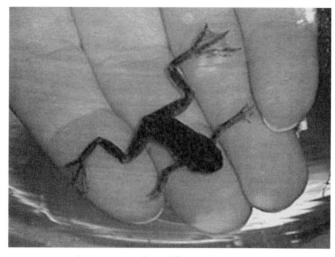

Dwarf Frog
Photo by Bob Brunke

"In the end, we are helpful to you in this way. We will hop along with you on your journey, but we are not here to simply give you answers. You must discover answers for yourself. We are the Frog People. We speak to digging deep, looking around while you sit on your lily pad. We speak to croaking and enjoying our sounds, our lives.

"Our advice to your young people is to find a quiet place and sit with a frog. This is another means of becoming more familiar with animals and all the animal nations of this incredible planet.

"We Frog People have been on Earth for many, many, many eons. We are a creative, fertile aspect of life and so we have been featured in many of your most inventive, creative stories, especially during times when fairies were alive and the world of magic was something to behold with a sense of wonder rather than derision.

"Now frogs are used by students to be dissected. Do you think you can know us any better that way than by fairy tales? Our answer is that each is a different type of learning. But neither view sees the Frog People for who we

really are. We do not believe you can understand us solely by the stories you tell about us or by slicing us open. That is your own way of seeing the world.

"If you want to know Frog People, come sit with us, listen to our songs. We speak about magical things happening under the water; about true, creative ideas and enterprises occurring right under your noses. If you want to truly see and experience the wonder and magic of frogs, then you too must become a Frog Person and listen—listen with all your inner ears and eyes. Center yourself in a froggy way. We speak to balancing inner thoughts with creating beauty and wonder in our world. We speak from an earlier time of human-animal interaction and we continue to hold that place for all to behold and wonder.

"We send greetings to all members of the human tribes.

"We are the Frog People of Dreams and Imagination, the Frog People of Planet Earth."

Those who dream by day are cognizant of many things that escape those who dream only at night.

EDGAR ALLAN POE

Dreams that Animals Dream

The dreams we have about animals may be symbolic, philosophic, or prophetic. They may present memories, telepathic connections, lucid encounters with animal guides, explorations of our inner world, or just plain romps of fun. But what of animals? Do they dream? If so, what kinds of dreams do they have?

Maya the cat told communicator Gretchen Kunz: *"Of course I have dreams! Often, when you think I'm dreaming, I'm spirit-journeying, doing a job, or catching up on local gossip. Or I might be thinking of past lives. I dream about flying a lot, because I used to be a bird once. I dream about flying and swooping down and catching things! I love it! Sometimes, when I'm sleeping, I'm just being—enjoying the pillows and the sun, or snuggling with my people. Sometimes I journey into their dreams with*

TRUST YOUR DREAMING SELF

Some dreams are scary. Some dream animals are not ones we like or expect to find, and some show us things we don't want to see. It takes a working relationship based on trust to accept our dreams for what they are. It takes courage to seek out the deeper understanding that our Dreaming Self has used precious energy to present to us. As we continue to dig, moving past judgment and fear, exploring our dreams on wider, deeper, more heartfelt levels, we may be surprised by what we find—the ferocious tiger who stalks us night after night is actually an ally; the huge mutant frog who chases after us brings us a message of confirmation and encouragement. Did you know that in some cultures, the dream state is considered a more "awake" version of reality? Shake loose your ego's judgment and welcome the message of every dream, no matter how it first appears. Trust the wisdom of your Dreaming Self.

Your vision will become clear only when you can look into your own heart. Who looks outside, dreams; who looks inside, awakes.

CARL JUNG

them and see what's going on. But, more often than not, I am spirit journeying. I have a lot of work to do. And I like it!"

Quan Yin, another cat who lives with Gretchen, had this to say about her world of dreams: *"I dream about lots of things. I dream about my mommy cat. I miss her. I dream of being close to her belly and heartbeat.*

"I dream about things that happened in the past. I've lived a lot of life-

times. My past in Egypt is very vivid. I was a little princess—just a minor one. Mostly life was very good. I wanted for nothing, and the Nile and the city were beautiful, when I got to see them. But I died very young. I was killed. That happened to princesses a lot in those days. Did you know that we worshiped cats back then? That's part of what gave me the idea to become one!

"I've also been a mouse, because I wanted to hide and not be found. I was pretty good at it, but it was sometimes hectic and sad. It feels very real to me when I dream about being a mouse. I run fast and I love my whiskers!

"I dream about cat spirits dancing. It is not always a dream; sometimes they are here with me. Humans don't always understand that. They don't understand that dreams and what is real can be the same. But they can be! The cat spirits dance around me. Sometimes they are slinky. Sometimes they dance on their hind legs and wave their paws. Sometimes

Quan Yin
Photo by Gretchen Kunz

we sing. I like singing. It reminds me of the old days, and dancing around the fire.

"To me, dreams and reality are not so different. Sometimes I see spirits in the air when I am awake. Does this mean they are 'dreams'? And sometimes I am thinking or communicating with someone like I do when I'm awake, when I'm really asleep. Does this make the dreaming 'reality'?"

MAX'S DREAM

While I was working on this chapter, my dog Max invited me to "come along" with him to experience one of his dreams. Intrigued by his proposal, I lay down on the floor beside Max, closed my eyes, got quiet, and waited for the show to begin.

The first thing Max showed me was an image of himself in a marsh. He told me that in this dream he was following a trail. As we moved along he pointed out small leprechauns and other creatures that jumped out and tried to divert him from his path. I had the idea that Max's dream was like a game, and he agreed. He told me he often traveled through the dream marsh and yet was continually waylaid by the shimmering flowers, teasing leprechauns, singing trees, and other things that prevented him from finding the end of the trail.

Max showed me other dreams as well. One was of running through a field that turned into a forest filled with incredible smells and shapes—soft pads of lichen; crunchy acorns; fat, smelly mushrooms; and chirping, burrowing woodland creatures. Another dream involved running very fast and taking a giant leap off a hill, sailing up high into the clouds, and race-flying through a misty, cloudy world. *"At first this is fun,"* Max said, *"but then not so fun because it is hard to get a footing,"* and as he said this I felt his legs twitch and shudder as they sometimes do at night.

When I asked Max to show me a favorite dream, he shared one

in which he sat at a dining table, like a human, eating all kinds of wonderful foods. I laughed out loud as he pointed out fancy dishes heaped with mashed potatoes, gravy, and different kinds of meat. Also on the table was a plate of chocolates—forbidden to him in waking life, but an obvious delicacy in the dream. He showed me a variation of this dream, in which many dogs sat around the table, as if playing at being humans and having a *"fine dinner."* Max said this was a funny dream, and I sensed it as a joke, like the silly painting of dogs seated around a table playing poker. Max told me he wasn't sure if this was a typical dream for dogs, but because he loved food—especially human food—it was a dream come true for him.

zak on Dreams

When I opened my eyes from sharing Max's dream, my dog Zak, such a wise old being, nudged me with his nose. He told me that he also dreams, as do many animals.

"Dreams vary according to animal species. Cats, for example, do a lot of dream work and are for the most part comfortable walking through dreams—one to another—and bridging that dreamtime to waking consciousness. Some animals actively travel in their dreams, and many animals spend much more energy and commitment in the dream world than humans do." Zak paused, as if considering. *"However, this is changing as more humans are opening to the resources of the dream world."*

When I asked Zak what he dreamed of, he replied that many of his so-called dreams are actually travels through space and time to meet with other beings, and that much of his dreamtime is spent there. *"There are many worlds coexisting with the one most humans know or accept as real,"* said Zak. *"There are countless worlds, in fact, each with its own unique properties. Traveling to different worlds—or channels of reality—through one's dreams is simply a matter of focus."*

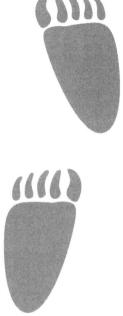

Zak, world traveler
Photo by Dawn Brunke

Like Maya, Quan Yin, and Max, Zak told me that he also dreams as humans dream. Sometimes it is for fun, he said—the sheer joy of running, chasing, jumping, or flying. There are many kinds of dreams, he pointed out: visionary dreams, travel dreams, meetings with other people and even with other parts of oneself. Zak felt it was especially important for humans to see our dreams as the meeting and coming together of the many different parts of our selves.

Zak shared with me a recurring dream he had of piloting a spacecraft. I was surprised when he showed it to me as a cartoon version of a dog in a small spaceship. When I asked if this was the same image he saw in his dreams, he said no, that the image was *"the meeting of your imagination with my dream."* He explained that while the cartoon image wasn't exactly how the dream experience was for him, it was a good way of understanding how dreams work— for they involve a translation or distinctive representation of how we see ourselves. Just like in animal communication, the way we understand our dreams is influenced by the framework we use to understand the world.

Zak then offered to dictate a message for this book, noting that it is especially for you.

WELCOME TO THE PARTY
Zak (dog) ~ Dawn Brunke

The dream world is vast and filled with many resources. My advice to readers is that you get out of a dream adventure what you put into it. Dreams are like having a conversation with your innermost self. They are gifts. Every dream is truly a gift that shows you something about yourself. What you choose to do with that gift is up to you—and that is a gift as well. Dreams do not demand of you. They only show you things that may be useful. They offer warnings, advice, suggestions, ideas, creative visions, and much more. If you want to get to know yourself, your true self—the self that sings the most beautiful song of the forest—you will listen to your dreams. The dream world is an invitation to a great party that is ever present. It is who you are.

LESSONS ON LUCID DREAMING
Dream Guides ~ Dawn Brunke

We are the Dream Guides. We work with connections, helping dreamers to become more aware of the subtle processes of your conscious, subconscious, and unconscious minds and the links between them.

For many it is easier not to be conscious when dreaming. If there is no seeming measure of control, then you can plead you are "not responsible" for your dreams. And, at one level of reality, this is true.

The area we focus on, however, is helping individuals to become more conscious of the dreaming process and your responsibility in manifesting your dreams.

By this we mean how your dreams are portrayed in the inner theater, and what you do with your dreams, what actions you take, how you "hold" them as you awaken and relate to them throughout your days. We look to the way you approach the sacred act of dreaming and dream interpretation.

There are different types of dreaming, just as there are different versions of reality that exist side by side, so to speak. It is not a geographical space that exists between the dreaming and waking worlds but a different vibration. So, too, the difference between unconscious dreaming and lucid dreaming is a matter of perspective.

Unconscious dreaming is often a lesson for the conscious mind to discern or learn from. It is a reflection of other dimensions—sometimes a reworking or re-imaging of problems with which the deep psyche is wrestling. You might think of it as an anagram for some aspect of your life. Prophetic dreams offer guidance by blending or merging times—past to present, future to present, or even alternate life to present life.

Lucid dreaming is in some senses a more advanced form of dreaming, but only from your present perspective. In other cultures and times, when lucid dreaming was widely practiced, unconscious dreaming was considered the more advanced because it was seen as a gift from the gods, from the deep nature of one's being.

With lucid dreams, you are intentionally forging a pathway or link between two states of consciousness. Everyone can do this; it merely takes patience, desire, intention, and some practice telling oneself before bed that one desires to awaken within the dream. (At times, dream guides may hold on this request, if it is deemed that lucid dreaming is not appropriate, but most who come to this form of teaching will be aided by their dream guides.)

One form of dreaming is not better than another; rather, they are different forms of the same process. One must learn to use the gifts of each.

PART THREE

Deepening in Relationship

7
Animal Healing

We think that the point is to pass the test or to overcome
the problem, but the truth is that things don't really get
solved. They come together and they fall apart. Then they
come together again and fall apart again. It's just like that.
The healing comes from letting there be room for all of this
to happen: room for grief, for relief, for misery, for joy.

PEMA CHODRON,
WHEN THINGS FALL APART

A few months after our big black Lab Max found his way into
our home, he hurt his eye while playing outside in the woods. The
lid was swollen and he could not easily see from the eye. Although
a situation such as this might normally warrant a trip to the veteri-
narian, something stopped me. On the surface, I worried that I did-
n't know enough to handle this problem. But on a deeper level, I felt
called to healing.

After cleaning and treating the wound, I centered and focused on
Max. He assured me it was a superficial cut and that what he needed
most was to close his eyes and rest. *"Trust yourself,"* he said to me as
we ended our conversation. Later, I was struck by the implication of
those words, for trusting the call to healing was something that
would bring about a much deeper change than I ever would have
imagined.

I did some neck massage and energy balancing on Max while he

rested. With one hand placed lightly over his forehead and eye and another resting gently at the base of his spine, I imagined soothing pink-white light bathing his eye and flowing easily through his body. Max slept deeply for a few hours. During the ten minutes or so while I was working with Max, my daughter, Alyeska, who was then four years old, watched intently. She wanted to know what I was doing, what energy was, and how to find the pink light. When she sat beside me and put her little hands on Max to help make him better, I was reminded that we are never too young to participate in a healing relationship.

Alyeska then wanted to make a "potion" to help Max. What kind of potion, I wanted to know. Like a magic spell? Laughingly, Alyeska said, "No, Mom. Let's make a potion of *real* healing things!" And so, together, we collected "healing things" for Max: a crystal (to see clearly), some tiny flowers (to observe beauty), a penny (for luck). As we looked around for more, I suggested that we make a pouch to hold these things for Max to wear. Alyeska liked the idea. We sewed a small pouch and Alyeska drew a red heart on a piece of paper to put in with the other healing things, which by this time also included some dried mint and lavender. Placing all of the healing things into the pouch, we sewed it shut and tied it securely to Max's collar.

From the moment we placed the pouch on his collar, Max moved with a new sense of pride. It brought tears to my eyes to see this change: it was evident throughout his whole body and demeanor. Clearly Max knew we had given him something special, that we had pierced beneath the surface in caring for him, and because of this, he felt "beloved" by our family in a deeper way. I was even more surprised to find my own vision shifting, too. Something had happened in just a few short hours, and suddenly I was seeing Max in a whole

Max and Alyeska
Photo by Dawn Brunke

A healing relationship between the animal and human kingdoms must be a co-creative one, and an important first step in any co-creative relationship is to examine our perceptions.

STEVE JOHNSON,
THE ESSENCE OF HEALING

new light. I was touched by what I hadn't seen before: the enormous amount of love this dog held for our family.

Of course, it wasn't the pouch or potion that brought about this change but the energy that was activated throughout the process of making the pouch. It began with the "call" to trust, to go with the flow of events, to welcome others (my daughter) into the healing venue, to open to unexpected ideas (the potion, the "healing things") and expand upon them (the pouch). Max's hurt eye was merely the symptom, and although we treated the symptom, it was what happened beneath the surface where true healing occurred.

And now here is my secret, a very simple secret:
It is only with the heart that one can see rightly;
what is essential is invisible to the eye.

ANTOINE DE SAINT-EXUPÉRY,
THE LITTLE PRINCE

sensing past the symptoms

Symptoms are our body's way of giving us clues, telling us that something is not quite right. Some symptoms, such as cuts, broken bones, or burns, require immediate attention. To treat only the symptom, however, and ignore the underlying problem that caused the symptom in the first place, is to miss out on the deeper nature of healing. Symptoms are often treasures, great mysteries that—if explored—show us more about who we are.

For example, was the reason Max hurt his eye (as opposed to his paw or tail) an indication of something that needed to be seen more clearly? Was the injury an invitation to become aware of another perspective, to peer beneath the surface of things? Or, was it a reminder that sometimes we need to pay more attention to ourselves when racing wildly through the forest?

Holistic healing is about digging deeper than symptoms, treating not just the clues but seeking and addressing the core causes of disease or imbalance that manifest the symptoms. For what is disease other than dis-ease, an imbalance within ourselves? Holistic healing focuses on the whole individual. In fact, the word *holistic* comes from the Greek *holos*, meaning "whole."

As we embark on any deep healing journey, we will inevitably discover an amazing interconnected network of thoughts, feelings, emotions, and bodily symptoms. Deep patterns are involved—from

If we approach this work with open hearts and minds we will be able to receive many valuable insights as to what is really taking place on the soul level within the animal kingdom.

STEVE JOHNSON,
THE ESSENCE OF HEALING

ANIMAL HEALER
MAURICE ~ GRETCHEN KUNZ

I am a healer cat. I balance energies, although I am not always a balancer. I balance energies, for example, when my human is sad or when she is communicating with other animals.

I do not mess with things on a grand scale. I am a healer in that I concentrate on the here and now and love and feeling good and goodness around me and you. By making people think of me instead of their problems, they feel better. Also, when they feel better and I am petted, I feel better, too. So what's to lose?

We should all be fed well and sleep and exercise and get lots of touching and love and good energy all the time, and that's what I focus on. With that, you can heal all sorts of wounds, whether they are in your spirit or in your brain or in your body. Don't you see?

Maurice
Photo by Gretchen Kunz

cellular to soul related, all reflected in who we are and what symptoms we have at any given moment in our life. The holistic approach acknowledges that our physical, mental, emotional, and spiritual facets all play an essential role in the totality of our being. We are not just a corporeal body or a collection of thoughts or impulses—and neither is any other animal. In all areas of healing, we need to listen to the body as well as the mind; we need to hear the call of feelings as well as the stirrings of the soul.

How do I know the world?
By what is within me.
LAO-TZU

finding center

So, what does it mean to listen to the body or sense the stirrings of the soul? How do we do such a thing? First, we must realize that we all fluctuate from moment to moment in the way we relate to the world. Our "center" can shift easily, and often.

For example, when we make cool, calm, rational decisions we are focused in our head center. This center is all about our thoughts, ideas, beliefs, and how we make sense of things. When approaching healing from the head center, we want to know the facts of a situation. We might list symptoms as signs or indicators and then search for patterns of correspondence between the mental, physical, and emotional aspects. We might seek insights from medical research, alternative healing studies, ancient cures, and home remedies to determine the best techniques to address the problem.

When we have a gut feeling or instinct, we are often sensing from our belly center. From the belly, we relate to the world in a visceral way. This center tells us how we "stomach" ideas or "digest" information. If we come to healing through our belly center, we learn to trust our instincts. With practice, we can sense when things are not right before physical symptoms appear, and we may even learn to pinpoint what those things might be. Coming from our belly, we are guided by hunches, instincts, intuitions, and feelings.

Our heart center reflects our emotional connection to the world. This center loves to have heart-to-heart talks and warm, meaningful, heartfelt interactions. If we come to healing from the heart center, we open ourselves to the deeper levels of another being—and we may even go so far as to meet at a soul level. A centered heart does not judge or discriminate; rather, it sees and feels what is, accepting the world with unconditional love.

To work effectively with others in a balanced, healing way, we need to find balance in our own centers. Drawing upon the wisdom of our head and heart and belly, we make use of all our resources and find the most appropriate responses for each situation. Using our mental abilities, we assess a situation and discern whether emergency care is needed or not. Using gut feelings, we sense underlying causes and are intuitively guided to appropriate healing therapies. Using our heart, we meet our patient in a profoundly caring, connected manner, thus encouraging self-healing to begin.

While this sounds like a wonderful plan, the truth is that we will all have moments of doubt and confusion. When I first saw Max with his bloody, wounded eye, I was frightened. That initial fear knocked me so far off balance that my head center seized up and began telling me that I knew nothing and could not properly treat a wound and what was I even thinking to imagine such a thing? Luckily my belly center did not jump into fear. Instead, my intuition heard a different call. That part of me was centered and strong enough to calm my thoughts. As soon as I let go of my worries and fears and began following the flow of healing energy, all doubt disappeared. My thoughts returned to center and even brewed up some brilliant ideas to make use of specific healing

First, do no harm.

HIPPOCRATES

techniques. As I allowed my hands to touch Max, our hearts engaged, and I felt a rise in consciousness to what was real and whole.

And that's really how it works: sensing our way with all facets of our centered selves, to simply "be" in that healing space of unity—with ourselves and with others. It's from that place of balance that we feel the movement of healing energy and begin to flow with it, thus becoming a tool of healing. As my dog Zak later told me, *"The point is to listen and trust. To find a space of centeredness and then be open to hear whatever you need to hear."*

LISTEN TO THIS . . .

Isn't it incredible how just talking with someone—be it human or animal—can be a truly healing experience? Many humans benefit tremendously from pouring out their feelings to their animal friends—whether or not they believe their animal understands. Similarly, many animals are greatly helped just from knowing their person cares enough to contact an animal communicator or try themselves. Most domesticated animals are extremely sensitive to our emotions. They know when we are attempting to help and when we show respect and consideration by listening to what they have to say.

It is by listening deeply—or being listened to—that we engage the energy of healing. We feel understood when others listen to us attentively, without judgment. In such a space, we are free to share parts of ourselves that we may not even have been aware of before. It is as if we are finding ourselves anew, unfolding ourselves, expanding in an exhilarating, healing way. In listening deeply, we open to another and are opened in return.

The power of touch

One of the oldest and most basic forms of healing energy is that which you hold within your own two hands. It's true. Touch is literally life-giving. Without touch from their mother or others, most newborn socially dependent animals do not survive. The power of touch is nothing short of miraculous. Not only that, it's completely natural!

With animals, touch can be a wonderful and truly moving form of communication. It is a gateway, allowing giver and receiver to commune at deep levels and set in motion the natural healing wisdom of the body.

There are many different forms of hands-on healing techniques. *Bodywork* is the general term used for various massage and movement-based forms. Some types address the muscles and soft tissues of the body; others work on structural alignment of the spine and bones; and still others focus on the flow of subtle energies within the body.

The benefits of bodywork are many. Different forms are good for reducing anxiety and tension; encouraging circulation and range of motion; increasing flexibility and energy flow; enhancing relaxation, health, and well-being. These are all terrific rewards. And yet, what truly allows any deep form of healing to unfold is the underlying connection we make within the healing process. By meeting another being (or a deeper layer of ourselves) in a shared space of communion, we can travel together to discover the energy that binds, knots, or obstructs. We can even travel *into* that energy, moving with it, unwinding it, following its natural ability to heal itself.

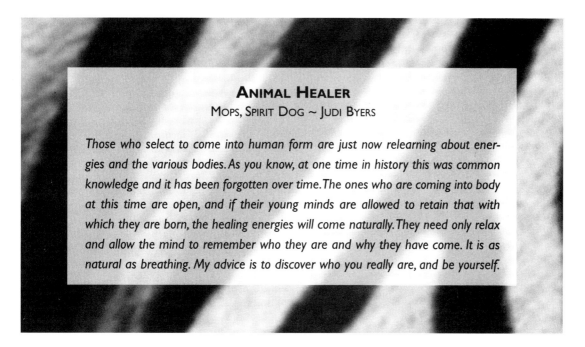

ANIMAL HEALER
MOPS, SPIRIT DOG ~ JUDI BYERS

Those who select to come into human form are just now relearning about energies and the various bodies. As you know, at one time in history this was common knowledge and it has been forgotten over time. The ones who are coming into body at this time are open, and if their young minds are allowed to retain that with which they are born, the healing energies will come naturally. They need only relax and allow the mind to remember who they are and why they have come. It is as natural as breathing. My advice is to discover who you really are, and be yourself.

meeting the Healer within

Our bodies all possess an inherent healing wisdom. In fact, some say all we need do is awaken our "inner physician" or "healer within" to begin healing. For, when returned to a state of centered balance, the body naturally heals itself. Blockages from stress, injury, or disease begin to release as the healing life force energy that surrounds us all flows through easily and effortlessly.

> *There is one way of breathing that is shameful and con-*
> *stricted. Then there is another way; a breath of Love that*
> *takes you all the way to infinity.*
>
> RUMI

Dr. Milton Trager, a physician who developed his own form of bodywork, used the phrase "hook up" to describe the remarkable feeling of becoming one with healing energy. Trager believed that by moving into a state of hook-up himself, his clients would naturally follow.

If you achieve hook-up while doing bodywork, you experience an undeniable sense of how to move, where to work, exactly how much pressure to use. You are in the flow and the energy is moving through you, guiding your fingers, using your hands as a tool of healing. You become part of an energetic dance, your centers merging in a flowing current of sensing and being. Your animal feels it too. You are both hooked up and attuned to the universal energy flow.

How to find hook-up in yourself and an animal friend? It starts with becoming aware of your body and breathing. You are shifting to that balanced space within all of your centers that is calm and deeply present. This is the same as the way you achieve animal communication, for as you deepen, you naturally open yourself to all beings, all energy around you. Like animal communication, hook-up isn't something you do; rather, it is a way to be.

The best way to learn how you work is to practice by sensing a lot of different energy fields. Just as in learning animal communication, learning to feel energy is a process of exploration and fine-tuning.

finding entrance

Linda Tellington-Jones discovered her famous TTouch healing method for animals unexpectedly. She was trying to teach students to intuitively listen to an animal's body with their hands. This is something that is very natural and easy to do once you experience it, though difficult to describe. When a student working on a horse became frustrated, Tellington-Jones told her to make circles on the horse's body and breathe into them. As Tellington-Jones relates, "It was something that came out quite spontaneously, without thought, but it turned out that the little circles allowed her to focus both her own and the horse's attention at the same time, and in a way that brought a deep sense of communion."[1]

This sense of communion is the key to all good bodywork. It is the same essence as Trager's hook-up—a connection so deep and central that all superficial separations begin to disappear. As Tellington-Jones puts it, "The TTouch always makes me think of the rabbit hole in *Alice's Adventures in Wonderland*—it looks so innocent on the surface, yet it is an opening to a whole new magical world. You make circles holding your fingertips, your fingers, or your hand in various positions using varying pressures. Simple. But these simple circles, like the rabbit hole, are an entrance, a doorway into a whole different dimension of relationship with your animal."[2]

Finding the gateway, sensing hook-up, sliding down the rabbit hole—these are all doorways to deeper connections. Every technique is a doorway. And it is wonderful that we have so many doors to choose from! The simple motions we make on the surface—be they circles or rocking movements, massages or healing pouches—are entryways to the energetic presence of healing.

ABOUT ANIMAL HEALERS
KC (cat) ~ Morgine Jurdan

Animals are capable of healing in many different ways. When there is stress in the home or when people are ill, animals do their best to restore balance by healing work. Some give healing energy, like a cat resting on your lap or snuggling up by your head. Some communicate with you and make suggestions about releasing anger, changing jobs, taking a workshop, and so on. Some work with you in dreams. Some transmute things with their own bodies after clearing your energy fields. A cat's purring is healing itself. Animals can send healing to you and others who live far away. Animals are capable of being in more than one place at a time. Sometimes they encourage you to play with them because you are the one needing to relax and unwind and release your stress. This applies to all kinds of animals, not just cats and dogs.

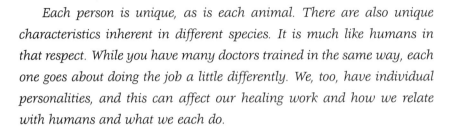

Each person is unique, as is each animal. There are also unique characteristics inherent in different species. It is much like humans in that respect. While you have many doctors trained in the same way, each one goes about doing the job a little differently. We, too, have individual personalities, and this can affect our healing work and how we relate with humans and what we each do.

Building and Expanding Your Healing Repertoire

If you feel called to the path of healing, it is useful to have a range of techniques to draw upon. By familiarizing yourself with a variety of modalities, you will discover different ways of doing things and gain insight on which methods work best for you, for your animal, and for particular problems. As you learn more about holistic healing, you will build a larger "healing toolbox" from which to choose the perfect approach for each situation.

Just a few of the many excellent healing methods for humans and animals alike include the following.

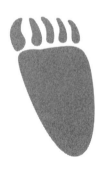

Acupressure: Developed in Asia more than five thousand years ago and similar to acupuncture, this method uses finger pressure to stimulate points on the energy meridians of the body. Easily combined with massage, acupressure encourages the flow of *chi* (energy) to promote the body's innate healing power.

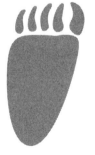

Massage: As an ancient form of healing, massage techniques vary widely: from kneading, tapping, shaking, and rubbing muscles to manipulating the deep tissues, joints, and organs of the body. Massage affects the entire body and supports the body's natural healing abilities.

Reiki: Discovered in the 1800s by a Japanese doctor, Reiki (the Japanese word for "universal life energy") involves transmitting healing energy through placing the hands on or above the body. Because Reiki is gentle and noninvasive, and can be done at a distance, it is often an excellent choice for animals.

Tellington TTouch: Linda Tellington-Jones developed her distinctive bodywork method of circular movements especially for animals. TTouch can calm animals, increase body awareness, encourage healing, and uncover solutions to behavioral and physical problems.

Trager: Created by physician Milton Trager, this system uses gentle rocking motions to help release muscle tightness and energy blocks along with the physical and mental patterns that may have caused the blocks. Although designed for humans, Trager movements are easily adapted to animal massage.

(For more information on these modalities, as well as others mentioned in this chapter, see the resources section.)

The following activity (primarily designed for dogs or cats) features some basic moves to give you an idea of the many creative things you can do in a bodywork session. As a former teacher of massage, I encouraged students to learn a technique well enough to make it their own. Once you have mastered a basic movement, have fun playing with it, combining it with other moves, and adapting it to fit your own style.

An Animal Communication Activity
A HANDS-ON HEALING MASSAGE
Beginning

- Choose a quiet place, away from distractions.

- Let your animal settle into a comfortable position. As your animal shifts positions, work with the area that presents itself. While you may encourage your animal to turn, never forcibly move an animal to accommodate your actions.

- Before touching your animal, take time to center: clear your thoughts, breathe deep, relax.

- Talk softly to your animal, explaining what you'd like to do. Use a gentle voice to calm your animal, but gradually let silence take over.

- A word on pressure: always start light and easy. Increase pressure gradually, as the technique and your animal's body require. Some animals love deep massages; others prefer a light touch. Trust your hands to sense the perfect amount of pressure.

- Begin with short periods of time. For some animals, two to five minutes is plenty. Let signs of anxiety or irritation be your cue to finish.

- It can be very helpful to familiarize yourself with the basic anatomy of your animal (bones, muscles, and energy meridians) before doing bodywork—see the resources section.

- Let the experience be a journey—not only an opportunity for you to practice massage and your animal to receive but a healing partnership in which you follow the flow of energy together.

Making Contact

With your animal resting beside you, begin with light petting strokes down the back, head, shoulders, and hips. Your palm is flat, fingers relaxed, and your hand is moving slowly, easily, gently along the fur line.

It is usually best to position yourself so that the majority of your massage strokes are made away from you (so that you are pushing rather than pulling your hand). Let your other hand rest lightly on your animal's side or shoulder. Your stationary hand is a support, a means of reassuring your animal that you are fully present and attentive.

Deepening

Gradually slow your strokes and slightly increase pressure, following the natural curves of the body. Move along the fur line—down the neck and back, around the curves of the shoulders, hips, and legs. As you stroke each area, sense a little deeper with your fingers and palm. Your touch does not necessarily become heavier, but your intention or focus sinks in and shifts to a listening, perceiving mode. Let go of thinking and doing and *feel* the connection. It may help to close your eyes. With practice, you will find that your

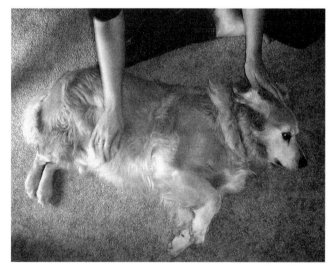

Ahh, Massage!
Photo by Bob Brunke

hands become incredibly sensitive tools, able to sense tight muscles, knots, sluggish areas that need more circulation, and points of blocked energy.

Playing with Technique

Palm Circles: With your palm flattened and fingers slightly curled, shift from straight strokes to lazy circles around the major muscle groups of the body. Now, instead of moving your hand over the fur, imagine your hand sticking to the fur, holding with just enough pressure to move the skin underneath. You are loosening, opening, and encouraging movement and relaxation. Let your hand move as you feel guided, varying circle size and pressure. Some areas need only light pressure, while your palm will naturally sink deeply into others.

The Crawl: Slightly cup your hand and curve your fingers. Now, using your fingertips as anchors, slowly pull your palm toward them, allowing the palm to slide or "crawl" along the body until your hand is fully curved. Extend fingers and repeat. This is a fun way to travel from one area of the body to another while staying connected to your animal.

Petrissage: For areas that feel heavy, blocked, or tight, try a little petrissage. This involves lifting, kneading, squeezing, or rolling the skin between your thumb and fingers. Start slowly and gently; then increase the pace and pressure as you feel moved. Scoop up the skin and muscle, gently rolling it between your fingers and the base of your palm. Petrissage is an invigorating action that can work wonders with tight, strained muscles.

Fine Finger Moves: Starting at the base of the neck, place your index and middle finger on either side of the spine and sink in while making small side to side motions down the back. Make small circular movements around the neck and head, jaw line and base of ears. (Some animals also like their ears massaged.) Let your fingers play, varying pressure and motions. Use all your fingers, just one, or any combination. Use fingers and thumbs to sink gently (don't push!) into muscle attachments and joints of the body; hold for a few seconds and sink deeper still. (When done correctly, the entire muscle may suddenly relax.) Experiment and discover what your animal friend likes best.

Rock-a-Bye Body: With your animal lying sideways, rest your hands on the spine and gently rock the body. As you push or pull with a very easy, encouraging movement, your animal's body rocks back in return. Your motions are light, effortless, accommodating. Gradually move your hands up and down the spine, rocking each part of the back and ribs. As your animal relaxes, his or her entire body is moved by the rhythm. This motion begs for creativity, so allow your animal to guide you, moving one or both hands as you are called. Some animals will turn belly up and invite you to rock them from side to side. Rock the shoulders, the hips, the legs. Vary your tempo; it's a dance of energy and movement.

Ending

It is nice to end a massage just as you began—with long strokes down the back. This is reassuring and calming, and it gives a good sense of closure. Let your hands rest at the base of the spine or upper back for a moment before disengaging. Thank your animal for accompanying you on this healing adventure.

Nobody sees a flower—
really—it is so small it takes
time—we haven't time—
and to see takes time, like
to have a friend takes time.

GEORGIA O'KEEFE

Every massage is different, for we are all in a constant state of change. The most important thing you can do, therefore, is to tune in and listen—listen deeply—to your animal, to yourself, to the energy that connects us all. Let the technique be a vehicle to bring you to that feeling of connection, of hook-up, of sliding down the rabbit hole. Allow your animal, your feelings, and the healing energy that is all around us to show you exactly where you need to go. Let all of these be your teacher.

Remember, the bodywork techniques listed in the activity above are basic suggestions and starting points. As you learn and practice, your abilities will grow and you will know how to position yourself, how much pressure to apply, and which techniques to use.

Before using any healing modality, it's wise to experience it yourself. Exchange neck and shoulder massage with a friend, or practice massaging your thighs or arms to get a sense of what the different pressures and strokes feel like. You might also schedule a healing treatment for yourself or your animal with a massage therapist or other bodywork practitioner.

The more massage you do, the more sensitive you'll become. Not only will you help your animal relax, but as you slow down and tune in to the flow of energy, you will also relax. You will learn how to listen with your inner ears and see with your inner eyes. You will deepen your intuitive skills and come to know the natural healing wisdom of the body. Congratulate yourself!

ANIMAL HEALER
TOBY (DOG) ~ JUDI BYERS

Healing is natural and we can all be doing it without the drugs so common today. Humans move too fast—always in a hurry, makes the physical body in a hurry and it wears out much too early.

I like to work with all forms of life, but humans are so funny. They have set up so many blocks—you call them beliefs—which make it difficult to accept the healing energies. Animals always accept the energies, although they may utilize that energy to transition rather than heal the physical body.

When I get on the table to help humans, I work with the meridians along either side of the spine, and then individual chakras. In this body, I am barely big enough to cover one chakra, so I have to expand my field to accomplish the full energy connection. I like to walk up and down the spine, aligning energies. Then I place myself at the root where I can clear the channel. If you saw me, you would just think I was asleep.

Toby on massage table
Photo by Judi Byers

other Types of Healing

In addition to bodywork, there are many other healing modalities. Some work with vibrational energy, such as sound therapy and chakra and aura balancing. In these, particular sound tones or vibrational movements are used to energize, calm, strengthen, or soothe the body's energy into balance. Other therapies, such as Bach flower remedies and gem and flower essences, enlist the healing properties of plants and nature to encourage healthier, more expansive vibratory rates. These essences (taken in a liquid form) work gently yet powerfully with the natural energy patterns of both humans and animals.

Healing can occur at any time, any place. And, if we open ourselves to the grand realm of possibility, healing can occur through us in the most fascinating ways.

For example, consider the way some healing fairies came to the aid of animal communicator Patti Henningsen while she was working with her rabbit, Horatio. Because hints of the fairies had previously appeared in Patti's life, their presence was available for her to call upon. She explained that while working to help Horatio she felt the need for some helpers and, "the fairies just sort of materialized.

"Although I'm not terribly in touch with my Celtic heritage, I think it has come into play with this. Joseph Campbell said that our mythic heritage is part of our psychological blueprint. Prior to working on Horatio, I had witnessed small balls of light dancing around the front door and in the flower garden. I later discovered this is often how humans see fairies—as dancing balls of light.

"It is also interesting that fairies and rabbits are often linked together. They are both crepuscular, most active at dawn and dusk. Through research, I learned that fairies love rabbits and will sometimes disguise themselves as rabbits. It is also said they surround

HORATIO, TOPAZ, AND FAIRY HEALING

I noticed my little rabbit Horatio's damaged tear duct was blocked again. Every time it backs up, he has to be anesthetized and have it flushed with a needle. This time, I lay next to him and imagined many little fairies dancing around his tear duct. I saw them pulling out the junk and repairing the duct. I saw them "kissing it with gold" by taking their tiny wands and tapping the duct, exploding it with fireworks of regenerative fairy dust. Sometimes after I imagined a repair, the work would be reversed and I'd have to repeat it. But eventually it was done.

Horatio
Photo by Patti Henningsen

The next morning when I checked on him, Horatio was bright eyed, with gunk all over his cheek—his tear duct was flushed! As soon as I saw that, Topaz, my little-old-lady rabbit who is twelve years old and has chronic renal failure, danced around. I heard her clearly say, *"If you can do that for him, you can do the same thing for my kidneys!"*

When I later worked with Topaz, I imagined little fairies working in her kidneys. The next day Topaz had cut her water intake and I had never seen her in such a relaxed state. Kidney disease can be devastating, but there she was lying on her side, happy as can be. It was miraculous!

The "proof" came from the vet a week later. Results from a blood test showed her kidneys to be in perfect shape! Isn't that amazing?

PATTI HENNINGSEN

rabbits to protect them, so maybe this is what happened when I scanned Horatio—I met his fairies!"

This is another dimension of animal healing, and many healers call upon helpers such as fairies, angels, spiritual assistants, and others to assist. Our animal guides may also play a role as healing partners or teachers. As Lewis Mehl-Madrona, a clinical psychologist, family physician, and author notes, animal guides can have deep, life-long teachings for us, if only we are wise enough to observe, listen and learn:

> Coyote has been my guide for years. Our animal helpers choose us more than we choose them. I've always been drawn to coyotes, and they to me. I wanted a wolf, eagle, or bear as my muse, but I got Coyote instead.
>
> Coyote has taught me the wisdom of making people laugh, of helping people to take themselves and their painful situation less seriously as a precursor to healing. I work like Coyote. I give people experiences that challenge their usual worldview. I introduce constructive chaos, trusting the inner healer in all my patients to reorganize perceptions and beliefs toward a state of greater healing. I teach people to welcome the unexpected, learning flexibility and resiliency.[3]

The Healing Space

One of the most important things we can remember is to be open to the flow of the healing, whenever we are called to it. The experiences that come to us—ill rabbits and healing fairies or a big black lab with a wounded eye—are the ones that are right for us, providing the perfect situation for us to deepen and discover more.

We must take care not to project our thoughts of how healing should happen or what constitutes healing for another being. Our

idea or image of healing may be completely unsuitable for the individual we are attempting to heal. In fact, as soon as we believe we are the ones doing the healing, we are in trouble. So, too, our own healing may not bring us what we envision. On deeper levels, a cure is not necessarily a healing. Sometimes, healing looks much different from what we imagine.

True healing is about relationship. We open to a space in which energy flows naturally, in the most perfect way for everyone. In allowing ourselves to *be* a healing space of love, we allow others to heal at their own rate, in their own time, in their own best way. So, too, we bring healing to ourselves.

You've heard it said there's a window that opens from one mind to another
But if there's no wall, there's no need for fitting the window or the latch.

RUMI

THE FIRST STEP TOWARD HEALING
Beau (dog) ~ Morgine Jurdan

Beau and Morgine
Photo by Marcie Bomarito

When you are centered and in a peaceful place, there are not a lot of things that can upset you. When you come from your heart, you tend to see and feel more deeply; you understand that there is usually something hidden underneath another's anger or pain. Receiving that anger or pain with love can be the first step toward healing.

Being a dog, this is part of what I do every day. When my person is upset and angry, she might forget to take me for a walk. She might not notice I am trying to get her outside for a moment so she will feel better. She might get angry at me for no reason. Anything could happen. I still love her despite it all. I still respond with love, regardless of what she is doing. This helps her heal and love herself more.

I am an inspiration of sorts, a role model you might say. And each one of you can be one, too.

As a cat named Ashah once told me, *"Never underestimate the power of a purr."* Certainly, it is widely known that some sound vibrations have an ability to boost the body's immune system, lessen pain, and reduce stress. In particular, the vibrations of a cat's purr are often recognized to soothe the nerves and encourage broken bones to knit faster.

Ashah advised that humans learn to purr, too, for *"when you purr, you recall inside yourself the energy of the earth. By purring, you can feel that healing, calming tone of the deep earth all through your body."* Purring can thus be used to center oneself and activate the energy connections needed for healing. The exercise on the following page is based on Ashah's recommendations.

As Ashah reminds us all, *"Breathe deep, purr loud, and remember what it means to en-joy life."* By taking joy into our bodies and life, we en-joy it—we become a carrier of that joy, shining it out to others and the world at large. Shining the love we have—or even the love we wish to have—is what magnifies love in the world. This is healing of the highest order.

An Animal Communication Exercise

THE POWER OF A PURR

Sit or lay down—preferably like a cat in the sunshine. Relax, breathe deeply, and exhale with a low, deep purrr or hummm. Continue breathing and purring, allowing periods of quiet when appropriate.

Feel the purrr go deeper, expanding throughout your body. Feel the sound as it reverberates within your skull. Follow the purrr as it travels down your arms, into your fingers; down your legs, into your toes. Feel it move throughout your entire body.

You can use this exercise to clear your head, ground your body, and energize your hands before doing any type of healing work. It is also a healing meditation in and of itself.

Ashah
Photo by Francine Curran

HEALING IS A SIMPLE MOMENT
Shanti (llama) ~ Tera Thomas

Shanti
Photo by Tera Thomas

I am Shanti. My name, Shanti, means peace. I bring peace and peace brings healing.

People view me as a baby llama, and that is physically what I look like. It is a very good visage for doing my work. Even when I am full grown, I will be small and have a baby's face. My own openness and innocence opens the hearts of others and helps them to feel their child self, the self that is whole and connected.

To be honest, I have never been a baby. I am a very powerful spirit, and I have incarnated in this particular body at this particular time for great purpose. I am a healer, and I will be so happy to speak to you about this gift and how I use it. All llamas are healers, you know. It is in our

DNA. We balance everything—the earth, the body—no matter what the species. And balance is health, of course.

The concept of healing is often misunderstood by humans, as if you can wave a magic wand and everything that feels wrong is miraculously turned to right. Some say that healing is an art, a gift, or a miracle. But healing is a very subtle thing. I say that healing is a simple moment of raising one's vibration to resonate with All That Is. A healing can occur from something very simple like a touch or a glance. If you are feeling down and you see someone who makes you smile, you have just received a healing. The reason that prayer heals is because the person praying in earnestness has let go of their individual self and connected with All That Is. It is not the words of a prayer that are important—it is the connection.

Humans tend to feel that healing is the repair of damage to the physical body. I say that healing is the repair of damage to the soul and that the body will reflect this repair if there has not been too much damage done to it. But, whether or not the body comes back into perfect health, healing can and does occur. We are all spiritual beings, here to experience the physical reality. If we remember this and understand that it is our spirit that needs to be healed and reconnected, then we can become whole. This is the goal for all humans—to remember your connection to all of life and so become whole.

I am a teacher of peace and oneness, a healer. Perhaps by looking at me and feeling my presence, you will connect to that part of yourself that is Shanti. Healing is a state of being that does not require a logical explanation or a scientific document. It just IS. So, don't look for healing in your mind, look for it in your heart. Breathe it in and let it expand your beingness to touch all others, to feel all others, to recognize your oneness, your belonging to the family of life. You are spirit in a physical body, looking to find your way home and to bring that home here to this planet, grounded in the love of All That Is and All That You Are.

8

A Look at Death

All goes onward and outward . . . and nothing collapses,
And to die is different from what any one
supposed, and luckier.

WALT WHITMAN,
SONG OF MYSELF

Rooskie was a seventeen-year-old black cat who lived with my friend Claire. When Claire asked me to talk with Rooskie, he had been ill for quite a while. Although he showed me that his lungs felt heavy and he was very tired, there was also a sense of deep contentment within this old cat. Rooskie said he was spending a lot of time resting and dreaming, and he would soon be ready to "fade away."

Approaching Death: Rooskie

It was clear that Rooskie was preparing to die and was using the dream state as a means of connecting with the after-death state in order to move onward gently. Sometimes a deeper aspect of an animal or human comes to talk as the physical body nears death. The body may be so tired that a higher (or deeper, wider, more expansive) self chimes in to convey information. Rooskie's higher self advised Claire that there was nothing she need do, that no intervention was needed. *"This is a natural process. Simply allow Rooskie to rest and have plenty of fresh, clean water."*

Although Claire was hoping Rooskie would pull through his illness, the talk helped to confirm what her heart already knew. "I don't want to lose my dearest friend," she wrote. "He is my Buddha Kitty, so wise and knowing. I know I can't keep him forever. I know his spirit-self is eternal. And yet he is so special to me, for he has been a part of my life for so long. I want his loving, physical presence to continue on and on and on. I know I will never be ready to have him pass over. It is so hard to let go when you love so much."

Letting Go

For many humans, it is the letting-go part of death that is most painful. It need not be, of course, but even as our mind reassures us that spirit lives on, we may still feel a good deal of sadness and aching in our hearts as a much-loved friend makes the transition to the great beyond.

Author and animal hospice director Rita Reynolds had the following experience with her beloved dog Oliver: "The day before Oliver died, he laid his head on my foot as I wrote down my thoughts about him. He communicated to me, *'Don't begin missing me yet. Share this moment with me, everything is as it is meant to be. And if you let me, I will guide you for all the moments to come.'*"[1]

Like so many animals, Oliver accepted the end of his time on Earth. He didn't want Rita to miss the experience of being with him—truly being with him—by losing herself in grief or worry. Oliver knew that to trust the process of life, and death, is to realize a great truth: all unfolds perfectly. We who remain on Earth may not always think the unfolding is perfect, but we may not be tuned in to the bigger picture.

Spirit, soul, consciousness, and miracle reside in everything. Animals teach us about life and death, if we let them. And in between, about love, hate, tenderness, anger, pain, ruthlessness, loyalty, friendship, craftiness, resignation—every possible feeling with infinite shades and tones. To love an animal truly, is to truly love, with no expectation other than to delight in that love. To see and believe that is simple, and yet it is the most radical world view. Tatti Wattles, a little black Norwegian rat with good karma, was here to prove it.

RACHEL ROSENTHAL, *TATTI WATTLES: A LOVE STORY*

When we let go of our own desires and surrender to the natural flows of life and death, we expand to a larger way of seeing the world. We experience *being* in the world in a different way. Instead of trying to control events, we release ourselves to a more expansive way of living. By letting go of our small designs, we become open to the deeper messages that are always available for us—be they from an animal's actions, a communication, or a simple turn of events.

This is what happened when Mike, a young man who was just learning animal communication, was asked by a cat he had never met to help convey a last message to his human family. He wrote to me,

What the caterpillar calls the end of the world, the master calls a butterfly.

RICHARD BACH

Well, it's been a long journey, full of trusting myself. Tonight I had a wonderful experience, though bittersweet. A friend of mine wanted an online animal medicine card reading for Cain, her boyfriend's cat, who was going to be put down. After I finished the reading, I got a persistent feeling from Cain. He wanted me to type a message, so I typed. This is what he said:

I just want them to know I love them very much, and they are doing the right thing. I know it seems hard, but I do have to move on. I feel very itchy and painful in some ways. It is definitely the end of a cycle.

For right now, just spend as much time with me as possible, and see if you can enjoy my physical body while it is still around. I really want to be free of this form. My lesson to teach has been enjoyment of simple things—being with family and friends. Also, the importance of having strong convictions and sticking to them.

When you think of me randomly, remember that I am there, and checking in. Sit in silence and hear my messages. It's not important to be enlightened—it's not important to be able to do any-

thing spectacular. It's most important to love, and to be loved. It is also very important to be who you are, enjoy the moment, and love your family. Remember, I will be around.

just be

Like Oliver and Cain, so many animals preparing to transition request such a simple thing of their humans: *be with me, sit with me, talk to me.* Many also ask us to deepen, to inwardly travel with our friends in a voyage of discovery.

A cat named Queen I once spoke with invited her person, Rain, to sit beside her and quiet her mind so as to better share her experience. *"I invite you to see,"* said Queen. *"Please don't feel bad for me. I had a great life as Queen. I know I was loved and I hope you know that I loved all of you, even the mice and birds and bugs. It was a great life and I learned many things. We all go on. Know that I am really where I want to be. My body is finished and will be gone soon, and that is how it is with all of us. But I am still alive and I will always be alive, just as you will always be alive. If you quiet yourself and go very deep inside yourself, there you will find me, and many others, too . . . even yourself. In this quiet space, you find the deeper you."*

Many animals impart similar messages of comfort in their final days. So, too, when we are calm and open to the natural flows of living and dying, does shared time offer some of the most profound moments of healing and elevated awareness. Rain was comforted and touched by Queen's invitation to take a more conscious role in the process of death. In doing so, she began to see both death and life with new eyes.

Animals in pain and distress can likewise benefit tremendously from our being present with them. Many healing modalities (such as those mentioned in chapter 7) can help to assist animals in their final

When the ten thousand things are viewed in their oneness, we return to the origin and remain where we have always been.

LAO-TZU

days. Bodywork is comforting, may relieve pain, and offers both animal and human a precious time to deepen in relationship. Flower essences can also be of great help in lessening fear, opening awareness, and offering support to animal and human alike. In addition, there are several essences that address death specifically (see the resources section).

In her hospice sanctuary for animals, Rita Reynolds uses cotton blankets in colors of deep blue, gold, and white to cover and soothe animals in their transition. Favorite music, special songs, soft chanting, and heartfelt prayer may also be calming and pleasant, not only for your animal but for you as well.

PRAYER FOR DYING
BY RITA REYNOLDS

(May be sung, chanted, or repeated to evoke a sense of peace.)
Beloved Friend:
I, with you,
resist nothing,
move in peace,
blessing this bridge.

Spirit we are:
unified always,
souls bonded
through our love;
now we are free.
Namaste.[2]

Be open to your animal's moods and needs as they shift throughout the day. Perhaps you will sense that quietly lying in the sunshine, feeling the earth beneath you, breathing in fresh air and resting a hand very lightly on your animal's body is just what's needed. Some animals prefer to be indoors, seeking out the warmth and comfort of their bed or favorite place in your home.

Each situation is different, and you may not know how or when or why you are called to participate. Listen; stay tuned; ask your animal how you can be of help. Some animals desire to die naturally while others ask for assistance. Making the decision to euthanize an animal can be difficult, but remember: you are not without resources. Ask for help if you need it. Draw upon support and suggestions from friends, family, healers, animal doctors, animal communicators, as well as your own animal guides and teachers.

Above all, breathe deep and trust your animal friend. Trust yourself, and trust the experience as it unfolds. As we shrug off ideas of what could be or should be, we open to what is. As we move beyond our usual frame of reference, we meet with greater levels of knowledge, experience, and wisdom. Whether we are talking, resting, or communing in silence, we enter a deeper place of communion—not only with our animal friend but within ourselves as well.

When one door closes another one opens; but we so often look so long and so regretfully upon the closed door, that we do not see the ones which open for us.

ALEXANDER GRAHAM BELL

Looking into Death: Rooskie, part II

As I checked in with Rooskie during the days following our talk, we began to spontaneously travel together, as if sharing one consciousness. I sensed Rooskie was exploring different ways of being from outside his body. He seemed curious to do this, without fear or

MAYA ON DEATH
MAYA ~ GRETCHEN KUNZ

If you are a human and your animal is dying, you may be sad. It is perfectly natural to mourn and miss your friend, and even to be angry that he or she is dying. Remember that your animal friend still loves you, even though it can be a confusing time for him or her, too. Think about it. If you feel sick or are hurting, you may feel "out of it" or not like moving or being nice to people. This can happen with animals, too. Generally speaking, animals are better at dealing with pain and sickness. We tend to ignore it or go sort of out-of-body so we're not feeling it much anymore, especially in the end stages. This is not true for everyone—each has his or her own path—but it is usually true.

A lot of people blame themselves when their animal friends get sick, which makes sense because they wish they could change or control it. Even some nonhuman animals will blame themselves or others. Nobody's perfect! But if you make yourself so sad, you are not only hurting yourself for something you cannot help but hurting your animal friend, who needs to feel love and positive energy from you. So—get over it! If you really feel at fault for something, you can work it out later.

Sometimes animals don't know what's best for themselves. They might want to stick around and suffer just to keep their person happy. Or a person might want to keep an animal living even though it's ready to die. You have to be careful and listen, both to what you want and need inside and what the animal wants and needs. And remember—wanting and needing are two different things!

While your friend is dying, take some deep breaths and see how you can help in the moment. Don't get caught up in the past. Your friend needs you now. Give acceptance and thanks and love: Acceptance for the path your friend is on and the need to move on to spirit, just as we all do. Thanks for being with you in body as your friend, and for being with you in spirit thereafter. And love for who your friend is.

Each animal may have a different way of dying. Your friend may want to be alone or be with you, to go with or without help. The most important thing is that you care and respect your animal. Trust me, if you love your friend, he or she knows it.

Death is both sad and joyous. Be understanding and strong for your friend. And remember, when they have passed, do not be afraid to talk to them and tell them you love them and ask them for love and comfort in return, as well. They will hear you, and you may feel it when they are near you! It's okay to both smile and cry, you know. The loss of the body can be a hard thing. But the continuing love of the spirit is a never-ending gift.

Maya
Photo by Gretchen Kunz

There is no death as most humans have conceived it and, from my point of view, leaving a physical body is not a negative occurrence. We are having a cosmic party. It has already begun. Dress in your party clothes, bring your festive spirit, your joy, your love, your exuberance. Dance and make merry. Magic is afoot and miracles abound. So be open to the miraculous and welcome what you don't know into your life!

INKA (LLAMA) ~
TERA THOMAS

worry, and I felt he was allowing me to share the experience with him in order to tell Claire and help both of us learn more.

One morning, I woke up with Rooskie very strongly in my thoughts. As I closed my eyes, I was with him as he "looked into death." The way this appeared to me was as a bright blue-purple screen that was the entrance to a cave, which was also filled with soothing blue and purple light. As I looked into the screen, I saw images of many animals in the process of living and dying. I understood that the screen could be used to glimpse into the past or the future—a way for any individual to review "past lives" or to consider possible "future lives."

As Rooskie and I watched the screen, we saw a young black panther in the jungle. The panther moved swiftly, softly brushing past dark green leaves and plants. The image became so vibrant and intensely real that Rooskie and I became the panther. I wondered if this was one of Rooskie's lives or one of my own. As soon as I thought the question, I knew it was a combination journey—something the two of us had created together as a way to explore and experience this energy.

I felt the strong, slinking motion of the panther as we moved. I saw jungle foliage and terrain through the panther's eyes in sharp details. The panther had a manner of swaying its head and body from side to side as it surveyed everything around it. At one point, we played with a stone and I felt our paw turning the stone, enjoying the energy in this simple game of play. The cat consciousness of Rooskie commented that cats have many such games. *"Humans may judge these games as meaningless,"* Rooskie noted, *"but if you actually watch a cat and really see, you will notice that they have many games with specific rules or goals."* He said that football, for example, seemed crazy to a lot of animals but that it has just as much meaning to some humans as cat games have to cats. With this understanding, Rooskie and I left the body of the panther, separating more clearly into our own consciousnesses, and said good-bye.

When I wrote to share this intriguing experience with Claire an hour later, she replied that Rooskie had died that morning.

Dreaming Ourselves Awake

It was only after rereading my talks with Rooskie and other animals that I realized how important dreams, daydreams, and contemplative states can be as a means of easing our transition to the world beyond the living.

For example, when Queen was preparing to die, she termed it *"dreaming myself away."* She explained that, for her, dying was like being on a road or path that she could explore little by little. *"I walk down part of the path to see what it is like,"* she said, *"and then I come back and feel my body."* As if to emphasize this, Queen shared a vision of other cats on this path, which looked like a golden trail through sun-dappled woods. She explained that in the past she had been afraid of death. In ending her life as Queen, she was working to lose that fear by easing herself into a deeper appreciation of death. Queen related that she wanted some time before her physical death to consciously move through the *"walkway of death,"* meeting friends and teachers along the way, then coming back into her body to ground the experience into her present consciousness.

"It all goes on," a cat named Ashah told her person, Francine. *"It all continues. Don't think of me as gone, but as still playing, just in a different way."* As so many animals want their people to know, Ashah reassured Francine that she was still available, both in spirit form and in her dreams. *"Trust yourself more,"* Ashah encouraged Francine. *"I can talk to you in your dreams and you know it."*

Indeed, Ashah's advice is something that applies to us all when losing a beloved animal friend: *"Go on with what gives you joy. Know*

An act of faith:
To view the end
as a beginning.

FORTUNE COOKIE

in your heart that I am okay, that we are all okay. What I most want to share with you is what you already know: we are all, always, okay."

Some say that the moment of death is also the moment of our greatest consciousness. For in that moment, we become deeply connected with our innermost being. We shed the masks we have worn to our parents and our children, our friends and lovers, and we open deeper, and deeper still, to the life force that lives through us. For a moment, our soul shines through—beyond time, beyond space, beyond the tiny confines of our body, emotions, thoughts, and ideas. We catch a glimpse of the immensity of who we really are.

SIMPLY A CHANGE

YOHINTA (CAT) ~ PENELOPE SMITH

There is nothing to be afraid of. You come and you go in different forms. You have to cast your body off when it's no longer useful and your job is done. That's all there is to it—simply a change in form. I know that I am eternal. I am huge; my space is enormous. When I'm in the body I focus on my body and its needs and my spiritual mission. When I am out of the body I will be free of all constraints, free to be anywhere that I wish, and be everywhere. It's very simple.

There's nothing complicated about death. It's all about bodies and forms changing. Earth takes back all that she creates. It's that simple. I look forward to my body being in the ground because that's how it should be. The earth is wonderful. I've always rolled on the earth and I want my body to be tucked in where it belongs, and then I, as a spirit, will do whatever I need to do. Don't worry. Life goes on. It goes on and on and on and on. It's limitless. Who would want a body that doesn't work right? Not me!

Chin-Lo's Teaching

For some reason, catfish can't live for long in our five-gallon aquarium. Bless their hearts, there have been seven of them that rapidly come and go, each helping me to "experience beyond knowing" how easy it is to leave the body and to know that the physical experience is not necessarily that of the soul. In other words, what may appear to be physical suffering to my human eyes is not suffering to the soul of the fish.

After several months without a catfish, I felt it was time to try again. At the pet store I was advised to try a Chinese Algae Eater. When the man who was helping me put the net in the aquarium, all of the fish swam away. I asked him to wait a moment while I connected with the fish. He humored me and was surprised when I greeted them and asked if any one would volunteer to come home with me. I pictured my aquarium as I said this. Two turned around and swam into the net. I thanked both, but told them I thought only one could live in the aquarium. So, one came home.

At home, I asked "What is your name?" I wondered if the name would be Chinese even though this fish didn't come from China. I then heard a musical, tinkling, laughing voice say, *"Chin-Lo"* in an Asian accent. The "o" sound in Lo sounded like toning—ooooo. She was floating with her back toward me. I said, "If your name is really Chin-Lo please turn around and face me." Immediately she swam around to face me!

Three weeks later, I knew she was dying. After celebrating her, offering her essences, prayers, songs, and energy work, I went to bed feeling sad, yet peaceful. At 2 A.M., still in bed, I had a vision as if I was kneeling close to the aquarium. I saw Chin-Lo lying on the gravel on her side. Usually when I see an animal that is in spirit, I see a silver, shimmering, sparkling light around the body. This time, I saw the silver light within her form and then suddenly a brilliant, huge flash of light. I understood that light was her true self. This vast beautiful light moved out against a blackness and merged into an enormous, pulsating, shifting gold and pink, cloudlike, nebula-like energy. I understood I was seeing Chin-Lo's true self merging back into All That Is.

Suddenly aware that I was in bed and seeing with ordinary vision, I went to the aquarium and there she was lying in the place I had seen her, yet still breathing. She left later that day. What a beautiful gift she gave to me!

POLLY LAZARON

saying good-bye

After my old dog Barney died, my husband, daughter, and I worked together to prepare his body and make a place for it to return to the earth. Although we had no real plan, we followed the ideas that came to us naturally.

First, we went to collect many large rocks. In our backyard, my husband, Bob, dug a hole while Alyeska and I gathered wildflowers. Remembering a baby blanket of hers that Barney had especially liked, Alyeska ran to find it. With the blanket wrapped snugly around his body, we lay Barney in the ground. Then, sitting in a circle around the grave, we told stories and memories of our friend and teacher. We were especially happy that we had just taken him to Hatcher Pass, a mountain area we all liked, and that he had played and run around like a puppy, barking at ground squirrels and paragliders. For every memory one of us told, we would add a flower. When all the flowers were gone, we scooped up handfuls of earth and filled the hole and made a stone circle over the grave.

It felt good to say good-bye in this way, and I was glad we did it all together. It made me wonder if it wouldn't help when anyone dies—beloved human or animal—to take a more active role in helping to return their body to the earth, saying good-bye with our hearts, not just pretty words, crying if we feel like it and laughing if we feel like it, and thus opening ever deeper to the experience of death and living.

Human cultures have many different ways of saying good-bye and honoring their dead. Some traditions include burying items that belonged to the deceased. For animal friends, this might include a leash, a collar, a favorite toy or blanket. The original idea behind this practice was to help the spirit be comfortable in its journey. On another level, the act of burying items along with the body is a means of releasing ties to physicality.

A pet's life is so much shorter than our own. We know this when we take them on. A pet is a lesson in letting go, a home course in Buddhism. To have a pet is to embrace impermanence and to say, Yes, I will lose her. She won't live forever. But I'll do it anyway, because of the love. The love between an animal and a human is like no other love in the world.

HELEN WEAVER,
THE DAISY SUTRA

THE GRAND RETURN
BARNEY ~ DAWN BRUNKE

The Grand Return! That is what it is like to die. To awaken to the idea that this is all a scenario designed to get you to remember. That is the point of this game—simply to remember. Because when you remember, you awaken to your true self—or at least a more conscious version of your true self than you have been led to believe was you.

Barney
Photo by Dawn Brunke

Most often, funerary rites are for the living. The things we do are ways to help us grieve, release, honor, and cherish our departed friends. Here are some ideas for saying good-bye:

Wrap the body in a favorite blanket or sew a special covering. Use markers or embroidery to decorate a sheet or blanket with words, drawings, or farewell messages. Or, write a letter to your animal and include it in the burial.

Make a marker for your animal's grave. Use wood and paint to create a traditional marker, arrange stones and rocks for a more natural marker, or plant flowers, a bush, or a tree as a living marker. If your animal will not be buried near your home, plant a seed indoors as a special tribute to your animal.

Build an altar for your animal. For an indoor altar, see ideas in chapter 4. For an outdoor altar, select a tree stump, flat rock, flower bed, stone garden, pond, or favorite area that was special to you and your animal. Mementos you might include in your altar: photos of you and your animal; a collar, tag, or toy; a snipping of animal hair tied with string; flowers; a written poem, letter, prayer, or blessing; a statue of your animal's form. Rearrange or change your altar as your feelings shift. Altars can be used to honor, remember, release, celebrate, or commemorate those we love. They may also serve as a meeting place between worlds.

Make a memory box or bowl. Find a special box or bowl to hold treasured memories of your friend. You might decorate the outside with photos, drawings, or written memories. Or place these inside, along with a clipping of hair, photos, favorite toy, or written stories of your time together.

Create a photo collage or album. Sometimes just looking at photos can help in sorting through feelings. Arranging pictures and designing a collage, adding a few words with metallic pens or in calligraphy, can likewise bring you closer to a sense of peace and closure.

Write a tribute to your animal. Creating a poem, story, or memoir about your animal friend can be a wonderfully moving experience. It is difficult to convey just how helpful this can be, though when you read the words of others who have poured their grief, affection, loss, and deepest love in tribute to their animal friends, you know without a doubt that something incredible has been expressed. Consider the following poem that Diane Pagel wrote when her much-loved sheep Calla passed away.

Nothing is more creative than death, since it is the whole secret of life.

ALAN WATTS

Calla

Wise ole ewe,
Keeper of peace.
She who steals my coffee.
She who is boss.

You showed me that sheep are human
With wool and four legs,
With humor and justice
And honor and peace.

Calla, you always were first
To greet me when I arrived,
First to offer me advice
When I worked on the flock.

Diane and Lily (Calla's daughter)
Photo by Conie Lodell

First to lay next to me
With your new lamb,
A proud mother you were
And mother to me, too.

I remember the last time
When we laid next to each other in the field
With your head in my lap
And my hand on your back

Talking of peace and friendship
While the sun beat down upon us

And clouds raced by at warp speed
And your lamb fast asleep.

We, too, fell asleep in the sun
And I awoke as if I were your child
With your head over me, your breath in my hair
Watching me as your other child.

Calla, you will always be in my heart
You will be by my side,
And I hope to make you proud,
As proud as I was of you.

In older times, families would often sit with their deceased all night long, ensuring the spirit was untroubled and content to travel to the next world. Staying awake until the early morning, friends and family would eat a hearty meal, reminisce, tell stories, and laugh and cry with each other. Drawing on this custom, you might create an all-night memorial for your animal, inviting family and friends to join in remembering your companion, pal, and teacher. For many, a funeral is not only a time to say good-bye but a celebration of life well lived.

So, too, may messages of farewell and signs of celebration come back to us from our beloved friends as they pass beyond the physical world. Consider the parting gift shared in the following story of Emmy Lou, a black Border collie mix with a white chest and white paws who had been diagnosed with cancer.

When I first spoke with Emmy, a higher self or healing guide began to speak through her, advising her people, Aaron and Kirsten, to trust themselves and not stay in fear, for "that is the least healing place to be." Emmy's guide also encouraged them, "Be open; listen deeply. Trust the signs and, most of all, trust your own feelings and inner intuitions and guidance."

EMMY'S LIGHTS

It was the night of the full moon in November and Emmy had been spending lots of time outside. The cold, the moon, and just being in nature seemed to comfort her. When I went outside to check on her, she wasn't in her usual spot. I called her name and she came to me from the bushes. She was moving very slowly. She sat down in her favorite place on the porch, and we sat with her, me on one side of her, Aaron on the other. She started to lose her equilibrium, her body swayed, and she plopped down on her left side.

We both put our hands on Emmy's heart. We said prayers out loud and in our minds and hearts, telling her how much we loved her, trying to help her gently pass. When Aaron said her heart was no longer beating, we stayed with her and cried and talked to her for a while. Our little Emmy had passed on.

It was about midnight. We gathered our gear and got ready to go to Hatcher Pass, a favorite mountain area where we had already dug a hole for her two months before. Before leaving, we brought her mother, brother, and sister outside to sniff Emmy, to let them know she died. She was already lying on the blanket we intended to use for her burial, and we wrapped her in it. Aaron took joy in lifting her body, as we both had done so many times before, picking her up like a puppy, which she had always loved, even at the age of almost four years.

We placed Emmy in the backseat and drove to the mountains. It was surprisingly clear and warm. Aaron carried Emmy in his arms, and the full moon lit the way as we walked on the snow-covered trail, heading for the site we had chosen. We remembered all the little nicknames we had for Emmy, and laughed as we said them out loud. She had brought us so much joy!

We found the hole we had previously dug for her, which symbolized our acceptance of her death, and reinforced our desire for her suffering to end. Aaron gently laid her in her place of rest in the earth. We burned some sage and blessed each other, and Emmy, too, encircling our bodies with the purifying, sacred smell.

We asked Spirit to help Emmy and us with her passing. We laid two twin crystals over her heart and covered them with our hands. We gave thanks for the miracle of her life and love and prayed for her sweet, gentle soul. We consciously put the intention of love and remembrance of Emmy's big heart into the crystals. One stayed with her and we kept the other with us as a symbol of Emmy's loving heart and spirit.

Aaron also put a piece of hematite, an important stone to him, by Emmy, and we each placed a piece of our hair in the grave, as pieces of us to help her on her journey. I took a piece of her hair and put it in my pocket.

I touched her one last time, saying, "It's going to be okay because I know I'm going to see you again." Right then, I looked up and there was a single green beam of the Northern Lights shooting over the mountain. "That's a good sign, Emmy!" I said.

We covered her body with dirt and when we finished, Aaron said, "We'll never forget you, Emmy." Then he gasped and said to me, "Oh, look!" I looked up and saw the sky bursting into amazing hues of green, purple, and white! The colors were vibrant! Despite the bright light of the full moon, a brilliant green beam formed around the moon and us and our surrounding area.

We lay down on the ground, each of us on either side of Emmy (her favorite place to be, between us), and watched the dancing lights. We both distinctly felt that these lights were intertwined with the expression and beauty of Emmy's spirit. When we said this out loud to each other, a shooting star flew by! We laughed, as we felt this amazing confirmation of our thoughts.

Emmy

It has been an emotional and difficult experience, losing our Emmy Lou. I move from feeling happy and smiling with memories to feeling sad, missing her so much, and feeling lonely without her. But, beneath that, deeper, we both feel the beauty of her life—and of life and death itself. She was such a blessing . . . and still is.

Now, whenever we see or think of those awesome Northern Lights, we feel comforted. We know our spirits are destined to be free and meet again.

AARON AND KIRSTEN

Drinking in the Light:
Rooskie, part III

Humans always want to know about the future!

ROOSKIE

What is life? It is the flash of a firefly in the night. It is the breath of a buffalo in the wintertime. It is the little shadow which runs across the grass and loses itself in the sunset.

CROWFOOT OF THE
BLACKFOOT NATION

Several days after Rooskie died, Claire asked if I would speak with him once again. Although I had spoken with many animals in spirit, each experience was unique.

The first thing Rooskie showed me was a bright cartoon image of a cat resting on his back atop a big, fluffy cloud. The feeling of this image was humorous and light-hearted. Rooskie's energy, too, seemed excited and happy. He directed me to feel his lungs, exclaiming how light and free they now were. He again showed me the cartoon version of himself breathing in very deeply, his eyes closed in ecstasy and a huge, exaggerated smile growing upon his face, as if to say he was taking in the fullness of life. *"Yes, tell Claire I am breathing in life!"* exclaimed Rooskie. *"It may not be the life we shared together, but it is important that Claire knows that this, too, is life. And I am living well!"*

Rooskie said he had much joy and exuberance for life—both his life in the spirit world and his life with Claire. *"I really loved it there a lot,"* said Rooskie. *"Everything was wonderful. I had great fun. It was truly a magnificent life."*

Rooskie shared with me such intense joy that I began feeling giddy myself. Once more showing me the cartoon image of the cat on the cloud, Rooskie said, *"I'm very high—and so this may seem silly, but there is such great love and light and pure joy."* As I felt the flow of this energy coursing through me, Rooskie said, *"You are now getting just a little taste of bliss. Magnify it to every cell in your being and then you will know how I feel!"*

Rooskie told me that he was resting and enjoying a healing time of his own design. A higher self aspect said, *"Rooskie did have a good life and met many interesting beings, some of whom he knew before. This life was more exploratory for him. There were no great goals other than to just experience—which is, of course, also a full goal of any life. He wishes to convey that he feels very much relieved and very light now. He wants Claire to know that all is well, as he knows she already knows deep within her being."*

Rooskie then asked if I would care to know more about his life in the spirit world. *"You wanted to know what happened after death,"* Rooskie told me, and this was true; I was very interested in learning more. *"I can give you a guided tour,"* he said. *"Come along."*

Rooskie first showed me a review of various animals he had been—a skunk, a snake, a little black puppy, a brown dog, a variety of cats. Rooskie told me that he had been human, too, though I felt some sadness around that life. Admitting that his human experience had been rather depressing, Rooskie said that his guides urged him to become a domesticated animal so as to relearn love from humans. He said that much of his life as Rooskie was about *"being basked in love from humans and others."* After a short, contemplative pause, Rooskie added, *"Don't think that we animals are always there for you. Sometimes you are here for us, too. It works both ways, and I appreciate all the love Claire showered upon me."*

Rooskie said it was too early for him to begin thinking of another life. Instead, he wanted to heal. What did it mean to heal in the spirit world, I wondered? Rooskie explained it to me as *"drinking in the light."* As he shared this, I felt a deep, wonderful warmth and imagined that "drinking in the light" was rather like sunbathing one's soul.

Rooskie said that in the spirit world he was free to assume any form and go any place he chose. As an example, he showed me a

You would know the secret of death. But how shall you find it unless you seek it in the heart of life?

KAHLIL GIBRAN

The smallest sprout shows
there is really no
death,
And if ever there was it led
forward life, and does
not wait at the end to
arrest it,
And ceased the moment
life appeared.
All goes onward and
outward . . . and nothing
collapses,
And to die is different from
what any one
supposed, and luckier.
WALT WHITMAN,
SONG OF MYSELF

version of himself with a different cat face. There he was, sitting on his haunches next to a friendly brown dog, near an elegant marble pond that was surrounded by tall white pillars, lush green plants, and colorful flowers. Although this appeared to be a twilight scene, the air held a sparkling quality of light, very different from that on Earth. The air felt cool and there was the faint aroma of flowers. The scene was like an enchanting children's book illustration, with bright golden fish swimming in the pond, the cat and dog drinking warm creamy tea from dainty china cups and saucers. Rooskie told me that any memory or reality could be created here. He added that he was enjoying quiet times talking with old friends and guides.

Rooskie noted that time didn't exist in the spirit world in the same way as humans know it. *"I think I'm here to enjoy the stillness, the sense of presence in the present,"* said Rooskie. *"I'm just resting and relaxing and enjoying every moment of Now. You should try this. We could have very long talks in this modality and it would be only seconds in your reality."*

Then Rooskie paused, smiled, and offered a final piece of parting advice to all.

A DAILY DOSE OF HEALING
Rooskie (cat) ~ Dawn Brunke

I would advise a dose of healing in the peace and joy of the Now for everyone. Animals should remember this too. As Rooskie, I did this occasionally, but never to the degree that I am doing now. There is a place in your heart where you can access this peace, this presence of Now-ness, and that is where true healing can occur.

When I look back at Rooskie, I see a love of curiosity, and this trait remains with me in the spirit world, though we don't call it the spirit world here! I encourage all humans to have some quiet time each day. Many will benefit from simply sitting still and listening to their inner voice.

Although I am different from Rooskie because I have shed that personality, Claire may still tune in to the form of Rooskie if she feels there is more for her to heal on that level. All forms remain since there is only the Now, though spirit consciousness is free to shift into various forms, and that is where I center myself—in the small now of this spirit form.

And as I pondered that, Rooskie-Spirit laughed, fading away on a warm rush of the ever smiling Now.

A JOURNEY OF BECOMING
Barney (dog) ~ Dawn Brunke

What is your relationship with death? How do you think about it and feel it in your body? Is it with a gasp of fear? A laugh of defense? Is it held with tension or lovingly, hand in hand? The way you think about death may greatly influence the way death occurs.

When you ask—What happens when you leave this world? Do you simply forget those on Earth or are you still tied with them? Where do you go? What happens?—I have to relate to you that most everyone knows in their heart and deep within their being the answers to these questions. Most beings have journeyed into death many, many times before.

If you ask me what happens at death, I say it is simply a passing into another mode of being. Many have said this before. Perhaps it would do well to take this into your consciousness at a deep level: death is merely a movement to another mode of being. Much like moving from one room to another, one state to another, it is really nothing more than that—a moving.

Just because you leave one room does not mean you forget it, does it? You simply are engaged in whatever you are now seeing and feeling,

though the reality and memory of that other room still survives. This is how it is with death to some degree, at least at certain stages.

There are many wonders out of spirit, many different dimensional levels to explore. You might compare it to moving to another country— once there, you are very excited by the newness and the different ways of the people and their land, their marketplaces, their art and language and culture. Death is a passage to another country—and there is very much to explore!

There are "schools" one can attend. Some choose to have personal guides. Others meet with family and friends. In truth, there are as many versions to this experience as there are beings—which is to say, infinite. That is why I remind you that your relationship to death is paramount. It is your movie, after all!

I am now preparing for my ending in this body of Barney the dog. It is like turning a page, shutting a book, momentarily turning attention away from Barney the dog to focus on another aspect of being. It would be best to think of this as a transition rather than as a finality or ending. It is like shaking off water, just as a dog shakes water easily from its fur when it is wet.

Death is a journey of becoming. In order to meet it in a conscious manner, you must become familiar with death, understanding of its nature and ways in the world. This is why I call death an art.

There are masters on the planet whose death is truly a magnificent spectacle to witness, for they simply whisper across the doorway, into another room, and sometimes you aren't even sure they were present to begin with! As one becomes more familiar and adept at this art, one soon becomes an apprentice to death. It is then she begins to reveal her secrets and her majestic smile.

9
The Art of shape-shifting

I was in many shapes . . .
I was an eagle . . .
I was a snake on an enchanted hill.
I was a viper in a lake.

TALIESIN, CELTIC BARD AND SHAMAN

In many ages and cultures, humans have embraced the art of shape-shifting—transforming one's bodily form or consciousness—in order to perceive the world with new eyes, feel the earth in a new and exciting way, and experience life from diverse perspectives.

In myths, fairy tales, and times of magic, shape-shifting is used in a wide variety of ways. For some, it is a means of holding or condemning one's enemy to a particular form, such as when the Greek goddess Circe lured lost sailors to her island and turned them into swine. For others, shape-shifting is a means of escape, of tricking others, or of alluding capture. In the Welsh tradition, for example, the cauldron-keeper Gwion and sorceress Ceridwen become hare and greyhound, fish and otter, in a transformative dance of shape and flight. For still others, shape-shifting is an instructive ability that allows one to learn about others by becoming them. It was this educational tool that the wizard Merlin introduced to young King Arthur, to help him experience the world of animals in order to rule with a compassionate heart.

213

The trick, according to Chiang, was for Jonathan to stop seeing himself as trapped inside a limited body that had a forty-two-inch wingspan and performance that could be plotted on a chart. The trick was to know that his true nature lived, as perfect as an unwritten number, everywhere at once across space and time.

RICHARD BACH,
JONATHAN LIVINGSTON SEAGULL

Shamans, magic practitioners, indigenous peoples, and explorers of consciousness alike may mimic animal gestures and sounds in dance, song, or movements in order to "become" an animal. By wearing skins, furs, hides and hooves; by using masks or donning feathers; by invoking the vision of an animal, making sounds of the animal or behaving "as if" the animal, one steps closer to becoming the animal itself, sliding ever nearer animal consciousness until at last there is no distinction, no separation. One *is* the eagle, the snake, the fish and otter, too.

True to its name, shape-shifting itself has many forms. For some, it may entail physically transforming one's body into that of a bear, leopard, or other animal. This type of shape-shifting is at the core of the werewolf legend, in which a human being's body actually assumes the shape of a wolf. Another form of shape-shifting involves shifting not the body but the mind. This includes the ability to move with an animal, to see the world through its eyes, to smell and feel and taste and hear everything around you through the senses of another. Imagine: speeding through the ocean as a dolphin, arcing up through the waves, into the sunlit air, flipping gracefully and diving back down into the depths of your watery home. How about hanging upside down in the dark, with acutely sensitive hearing, "seeing" through sound waves as you flap your long leathery wings to fly off into the night as a bat? Or perhaps you'd like to experience life as a lion on the African savannah, a lemur in the forest of Madagascar, a polar bear roaming the Arctic circle.

Is it truly possible to shift the shape of one's consciousness? How do we begin to shape-shift? If we do shape-shift, what does it feel like? How is this information useful? What does it show us about animals? And, deeper still, what does it show us about ourselves?

travels with shark

One night I dreamed I was a shark that had just been born. Aware of both human and shark consciousness, I swam aimlessly in a grayish green area. As a human, I wondered where the mother shark was, though this didn't seem to matter to me as the shark.

After swimming for a while, we began to notice lines on the ocean floor. The lines were made of a nearly invisible light that shimmered slightly and emitted high-pitched sounds. As a human I thought the lines were related to electricity or magnetics. As a shark I felt the sound lines vibrate through my belly all the way to my spine. When we swam over or along the top of the light lines, it was as if they sang, reverberating in a high, slightly tinny sound, which was not unpleasant to hear or feel. As a human I had the idea the lines were maps—but maps of what? Would they lead to the mother shark? Were they created by other sharks? As a shark I followed one sound line for quite a while but then lost it—or perhaps it faded—and I turned back around in a circle.

As a human I probed the deeper consciousness of the shark, to see what I could learn. It wasn't much, for as a shark, I didn't have a very clear idea who I was or what I was supposed to do. I operated out of instinct, though this instinct was not dumb, without awareness or consciousness. Rather, it guided me and had a life all its own.

Time passed quickly then, as it often does in dreams. The shark was older now, had been around and knew more things. As the shark I was more confident of my abilities. I ate fish mostly, sometimes live, sometimes dead. Once I traveled north to colder waters and came up from beneath the waters to eat a seal. It was resting on the fringes of a group of seals. I swam below it and lunged upward to chomp down half of it in a gulp.

As a human I began talking with the shark, asking if it had spoken to the seal before eating it, or offered a prayer, as other predator animals have told me they do. As a shark I had never heard of this idea of asking permission to eat something, and prayer was not something I knew. But neither was there any personal feeling about the seal—no revenge, no sense of destruction or anger. The shark showed me how it was led to the seal, how that seal was "open" to be taken. *"Some animals are open to be taken and others are not,"* the shark explained, indicating that some animals had a different purpose and could not—or should not—be taken.

The shark's awareness was now more familiar to me, and I wanted to know more about the history of sharks. As I sunk into the shark's consciousness, I sensed knowledge that seemed to exist behind this shark's conscious awareness. At this discovery the shark also became curious, as if my inquisitiveness had awakened similar feelings within him.

Together, in joined consciousness, we swam quite far until we came again to the grayish green place where we were born. From there, we turned and followed a particular sound line of light, swimming farther still until we came to a cave that really wasn't a cave at all. It was more the idea of a cave, and, as both human and shark, we realized we had entered a different sort of water.

As we swam into the cave that wasn't a cave, we sensed it was here—within this place or state of consciousness—where sharks learned more consciously about their history. But that was not what held our attention. Rather, it was the calmness—the silence of the place. We suddenly realized how noisy it had been in the waters outside, and how noisy it had always been throughout the shark's life. We recalled the multitude of sounds we had heard since our birth: the squealing of the electric lines; the sounds of so many fish; the songs of whales and other creatures; and the deep humming that was ever present, so much a part of us that we didn't even realize it until now, when suddenly it was gone. We swam and waited in this place of emptiness, not sure what we were waiting for.

As a human I expected there to be a lesson, some kind of teaching or maybe a holographic movie with a message. I then recalled a shark dream I once had in which I found myself in a classroom, watching a film about human-shark evolution. This wasn't like that at all, however. What was now taking place was like a distant remembering. It wasn't orderly, one, two, three, but more a whole, huge picture that you already know but are now remembering, excitedly, detail by detail. The memory had more to do with feelings than thoughts, and it felt as if something dim was becoming brighter and brighter.

If the portals of the perceptions were cleansed, everything would appear as it really is—infinite.

WILLIAM BLAKE

And then, suddenly—just like that—we both knew everything about sharks: a whole history from our beginnings to our connections all over the planet, all over the cosmos. We were now a special shark because we held conscious knowledge of this, and we understood that not all sharks are opened in this manner. We understood that, as with humans, enlightenment about who we are and who we may become is thrilling information, though it also carries the weight of responsibility. And now we would never be the same.

Dreaming a New perspective

Did you know that when you watch a shape-shift occur—be it in a dream, vision, or ordinary reality—that you, too, are part of the experience? This is what a group of animal teachers told me not long after I had the dream of traveling in consciousness with the shark.

Quite often, witnessing transformations in our dreams (such as dreaming a friend becomes an animal, a plant, a star in the sky) or strange events in everyday life (observing from the corner of our eye a cat who seems to suddenly shift in space or even disappear) may signify an initiation to the art of shape-shifting.

Just as it may be easier to talk to animals in our dreams before actually conversing with a whale or giraffe in everyday life, many humans are first introduced to shape-shifting within the dreamtime. Dreams provide a safe, adaptable, and creative world in which transformations of all kinds can occur. We are often more comfortable with the bizarre changes and slippery merging of forms that occur within our dreams, so it is only natural that this may be the first stage for many to apprentice as a shape-shifter.

But observing shape-shifts within dreams is just the beginning. As we deepen in focus, we may experience more variety—and ever more possibility—in the art of shape-shifting. We may be more lucid in our dreams, choosing the particular animal, plant, or aspect of nature that we wish to "see" through: coyote, cactus, rainstorm. Or we may blend with another consciousness, such as in the shark dream, retaining our own awareness while traveling within the body of another. A group of animal teachers shared with me the importance—and fun—of such shape-shifting adventures within our dreams:

"Many times you are not aware of how conscious you actually are or can become in your dreams. As you become more aware, you realize there are many versions of reality, many layers of reality that exist side by side, so to speak. It is not a different geographical space that you must enter to shape-shift, but a different vibration.

"Shape-shifting dreams are designed to help show you—to help 'feel you'—into the experience. They are no less valid than experiences in waking life. In fact, they offer a measure of safety and security because they

An Animal Communication Game
SENSING SYNESTHESIA—SALSA OF THE SENSES!

When exploring new modes of being, such as shape-shifting with animals, it's a good idea to practice shaking up our senses from time to time. Why? Because so many animals experience the world in ways we can't. We don't have gills or wings, whiskers or claws. What would it feel like to breathe through water or hover in the air? By stretching our imaginations and adapting our own senses, we can learn to experience the reality of another in deeper, wider, more meaningful ways. Ready?

Have you ever looked into the deep blue of the twilight sky and felt or heard that color? Have you ever tasted the sound of a howling dog? If you are able to combine your senses in this exciting way, you are experiencing synesthesia. Though hearing the colors of a cat's fur or feeling the sounds of a coyote's song cannot be easily understood by most of us, it is entirely real for some humans. In fact, several researchers suggest that synesthesia may be a more holistic way of perceiving the world.

You can have fun with this exercise in your everyday life, for it is simply to play with swapping and merging your senses. Imagine your eyes can taste the grass and sky. Your fingers are tiny ears, and you can hear the subtleties of all you touch—your clothes, your skin. Imagine you can smell feelings, such as sadness and love, or feel the texture of pale blue. Practice hearing flowers, tasting clouds, smelling sunshine.

This won't make sense to your normal way of perceiving the world—and that's exactly why it's valuable. By blending your senses in different ways, you are building an internal repertoire of sensory translations. Now when an elephant explains to you what it's like to trumpet through his trunk or a hummingbird shares the feeling of fluttering wings, you will already have an idea of how to ease yourself into expanding your senses to more fully appreciate the awesome ways in which life is experienced by others.

occur in the dream world. It would be wise to use such dream sensations as a template or physical reminder of how to 'feel into' a shape-shift, how to feel into the body of an animal or person with whom you are experiencing a shape-shifting experience.

"One of the prime directives of shape-shifting is to experience the shift—not merely to talk about it or study it—but to feel it within yourself. That is the crux, after all, of shape-shifting itself!"

A dream experience of shape-shifting offers a very detailed representation of what it is like to experience reality from the point of view of another. After having the experience many times in the dream world, we are naturally more capable of shifting our consciousness within the everyday world. Just as learning to communicate with animals may first entail imagining a conversation or even seeing, feeling, and experiencing the world through the perspective of animal eyes, so, too, is shape-shifting a simple step fueled by the power of our imagination.

Lend your ears to music, open your eyes to painting, and . . . stop thinking! Just ask yourself whether the work has enabled you to walk about into a hitherto unknown world. If the answer is yes, what more do you want?

WASSILY KANDINSKY

Having New Eyes

The only real voyage of discovery consists not in seeking new landscapes but in having new eyes.

MARCEL PROUST

One day, long after the dream of the shark, I was walking in a mountainous area and saw an eagle soaring overhead. As I gazed up into that brilliant, bright blue Alaskan summer sky, I wondered what it would be like to see from the eagle's eyes. And suddenly—without any thought of shape-shifting, without any plan at all—I "saw" from the eagle's point of view. I was so excited that I gasped and blinked my eyes in amazement, thus losing the vision almost as quickly as it had come. But for one incredible moment, I was both me, looking up at the sky above, and the eagle, looking down upon the green-brown earth. And then I knew, from actual experience, that the world we see is not nearly as firmly fixed as we believe it to be.

So, how to begin? How to experience a shape-shift of consciousness? For some, a shamanic journey might be most appropriate, while others may open unexpectedly through dreams, or be inspired by films or books. As in most everything, you'll need to experiment

STEPPING INTO YOUR ANIMAL'S LIFE
ZAK (DOG) ~ DAWN BRUNKE

Many animals come to visit, teach, or interact with humans for particular reasons. So many animals work in different ways than you are used to perceiving. Some of us find this amusing. You think you are very important at times and we are "just dogs," "just cats," "just fish" and yet—if only you could see it from our perspective!

My invitation to readers is to consider stepping into your animal's life for a time—at least once to be sure, though perhaps many times as well. Allow yourself to open on deeper levels—you will read that phrase a lot within this book—but that is truly what it is: allow yourself to feel a deeper way of seeing the world. Not so much skating around quickly on the surface as sinking down and feeling, sensing, knowing the world from a different channel, a different vibration, a different perspective. This you need to feel—not just to talk about or intellectualize, but feel around your body and in your body.

Allow yourself to merge with any aspect of the Universal One. You are still "you" but you are also expansive and one with all. From this point, there is no need to explain anything, for everything you need to know is present. In the oneness of connection you can feel the growth of plants, the movements of animals, the singing of the stars.

An Animal Communication Exercise
Two Approaches to Shape-Shifting

For either approach, find a quiet, undisturbed place where you can get comfortable, close your eyes, breathe deeply, and relax.

The first approach involves visualizing an animal species you wish to experience. You might choose elephant or orca, parrot or frog. With your inner vision, see the colors, form, and details of your animal with clarity. Now imagine slipping into this animal form as easily as if trying on new clothes. With your consciousness, step into this animal body. Begin to move and stretch. Feel your fur or feathers, the shape of your paws or tail. How do you see the world? What do you sense? As your body shifts into a new shape, so does your consciousness. You may feel a mind connection with your animal species, or you may be guided by an animal spirit to learn more. Enjoy your experience, knowing that when you are ready you can step out of the body just as easily as you stepped in.

The other approach involves visualizing a specific animal—your dog, the bird in the tree, your friend's horse. Tune in to that animal and ask if you may travel with it. If the response is positive, breathe in deeply and allow your consciousness to move beyond the confines of your body. Feel your energy spreading outward, merging into your animal friend. You may suddenly see through your animal's eyes or feel as if you are in the "passenger seat" of consciousness, alongside your animal. What is it like to see, hear, and feel from this perspective? You may be able to share thoughts with your animal, or you may simply be along for the ride.

On ending your journey, remember to give thanks. You may also want to record your experience with notes or sketches for later recall.

and find the way that works most powerfully for you. And, just as in learning animal communication, remember that it is not so much a matter of doing as being.

Many animals are experts in the art of shape-shifting and are happy to share their knowledge, if only you ask. For example, ravens are often venerated both as teachers of flight as well as skilled shape-shifters. In the following talk, a group of ravens explained to me how they see the relationship between shape-shifting and communication. They also offer an invitation to all who are interested in learning more.

ACTS OF TRANSFORMATION
The Ravens ~ Dawn Brunke

In early days, shape-shifting was used by shamans in order to receive a message—perhaps from the gods or from animals or plants, in any case, from a world that was different from their own. Shape-shifting was the vehicle to travel to the other world, but communication was essential to both receive the message and later convey it to the people who needed to hear the message.

Shape-shifting and communication are part and parcel of the same overall act of transformation. We see this in a large sense. Just as communication between humans and animals may be translated through images, feelings, and sensations or, as we are speaking now—mind to mind—so, too, does shape-shifting have many different shades or flavors.

If you deepen your work with shape-shifting—actually coming into the body and sharing the consciousness with another being—you will quickly learn that many species think in very different ways than you do. Perception may be vastly different and the variance in sensing mechanisms (hearing, smell, and many senses that you do not have) become apparent.

At present, in order for you to understand us and we to understand

Raven . . .
Black as pitch,
Mystical as the moon,
Speak to me of magic,
I will fly with you soon.

JAMIE SAMS AND
DAVID CARSON,
MEDICINE CARDS

you, a common translation occurs—both from you to us and we to you. Think of it as the "universal translator device." Thoughts from us are downloaded into you and then make sense through your unique language abilities, metaphors, and familiarity with certain ideas and things; our thoughts are translated in that manner. Your ideas could also download to us in a similar manner. Since we are a species who work to a high degree with communication, we work in a slightly different way than many animals and at this time often have more access to your thoughts and ideas than you to us. In time, this might change.

Students of shape-shifting seem to grow quickly and we are often surprised by information that is new to us and worth exploring. We are thus most always accommodating to new students and would like to encourage all humans to explore this arena.

We have much information to convey to humans. We invite you—and all those reading this—to travel with us. This is the quickest manner of learning more intimately about our kind. We encourage you to keep your connections open; to keep your awareness extended. If you like, we will take you on a voyage. You can ride with us and learn how we see the world through our eyes in order that you will communicate it back to others—so that you can learn to better understand and see your own world as well.

As the ravens—and many other animals—note, shape-shifting is a matter of shifting not just the shape of our body, but the shape of our thoughts. It is about shifting the shape of our perceptions, our experience of who we are. As with everything in the Web of Life, all is interconnected. If you dedicate yourself to exploring the art of shape-shifting, you come to realize that shape-shifts into other forms of consciousness, besides being interesting in themselves, also hold a higher purpose: to shake you up a bit and loosen your hold on who you thought you were.

At the same time, it is the smaller shape-shifts—the gentle beginnings of seeing through the eyes of another, even if only for a moment—that move us deeper. To experience life as a dolphin, a wolf, or a bear can change our own life dramatically. But, just as with animal communication, we are often asked to open larger still. What is it like to see the world through the eyes of a snake, a rat, a mosquito, or a fly? Are you ready to confront the resistance that so much of humanity has to the very idea of shape-shifting?

The Nature of Fear

As Gregor Samsa awoke one morning from uneasy
dreams he found himself transformed in his
bed into a gigantic insect.

FRANZ KAFKA,
THE METAMORPHOSIS

A mind once stretched by a new idea never regains it original dimension.

OLIVER WENDELL HOLMES

While I was working on this chapter, a flying creature—something like a fly, but with a longer, slimmer torso and a curious red head—landed in front of me and paused upon my keyboard.

"I'm a different form of consciousness," the little bug declared. *"I'm a form you don't know well and are slightly repulsed yet intrigued by."* Flying up and landing on my arm to be extra close and personal, he indicated that his presence and actions show me something important. And here is what this most extraordinary teacher had to say: *"I come to remind you of the constant moving back and forth between forms, of this never-ending dance in shapes, bodies, forms, and masks. I come to say that the reason frightful creatures come so close to you (or others) is to push you just a tad closer to the face of fear. Because when you are facing fear, you are facing a more intimate self, a self that needs*

love more than many, a self that brings you closer to an understanding of who you and all of us truly are.

"Why do so many humans fear insects? What is it about insects you fear when we are so little and you are so large? Why do you give us the power to frighten you? What part of yourself—what small yet powerful part of yourself—are you so afraid of? These are my questions to you. This is what I bring to mind when you write about loosening your hold on who you think you are. This is why we flying creatures can be so valuable to humankind. We pollinate your fields, and we pollinate the darker soils of your being, so that small things can germinate and grow into lovely flowers of awareness and becoming.

"Never underestimate the small in your life. It holds the vastness of treasures beyond reckoning—my wisdom, your wisdom, our collective wisdom—me to you, you to me, and so between us all."

One should pay attention to even the smallest crawling creature for these, too, may have a valuable lesson to teach us.

Black Elk

In his book *Shapeshifting*, author John Perkins discusses the human fears about this transformational experience with Viejo Itza, a Mayan shaman and teacher. Itza points out that the biggest fear humans hold is that if we truly shape-shift our body, we won't be able to return to our original shape—or, more daunting still, that we won't want to. As Itza comments, "In a way you have to shapeshift yourself out of it. . . . You have to accept that you already *are* the same as the thing you're going to shift into—that your separateness is only an illusion. You must also believe that there is no hierarchy, that you as human being are no higher on some evolutionary chart than you as tree or jaguar."[1]

And that is the key at the core of shape-shifting. If we can accept—if we can know by feeling it deep within ourselves—that our separateness is illusion, then we can finally let go, breathe fully, and allow ourselves to attune to the deeper energy that pulses through all creation. Feeling that energy within ourselves, we can ride it like a wave and emerge through the consciousness of any being—dog, camel, rabbit, mountain lion—that is open to sharing.

Shape-shifting is mostly a matter of allowing our own energy body to combine with another, to shift our awareness so as to "ride along" or inhabit the consciousness of another. Whether momentarily seeing through the eyes of an animal, or sharing thoughts, feelings, and experiences in a blending of energy, or even seeming to take control, as if becoming an animal, the basis of all shape-shifting is the same: it is about moving energy, shifting our consciousness to alter our perception or perspective and thus to gain a new appreciation of the world.

A group of finches shared their take on this in the following way: *"Part of the shape-shifting adventure is to travel beyond your own perceptions of what you see as bird and begin to see with bird eyes—or any animal's eyes. This adventure is a moving outside of your own perceptions and sharing the perceptions of others around you. In order to do this you must truly know—deep within you—the essence of our mutual interconnection, our essential oneness. It is only by following that thread of connection that you can truly enter the being of another and have the chance to see from their perspective.*

"Birds reveal a fascinating aspect of this ability, as in your expression 'a bird's eye view.' Our ability to fly is a method of transportation as well as a means of seeing from different perspectives. We can soar high or low; some of us can glide and some of us can hover. As a group, we offer many ways of seeing the world—both our world and your world—from varying perspectives.

"Our belief is that birds offer humans a unique manner of shifting from their present perspective to a much larger perspective. In the human world you have accomplished this in your own way—through planes, rockets, satellites, and many other machines that help you to see from a higher perspective.

. . . I am circling around God, around the ancient tower, and I have been circling for a thousand years, and I still don't know if I am a falcon, or a storm, or a great song.

RAINER MARIA RILKE

"We assure you, however, that it is a unique experience to fly with a bird, to see the beauty of the world from our eyes. We invite you—and others who are interested—to travel with us. Follow your connection portal to feel our oneness. Come aboard the Finch Express and see your world anew! Most any bird will be happy to guide you. All you need is to express your desire. We will be waiting for you."

Explanation separates us from astonishment, which is the only gateway to the incomprehensible

EUGENE IONESCO

By seeing through the eyes of another, we learn something new—not only about the other, but about ourselves. By being "shaken up" through shape-shifting experiences, we come to realize that our experience is simply one way of seeing the world. It is not the only way, and certainly not the best way for all. For some, this realization is dangerous territory, for it reveals that the world we know is simply one version of reality, not reality itself.

The Teaching

If I were to begin life again, I should want it as it were. I would only open my eyes a little more.

JULES RENARD

Shape-shifting teaches us many things while offering a vast array of creative possibilities. Learning to merge our consciousness with any aspect of life we choose can be exhilarating, enlightening, educational, extraordinary—and fun.

Shape-shifting also reveals a fundamental truth: that a living flow of energy passes through and unites all things. It is by tuning in to this energy—this Universal Mind or Flow—that we are able to shift the shape of our consciousness. We can experience life and death, time and space, eating, flying, sleeping, thinking, and loving through the thoughts and senses of an incredibly wide diversity of animals. We can learn about worlds we don't know as well as how the world we do know appears differently to different beings.

Shape-shifting shows us that things never really die. Water in the ocean evaporates, becoming a cloud that bursts into rain, saturating plants that are eaten by animals, traveling through moving bodies until expelled, soaking into the earth, becoming part of a stream that becomes a river that flows to the ocean once again. All death is

ON SHIFTING SHAPES AND REALITY
A Sampling of Books and Films

The View from the Oak: The Private Worlds of Other Creatures by Judith and Herbert Kohl. Focusing on the unique ways different animals experience the world, this book offers a more scientific approach to understanding the consciousness of others.

The Catswold Portal by Shirley Rosseau Murphy. A captivating adventure involving the shape-changing Catswolds, who move between worlds and shift between cat and human form.

The Golden Compass by Philip Pullman. In the strange yet somehow familiar world of Lyra Belacqua, every human has a daemon—a version of his or her soul in animal form—which, for young people, can shift shapes to suit one's needs.

The Witches (1990). This funny, frightening, magical film, based on Roald Dahl's book of the same name, stars Angelica Houston as the Grand High Witch who wishes all children to be turned into mice.

Pay It Forward (2000). Based on the novel by Catherine Ryan Hyde, this film with Kevin Spacey, Helen Hunt, and Haley Joel Osment looks at how one small vision can shift the shape of collective consciousness.

A LESSON FROM LION
Journal Entry

I merged with an old male lion this morning. I felt his mane around my face, his claws and paws, body resting, two front legs stretched out before us. I felt the roar that came from deep within, and it felt good. It was a declaration, an affirmation, an announcement: *"I AM!"*

The old lion showed me many things from his perspective. I was able to see the land from his eyes—dots of antelope in the distance. Everything was yellow and brown and golden. Movement was the key to his vision, for it was as if movement were part of the color, part of the landscape. This is hard to describe in human terms for it was so different from the human way of seeing. I could smell in different tones as well—layers of smell, subtleties that had no words. It was as if the smells were emotions. The scent of fear was the strongest, the lion showed me. If an animal puts out fear, that scent is stronger than movement and most likely that animal will be taken, whether it runs or not (though most animals will freeze and then run, the lion added).

"Lions can be gentle," he tells me—allowing me to feel the movement of softened paws, delicate licks of the tongue, gestures of nuzzling—*"but we can also kill in an instant"*—and he shares what it feels like for claws to jackknife and flex from their hiding places beneath velvet paws.

Lion in Africa
Photo by Dawn Brunke

The lion tells me that even within the pride he hunts by himself at times, and as he was growing up he also hunted prey. He likes the hunt—sharing with me the movement involved—the moment when his teeth sink into flesh and muscle and the warm blood flows. He shares this as a delicious taste—salty and warm and nourishing, full of life. When he shares my thoughts and looks into my experience of eating meat, he says there is no comparison. *"You have never eaten life in this way,"* he tells me.

The old lion goes on to say that humans like me have no real sense of presence, such as lions do. *"Lions claim their presence. It is rare that a lion feels fear,"* he says. He tells me lions are indeed "royal" and "regal" and they do have "pride" and it is no mistake that humans use those words in association with lions.

After several moments of silence, the lion informs me that he feels most humans allow fear to control them, or at least allow fear to be overwhelmingly present in their lives. He tells me he doesn't know much of humans but now has a sense of them by sharing thoughts and feelings with me, just as he is giving me a sense of lions by allowing me to share his world.

"Humans need to learn to eat their fear," he says. *"To claim their presence"*. He tells me I worry way too much about whether I am right or wrong, and that I don't spend nearly enough focus or energy on claiming my presence in the world. He shows me that by claiming one's presence one puts fear in its proper place.

This reminds me of a story about J. Allen Boone, who once traveled into the jungles of Africa without a weapon, believing that "all the jungle creatures he met, despite their bad reputations, would be friendly if his thoughts about them were friendly."[2] For a long time, I felt that Boone was foolhardy in this respect. What if he caught a tiger on a bad day, or met a gorilla with a temper? Just because you can talk with animals doesn't necessarily mean you can convince a hungry one not to eat you, after all.

And yet the way the lion echoed his statement—*"by claiming one's presence one puts fear in its proper place"*—shifted something in my thinking and I began to see in a new way. Boone believed that "right relations are possible outwardly only when they have first been made so inwardly."[3] For Boone, sitting in the jungle without a weapon was more than mere confidence or bravado, and it had nothing to do with the other animals. Rather, by claiming his *presence*, Boone had found "right relations" within himself. By shifting the shape of his consciousness to a new way of being, he also naturally reshaped his relationship with others—the lion, the jungle, the world.

How simple! How powerful! As I think these thoughts, the old lion listens and tells me this is so—that it is never a matter of the other beings in our life. It is always about claiming presence for ourselves. And only we can welcome that presence into our being. By claiming our presence, we also claim the world.

I feel the old lion nodding as I think these thoughts. For a flicker of a moment, I feel his satisfaction as well. He tells me then that he will be happy to talk and instruct me again. And for that I thank him very deeply indeed.

merely a change of form, for all life is continuously reshaping itself—be it the nature of water, the ever shifting geography of the land, or the cycle of birth to death and back again of animals of all kinds. If you look, you will see this everywhere on our planet—everything shifting in shape and form and idea and consciousness—causing you to wonder, perhaps, how you could not have noticed this all along.

As my dog Zak once related, *"At a certain point, you may ask, 'Well, what can I do with this? How does it serve me? How does it serve humanity? What is the real value of shape-shifting?'*

"Surely there is value in seeing the world from the eyes of another—be it animal, plant, or human. There are nearly limitless possibilities, and you can learn many, many things about the world through talking or merging with just one animal.

"At another level, shape-shifting allows you to see your own species in a new light. The views of other animals help you to expand yourself with new perceptions so as to reevaluate your thoughts and beliefs, and those of your species. It allows you to add some depth and texture to the fullness of who you are and to see more clearly the magnificence of the world around you.

"At still another point of being, you come to appreciate the fact that what you are doing is opening to a larger presence. In a sense, you are rewriting what it means to be human."

As we familiarize ourselves with the ever shifting shapes of our perceptions, we open to a larger version of ourselves. We step beyond the limits of who we thought we were. As we open more deeply to this Universal Mind or Flow, we begin to see not so much from inside ourselves but *through* ourselves. With that small *Aha!* we move from the experience of a limited "I" to a larger awareness of life living through us. It is a final gift from the art of shape-shifting, for we realize we are this and that and the other, too—lion, jaguar, human,

I am the Poem of the Earth,
    said the voice of
    the rain,
Eternal I rise impalpable
    out of the land and the
    bottomless sea
        WALT WHITMAN

raven—all things pulsing with the flow of One. And then we see: we are all shape-shifters, each and every one.

> *In a sense, everything in this world is about shape-shifting. We are all shape-shifters, for we are all constantly changing. Our life is a shape-shift, our creations are shape-shifts. Everything we do or make is seeded in thought, which is a kind of shape-shift. This is the deeper sense of shape-shifting, the deeper essence of All That Is.*
> ANIMAL GUARDIANS OF THE EARTH

THE ANCIENT ART
The Ravens ~ Dawn Brunke

Greetings! We are the Raven Folk, the Raven People, shape-shifters of old and friends to humans throughout our many eons on this planet together.

The history of human-raven affairs is deep, and there are so many chapters that it would be impossible to encompass them all. But let us tell you, the young readers of this book, that Ravens have long watched and observed the ways of humans. Our efforts at being in this world have often coincided with your own. And we have been teachers to many humans, especially those who have desired to learn the ancient art of shape-shifting.

For us, shape-shifting is a vehicle of education. And yes, of course it is fun—for we ravens are experts at both fun and learning!

Many of the various bird tribes journey while we sleep, or while standing still and calm, hiding within the boughs of protective trees. In fact, we often journey into the trees, partaking of their wisdom and viewing ourselves through the "eyes" of the trees, which are of course not eyes at all but another means of perceiving the world.

We also journey on what you might call dreams or journeys of consciousness in which we fly with other ravens, or with the ravens of old— yes, shape-shifting can be used to access both past and future times! There are many, many possibilities! Sometimes we project our vision to high above the earth, to the moon or to passing clouds. This is often how we plan our days or to know of weather patterns that are coming our way. We teach this to our youngsters at an early age, and many youngsters learn by traveling in consciousness with a parent or elder.

Even our hopping movements reveal a kind of shape-shift, an observation for humans of how Ravens travel not just in the air but on the earth as well.

Our advice to you is to try on this skill from time to time, incorporate it into your life. It is a wise being who discovers and uses this wonderful talent of moving between forms, trying on the world from different bodies, different eyes, different minds and states of being.

We Ravens offer you tutelage, if you are interested. Ravens, crows— many of us are happy to help. Or, seek out your own animal teachers and ask to learn of the shape-shifting days of old when many animals— including the human animal—feasted together on this splendid repast of knowing the world through so many different eyes and ears and ways of perceptive feeling.

Lastly, our wisdom to you—our gift to you—is one of attention. To know that as you shift shapes you are accessing greater and ever more aspects of yourself. At the deepest levels, there is only One tone, One being, which lives through all life. That is you. Tat Tvam Asi, to quote a very old truth—Thou are that. As are we all, in the One.

10
center being

At the center of your being you have the answer;
You know who you are and you know what you want.

LAO-TZU

When I first began communicating with animals, I was thrilled and amazed, and yet, for a long time, I wondered if what I was hearing was "real." Even with my doubts, I practiced as much as I could, intrigued by this long-forgotten ability that seemed to become more "real" with each day.

I talked with many different animals—my dogs and goldfish; the spiders, flies, mosquitoes, bees, and butterflies in the backyard; the ravens and moose passing through the forest; neighborhood cats and rabbits; animals living with friends and acquaintances; and many others. Most often, I would sit with a notebook or computer, close my eyes, tune in to the individual animal or species, ask questions, and listen. I would then type or write what I was hearing and sensing. This method worked well for me as my logical brain was too focused on recording the experience to judge it, thus freeing my intuitive side to enjoy itself without worry of whether the conversation was real or not. I also discovered it was very helpful to have a written report as I would often not remember details of the talk until reading it later.

After gaining some confidence and feeling more at ease with the deeper nature of the messages I was receiving, I wondered where this newfound ability might lead. Why was I being opened to animals in this way? In rereading my growing collection of talks, I noticed that several different animals had referred to me as a "scribe." *Yes,* a voice within me responded. Being a scribe—someone who is called to listen to animals and share their stories with others—felt right and true and real for me.

On a simple level, a scribe is someone who copies or transcribes information from one medium into another (the spoken word into the written word, for example). On deeper levels, scribes help to shape ideas and thoughts into words or other means of expression. For myself, I often felt a surprising multilayered partnership while talking with animals in which our mind-to-mind and heart-to-heart or even soul-to-soul meeting allowed a cocreation of ideas, feelings, unique perspectives, and experiences to flow between us and emerge—magically somehow—into a written expression of collaboration. *Yes,* I felt again and again: a scribe—this is part of who I am and want to be.

I only went out for a walk, and finally concluded to stay out till sundown, for going out, I found, was really going in.

JOHN MUIR

> *Know what you want,*
> *know what makes you feel good about yourself,*
> *know what brings you into harmony with others.*
>
> I CHING

TO ACCOMPLISH GREAT THINGS

Perhaps you are wondering, as you near the end of this book, how talking with animals, working with animal guides, or deepening your connection to wildlife and nature will fit within your life. How might you use your abilities in everyday life, or in a professional capacity? What is it that calls to you most deeply? Can you see the path that shines most brightly for you?

BE TRUE TO YOUR SPIRIT
Barney (dog) ~ Kat Berard

We are here to bring your heart out—to help you feel what you know deep inside to be true—that you are worthy of the love that you show to us. We show it back to you; look in our eyes, you see it there. We do not lie. What you see is what you get. Sometimes you do not look closely, you are too afraid. You do not want to see yourself, to give acceptance and love and graciousness and compassion to yourself. We hold it for you to see—and that is the truth.

Be true to your spirit, your self, your way of being. Do not walk as another does. Walk as you are meant to walk. Be who you are. You are here at this moment, in this lifetime, to accomplish great things.

Twenty years from now you will be more disappointed by the things you didn't do than by the ones you did. So throw off the bowlines. Sail away from the safe harbor. Catch the trade winds in your sails. Explore. Dream. Discover.

MARK TWAIN

Barney and Kat
Photo courtesy of Kat Berard

Careers with animals can be as familiar or as unusual and creative as you like—from doctor of veterinary medicine to holistic animal healer specializing in energy work; from wildlife biologist to animal telepathy teacher; from training search and rescue dogs to rehabilitating injured wildlife; from directing a sanctuary for homeless animals to increasing public awareness of animal welfare by speaking in classrooms or civic groups. Sometimes we have an inkling of what path we might choose, and other times our path seems to find us in the most curious of ways.

As a young college student, Carol Buckley fell in love with a baby elephant that had been bought as a mascot for a tire store in her neighborhood. Dedicated to learning all she could about elephants, Carol made friends with the pachyderm. She watched her, fed her, played with her, and finally adopted the little elephant she named Tarra. Carol and Tarra worked in a theme park and circuses, traveling the world, during which time Tarra became famous in stage shows, parades, television shows, and films. After nearly fifteen years, however, the thrill of performing paled for Tarra, and Carol searched for a way for her beloved elephant to be with other elephants, to grow old in a natural setting. As Carol wrote in her book, *Travels with Tarra*, "I knew Tarra could not go back to the wild—but what about bringing the wild to her? I dreamed of a place where many elephants like Tarra, from zoos and circuses, could live together as a family. It would be a sanctuary for captive elephants, a place built just for them. I knew I had to make that dream come true."[1] And, in 1995, Carol did just that by cofounding the Elephant Sanctuary, the nation's first natural habitat refuge specifically for endangered elephants such as Tarra. (For more information on the Elephant Sanctuary as well as all of the groups and programs listed in this chapter, see the resources section.)

Wheresoever you go, go with all your heart.

CONFUCIUS

Carol and Tarra
Photo courtesy of The Elephant Sanctuary

Whatever you do, or dream you can, begin it. Boldness has genius and power and magic in it. Begin it now.

GOETHE

Be the change

Never doubt that a small group of thoughtful, committed
citizens can change the world. Indeed, it is the only thing
that ever has.

MARGARET MEAD

In the late 1980s more than fifteen million homeless dogs and cats were destroyed each year in the United States. In the late 1990s that figure dropped to less than five million a year, and the number is dropping still. In most part, this is due to the success of spay/neuter efforts and adoption programs, all begun by small groups of "thought-ful, committed citizens" wanting to see a change in the world.

No matter how small a single change begins, it can easily and quickly expand, inspiring other changes, creating new ideas and models for the world. When groups of animal lovers questioned the conventional belief that humane societies had no choice but to destroy their "unadoptable" animals, some formed their own no-kill sanctuaries. Today, many more shelters, humane societies, and animal control groups are becoming no-kill facilities, emphasizing adoption and increasing public awareness through volunteer, internship, and educational programs. One of the largest is the Best Friends Animal Sanctuary in Utah, which houses about 1,500 animals daily (including dogs, cats, horses, burros, rabbits, goats, and more), produces a magazine that prints "all the good news about animals, wildlife, and the earth" and focuses on how we *can* change our world.

Other centers offer rescue, rehabilitation, and relocation to wild or exotic animals. Some, such as Wildlife WayStation in California, offer sanctuary to animal species from all over the world, while others focus on specific species—anything from abandoned potbellied pigs to chimpanzees no longer used in medical research. Still other sanctuaries provide lifetime care for abused, ill, or elderly animals, or those with special needs, while animal hospice facilities, such as Angel's Gate in New York, offer therapy, comfort, and companionship to animals in their final days. Without exception, each of these centers began with one individual's or small group's desire to make a difference.

We must be the change we wish to see in the world.
MOHANDAS GANDHI

Your decision to evolve consciously through responsible choice contributes not only to your own evolution, but also to the evolution of all of those aspects of humanity in which you participate. It is not just you that is evolving through your decisions, but the entirety of humanity.

GARY ZUKAV,
THE SEAT OF THE SOUL

How Can I Help?

Adopt. Looking for an animal friend? Adopt through your local shelter or an online adoption group. Or, foster care an animal until a permanent home can be found. If your community does not have a foster care group, consider creating one. Help promote adoption with photos and written descriptions of animals in need for newspapers, bulletin boards, or adoption Web sites.

Volunteer. Assist understaffed shelters by offering to walk, feed, groom, clean, or spend time with the animals. Use gentle touch or massage to calm animals; use communication skills to explain where they are and what is happening. Some communicators write up descriptions of each animal's likes, dislikes, and family preferences to help place them in the best possible home.

Donate. Help raise money (and awareness) for sanctuaries, shelters, search and rescue, or animal care groups by holding fundraisers or neighborhood garage sales, or using donation cans placed at local businesses. Pass on animal equipment you no longer need (doghouses, grooming equipment, blankets, or towels) or check out yard sales and thrift stores for low-cost bedding, toys, or leashes to donate.

Educate. Teach young children to respect and care for animals by speaking at elementary schools. Help friends discover their animal guides through sharing your experiences. Educate others by writing of your encounters or communications with animals for school or local papers. By cultivating awareness of our deeper connections with animals and nature, we raise collective consciousness and encourage the world to treat all living things—animals, plants, the environment, and each other—with consideration.

working partnerships

There are many innovative programs that bring humans and animals together in ways that visibly benefit all. For example, offering young inmates or troubled teens in rehabilitation centers the chance to care for abandoned or abused animals promotes mutual trust and friendship between humans who have been hurt, neglected, or mistreated and animals who have experienced the same. Likewise, programs that team special needs youngsters with injured dolphins or lame horses provide therapy for both humans and animals.

Life presents us with cycles of give and take. At times humans dedicate their efforts to helping animals, such as through rescue and rehabilitation programs. At other times it is animals—dogs guiding the blind or Capuchin monkeys aiding quadriplegics—who seem to be the ones dedicated to helping humans. And yet, as we peer deeper beneath the surface, we find there is always the relationship, always the interconnected needs and learning experiences for both human and animal.

Therapy animals, along with their handlers, visit patients in hospitals, nursing homes, and special learning centers to promote healing and emotional well-being. Simply by their presence, these animals can make a remarkable difference in recovery. Similarly, therapy dogs or horses may help children with autism or learning disabilities to become more responsive and communicative.

Many studies show the value to humans of such interaction. But how do animals in such situations feel? I once spoke with a guide dog who told me about her "mentor," a dog working in spirit form as counselor to canines choosing to interact with humans in this way. Here is what the guide dog mentor had to say: *"The animals who work with me—specifically, dogs who work with humans needing visual help—often choose this role as part of an overall spiritual training. A comparison for humans might be young doctors who learn about different branches of medicine by training with different types of 'specialty' doctors for short periods of time. Most of the dogs I work with come to learn about forming a partnership with an individual human, developing their senses very keenly and then translating that information to their human partner.*

"Many beings in the spirit world believe at first that this will be an easy task, though once they come into form, they find this is not always the case! For example, some find it difficult to balance the instinctual nature of a dog with the part that strives to remember, stay clear, and focus on the task at hand. Others come to work on fine-tuning their sensitivities and discover it is rather like learning to do very minute operations while wearing large furry gloves.

"It will benefit humans to engage the silent language of communication more consciously. Humans can also learn quite a bit from the spirit beings who come into form as service animals. Some enjoy speaking of their experiences and, truly, have much to share."

Barney, a rescued male Weimaraner currently in training to become a certified search and rescue dog, told his person Kat Berard what it means for him to work in this way.

"Was I born to do this? It is my job; it fits me well. This is elite work, and we have to work hard and pay attention. And yet, it is easy when I just flow with myself, with how my body works. It is a powerful feeling, knowing I can be of service in this way. It means that I get to be who I am, all the way. Every part of me gets to be a part of what I'm doing. It makes me feel big and full, and I feel everything about me intensely. It is challenging, yet it is natural for me. It lets me be all of everything around me, and of you, and part of the team. We are very close now in what we do together, looking in the same way, being better at who we are. I like what we do together—a lot!"

More humans are considering the needs and desires of animals by consulting with them and, if appropriate, forming working partnerships. A

Out beyond the ideas of right and wrong there is a field—meet me there.

RUMI

new wave of animal trainers has shifted from the old mentality of domination to an attitude of equality. Those with this newer mind-set seek the challenge of learning new skills and fine-tuning abilities for both partners. Some groups of animals and humans work together brainstorming fresh ideas for human-animal interaction in the world, or collaborating on projects to expand our collective vision of life on planet Earth.

For example, whale naturalist Mary J. Getten drew upon both her science background and her animal communication skills while interviewing orcas for *Communicating with Orcas,* a book that presents the whales' perspective. Some of what Mary learned was in keeping with what humans already knew about whales; however, Mary's friend Granny (the matriarch orca of the whale pod Mary knew best) and other whales that she worked with gave Mary new information that expands our understanding of how whales experience the world. Similarly, by talking with Mary, many of the whales learned something about how humans see the world.

Some fish I once met suggested creating Exchange Centers—places where animals and humans might both come and go freely, meeting for short periods of time to share thoughts, swap perspectives, exchange knowledge, and learn from each other's experience.[2] The creative range of possibilities to form exciting, mutually beneficial partnerships with animals is as open to us as we are willing to be.

We would like for humans to talk to us, to exchange thoughts, to question us as well as themselves. Think of our interchange as an opportunity to learn about different cultures and species. We are here as teachers, spokesbeings, ambassadors of knowledge as well as goodwill.

FISH AT SEALIFE CENTER ~
DAWN BRUNKE

Ambassadors of Deeper understanding

Numerous individuals and groups (composed of both humans and animals) work to promote awareness and deepen our collective understanding of how we might live better with all species upon this little gem of a planet. Many serve as role models, revealing by example positive ways we can open to the rich diversity and intelligence of all life, and become better environmental stewards of our world.

Consider Jane Goodall and her dedication to wild chimpanzees. It is important to note that Goodall's efforts focus on aiding both chimp and human populations, for lack of forest land is often just as much a problem for humans as for chimpanzees. How can there be balance or health of the whole if any group is in need? The Goodall Institute thus seeks to foster positive relationships among animals, humans, and the environment.

> *Let us develop respect for all living things. Let us try to replace impatience and intolerance with understanding and compassion. And love.*
>
> JANE GOODALL

If you are interested in helping to care for wildlife or the land and water, or in helping to make the planet a healthier place for all living beings, you might consider joining, volunteering, or contributing to a group that focuses on protecting endangered species and habitats. As in all things in life, it's wise to research the groups you are interested in. Do they consider a wide range of perspectives, offering possibilities of change through education and tolerance? Do they offer informed, well-grounded ideas that resonate with you? Are the proposed solutions in the best interest of promoting healthier conditions for all beings on our planet? There is a vast difference between using scare tactics, anger, or an "us versus them" mentality and honoring a diversity of viewpoints, encouraging dialogue and the inspired solutions that come from it, and working together to seek ways in which all living beings will benefit.

Our task must be to free ourselves by widening our circle of compassion to embrace all living beings and all of nature.

ALBERT EINSTEIN

Thank you for allowing our voice to be heard. Thanks to all who are reading our words and feelings. Often just by listening to others, we learn not only about ourselves but also about our role in the world. We learn how we can understand others better as well as ourselves. We moose do not wish to harm others. We try to respect your ways. We only ask for you to be considerate of our ways, and to honor us when we come into your world to help you learn. We also learn from you.

A GROUP OF MOOSE ~
DAWN BRUNKE

A wise llama named Inka reminds us of this most important point: *"All of us must embrace the whole and shine our light and offer our love to everyone. Yes, speak out against cruelty and injustice. Do it with love and compassion. If you are forgetting the love, you are adding your hatred, your anger, and your judgment to the situation you want to transform; then you are contributing fuel to continue the circle of abuse. Love is the answer to every question. Let love embrace you when you are feeling despair about the state of the world, let love heal your own wounds, and let love spill out of you to heal others. Let your own life be an example, a role model, for a compassionate way to live. All the animals will support you in this and assist you when you need guidance or an extra dose of love."*

Inka and Tera
Photo by Ducka Kelly

WAYS TO DEEPEN

Join others. Form practice groups with friends to fine-tune animal communication skills and share dreams, magical meetings, and teachings from animal guides. Support each other by listening and offering constructive feedback. Or, join an online group or forum to exchange tips, ask questions, offer help, and practice long-distance communication with others.

Help and learn. Many sanctuaries, shelters, rehabilitation centers, and other groups offer apprentice and internship programs (some especially for young people), where you can learn practical skills as you help animals. Service and therapy animal organizations often look to volunteers to raise and foster pups. Be creative as you pursue what interests you. Contact practicing wildlife rehabilitators, feral cat caretakers, animal healers, or search and rescue groups to learn how you can help and learn.

Make informed, healthy choices. Keep local animal populations low by spaying or neutering your animals. Learn about the dangers of declawing cats or debarking dogs, and enlighten others. Always consider the impact your decisions as a caretaker will have on your animal's well-being as well as your community and the world at large.

Feed and eat well. Many ancient people lived in harmony with the animals they raised, hunted, and ate. Connecting with animal spirits, they honored the gift of life provided. We have moved away from this deeper connection and, as a result, much of the packaged meat sold at groceries holds precious little nutrition for our body or spirit, and often many dangerous chemical additives as well. Packaged food for our animal friends is similarly lacking. Eating animals raised production style in cramped, dirty cages with no regard for their life force causes entire animal species to become sick in body and soul, as it does us.[3] If you eat animal products, find local farms or companies that promote wholesome feed and healthy living conditions for their animals. Become more aware of what both you and your animal friends eat.

Listen. Remember that the messages you need to hear are all around you, all the time. Allow yourself some quiet time each day to listen to those around you—your family and friends as well as animals you live with or meet. By sharing your feelings and thoughts at deeper levels, and by providing an open and quiet space to really listen, you encourage others to do the same.

As ambassadors of deeper understanding, we are called upon to dig beneath the surface and bring our own buried truths to light. In order to do this, we must be true to ourselves, honoring all of our experiences by looking at all aspects of who we are—the good and helpful as well as the fearful and petty. By seeking a more genuine understanding of ourselves and accepting what we find, we allow change to occur, both in ourselves and in others. By shining our truth we come closer to being who we really are.

You can't take sides when you know the earth is round.

PATRICIA SUN

There are big changes coming. Humans are—finally!—beginning to see that it's okay to talk with animals.

There are some humans who are making room in their lives for animals to advise them and to converse, for living in harmony. This is not true of all humans, for many are still afraid. So, if you want to help animals, it helps to help humans as well, because as long as humans are afraid, they will hurt each other, and hurt us animals, too. You have to remember this, too, when it comes to how you treat yourselves. If you are mean to yourself and are afraid, if you beat yourself up and tell yourself you cannot talk to animals or hear them, then it will be hard for you!

MAYA (CAT) ∾ GRETCHEN KUNZ

everything you need

My world is one of quiet contemplation, and moments of great joy. I am not here to prove anything or to be the "best" at something. I Am Who I Am, and that means that whatever I do or exhibit or feel and share with my beloveds is the core essence of me. Honesty, Courage, Honor—these are important to me. That is what I am

about. I am also Love—big Love. And I am exactly where
I am supposed to be. My life is a good place to be.
Everything you need to live your life harmoniously, peace-
fully, joyfully, is already within you. You just have to
choose it. So look at the buffet of life and pick what sounds
and feels and smells and tastes good to you, and load up
your plate. Find the joy in what living here is about.

MAX (DOG) ~ KAT BERARD

Max
Photo by Kat Berard

I could give you no advice
but this: to go into yourself
and to explore the depths
where your life wells forth.

RAINER MARIA RILKE,
LETTERS TO A YOUNG POET

As Max notes, everything you need to live your life in harmony is
already present. What do you choose? "Follow your bliss," advised
Joseph Campbell. Find what sparks your interest, touches your
heart, ignites your thoughts, and blazes your passion.

We all play a part in the work that is done. We are all
connected to an energetic web of life and can sense when
something is needed and then do our part to fulfill the
request. Each part enjoys being whole and balanced, and

enjoys it most when it can be itself. Humans, animals,
nature, insects, even energy itself occurring
in myriad forms—we each seek this natural
state of being and assist one another to achieve this goal
by the very nature of our being.

KC (CAT) ~ MORGINE JURDAN

Indeed, it all goes back to being—most specifically, being true to who we are. "Do little and be" is just as much a key to learning animal communication as it is a helpful path to finding our center, tapping in to the flow of all life, and expressing our unique presence within that flow. This is not to say we shouldn't do things, of course, for it is often the doing that brings us to being. Fully engaging ourselves in what we are doing—especially what we love to do—can become a meditation, a way of stilling our mind and recentering our awareness on who we are, right here, right now.

As a Zen Buddhist proverb explains, "Before enlightenment, chop wood and carry water; after enlightenment, chop wood and carry water." Shifting to a deeper sense of being doesn't necessarily change what we do, though it may certainly change our awareness of how we do it. It is a shape-shift of consciousness, a way of allowing the momentum of doing to carry us into the stillness and mystery of being.

When we come to a point of rest in our own being,
we encounter a world where all things are at
rest, and then a tree becomes a mystery, a cloud
becomes a revelation, and each person we meet a
cosmos whose riches we can only glimpse.

DAG HAMMARSKJOLD

In such moments we are in balance, feeling the flow of life moving through us.

Life is a balancing act. Remember, communicating
is all about balance. When you are in balance
with yourself, you feel good, take good care of yourself and
love yourself. Things could be falling apart around
you—people upset, chaos occurring—and
you remain peaceful and calm, doing what you need
to do. This is a form of communication between you and
your body and your mind, all blended into one.
You feel at peace inside yourself and can
handle whatever happens around you. When you are
in this place, you can communicate clearly.

KC (CAT) ~ MORGINE JURDAN

KC
Photo by Morgine Jurdan

Here and Now

"Here and now, boys," chanted the bird. "Here and now . . ."
ALDOUS HUXLEY, ISLAND

It is easy to feel a loving connection with all beings when we are in balance. And life can be like this. It's great. But what happens when we lose our balance, when the currents of life seem to dash us on the rocks? How do we stay centered in being when there are so many things that divert us, so many ways to lose our center? How can we find being when all we seem to be doing is running into walls and obstacles?

While thinking these questions, my wise dog pal Zak responded from his napping place beneath my desk:

"Thoughts, thoughts, thoughts—that is what I hear when I tune in to humanity at large. Even to those whose thoughts are directed toward working on higher aspects of oneself, I say: thoughts, thoughts, thoughts!

"Your thoughts build the very walls you ask about. The problem is not the walls, because the walls do not exist; the problem is the thoughts of 'walls' and 'running into walls.'

"When you are quiet and centered all is well. Is this not true? How can anything not be well when you are centered and connected to All That Is? What I hear you asking, at a deeper level, is how can I 'be' in this place of centeredness throughout my day?

"The answer may be found in continually moving back to the space of centeredness. In truth, you never left, though you often get caught up within the illusion (or thought) that you have.

"On practical levels, the best suggestion I have is to consciously return your thoughts to the place of quiet centeredness. It will become habit after some time. And soon you will begin to operate from a much larger field

It would be very good if we would wake up before we die.

HINDU SAYING

Zak
Photo by Dawn Brunke

of feeling, thought, emotion, and creativity. It is all about opening to the fullness of who you are."

Finding a home in quiet centeredness is the same as attuning ourselves to that state of inner calm in which we are able to communicate with animals, nature, and all the world. You remember—it is about expanding consciousness by breaking free of what we think we know or what others have told us. It is about letting go of assumptions, letting go of trying to do, or even trying to be. It is about opening to the sacred space of allowing life—with all her wondrous surprises—to live through us.

We carry our reality with us wherever we go. The energetic vibration of our thoughts and feelings are way more powerful than we have been led to believe. So remember to choose wisely. Breathe deep and consider that the world you see is the world you help to create, every day, anew.

When, before the beauty of a sunset or a mountain, you pause and exclaim 'Ah,' you are participating in divinity.

JOSEPH CAMPBELL

Goldfish
Photo by Dawn Brunke

By believing in miracles, you inspire the miraculous. By creating and seeing beauty, you elevate its vibration in yourself, and others, and the world at large. We are goldfish and we inspire beauty in the world. Our message is to inspire, uplift, elevate, and touch the heart of all beings. In beauty you move to a deeper love, for you touch another and find yourself—you discover the place of oneness, of inherent connection, in all.

GOLDFISH ∽ DAWN BRUNKE

Discovering the fullness of who we are is an opening to what calls us. It is sharing laughter and wisdom as we talk with animals, feeling comfort in the trees and plants and land, finding beauty in the water and sky and stars, and believing in ourselves by appreciating our own small, still, precious voice within. It is using our intellect to gather information and learn. It is developing and trusting our intuition, honoring the wonderfully creative ways in which we sense and feel and know. It is igniting our imagination to undreamed possibilities. It is using our experiences to fine-tune ourselves, to feel deep down into the nature of all Being and know that we are home.

When you feel that flow of connection within your heart and mind and bones and soul, you align yourself with Center Being. And then you see: here we all are—lion, moose, human, whale; cat, wolf, goldfish, snail—each and every one unique, each and every one connected. There is nowhere you need to go, nothing you need to do. Everything is right here, right now. The central pulse of All That Is flows through all creation, speaks in all manner of voices, awakens those who hear the call. So trust yourself, welcome your experiences, share your truth, and enjoy your life. The Bird of the Most Beautiful Song of the Forest sings through you.

 ## NOTHING TO SAY, NOTHING TO FEAR
Gray Whales ~ Penelope Smith

There's nothing to say. We are one in oceanic majesty. We hold the space of oceanic majesty for all beings to remember who we are as one being in the light of life. There's nothing to fear; there is only love here.

We are the great love, taking all beings in our great arms of love, into the greater love. The message is always about the greater love. There is no other reality. It is all about the soul contained in love, expanded in love, giving love, being love, holding love, loving love. We are a love that knows no bounds; we are the greater love ascending, descending, expanding into greater and greater fields and oceans of love.

Join us in the majesty that you are—that we all are—and never fear. This time of pain will pass into the great ocean of time, form, and timelessness. We hold it all in one breath—the Great Breath of the Great Whale expanding to oceans and spaces beyond the imagination. Open and hear your heart space and this greatest of realities that knows no bounds.

Notes

Introduction

1. Coleman Barks, trans., *The Essential Rumi* (Edison, N.J.: Castle Books, 1997), 36.

Chapter 1

1. Edward Field, trans., "Netsilik Eskimo Song," *Eskimo Songs and Stories: From the Fifth Thule Expedition,* collected by Knud Rasmussen (New York: Delacorte Press, 1973).

2. Joseph Campbell, *The Way of the Animal Powers,* vol. 1 (London: Summerfield Press, 1983), 8.

Chapter 2

1. Irene Smith, *A History of the Newbery and Caldecott medals* (Viking Press, 1959).

2. Patricia Jepsen and Delphi, *Six Lessons with Delphi: How to Live Happily with All Life* (Patricia Jepsen Chuse, 2002), 64–65; adapted with permission.

Chapter 3

The lines of poetry by Jelalludin Rumi quoted in this chapter are from "The Guest House," which can be found on page 109 of Coleman Barks, trans., *The Essential Rumi.*

1. Carl Gustav Jung, *The Structure and Dynamics of the Psyche,* in *Collected Works of C.G. Jung,* vol. 8, 2d ed. (Princeton: Princeton University Press, 1970).

2. Ted Andrews, *Animal-Speak: The Spiritual and Magical Powers of Creatures Great and Small* (St Paul. Minn.: Llewellyn Publications, 1997), 338.

3. See Joanne Elizabeth Lauck, *The Voice of the Infinite in the Small: Revisioning the Insect-Human Connection* (Boston: Shambhala, 2002), chapter 4. Much of the association between flies and disease is not based on fact but on skewed information.

4. Ibid., 55.

5. J. Allen Boone, *Kinship with All Life* (New York: Harper & Row, 1954), 144.

6. Ibid., 55.

7. Condensed and edited from "Command Performance" by Karen Lee Morrison, reprinted with permission from author and *The Brayer Magazine,* Journal of the American Donkey and Mule Society 34, no.3 (May/June 2001), 74.

Chapter 4

1. Chief Letakots-Lesa of the Pawnee Tribe to Natalie Curtis, circa 1904, as cited in Joseph Campbell, *The Way of the Animal Powers,* vol. 1 (London: Summerfield Press, 1983), 8.

2. Jean Houston, *Mystical Dogs—Animals as Guides to Our Inner Life* (Maui, Hawaii: Inner Ocean Publishing, 2002), xviii.

3. Jean Houston, *Mystical Dogs,* xix.

Chapter 6

1. Siegfried and Roy, Web site: www.siegfriedandroy.com.

2. Carl Gustav Jung, "The Meaning of Psychology for Modern Man" in *Collected Works of Carl Jung,* vol. 10, 2d ed. (Princeton: Princeton University Press, 1970), 327.

3. Victoria Covell, *Spirit Animals* (Nevada City, Calif.: Dawn Publications, 2000), 45.

Chapter 7

1. Linda Tellington-Jones, *The Tellington TTouch* (New York: Penguin Books, 1993), 19.

2. Ibid., 21.

3. Lewis Mehl-Madrona, *Coyote Healing* (Rochester, Vt.: Bear & Company, 2003), vii.

Chapter 8

1. Rita Reynolds, *Blessing the Bridge* (Troutdale, Oreg.: New Sage Press, 2001), 3.

2. Ibid., 54.

Chapter 9

1. John Perkins, *Shapeshifting: Shamanic Techniques for Global and Personal Transformation* (Rochester, Vt.: Destiny Books, 1997), 44.

2. J. Allen Boone, *Adventures in Kinship with All Life,* ix.

3. Ibid., 32.

Chapter 10

1. Carol Buckley, *Travels with Tarra* (Gardiner, Maine: Tilbury House, 2002), 36.

2. For more, see Dawn Brunke, *Animal Voices* (Rochester, Vt: Bear & Company, 2002), chapter 22.

3. For more on this subject and a deeper exploration of animals eating animals and the predator/prey relationship, see *Animal Voices,* chapter 23.

Resources, References, and Recommendations

For those who want to learn more about animals and about experiencing deeper ways of being, there are many excellent resources. The books and Web sites listed below are just a beginning. Some provide additional information to topics discussed in this book; others are simply great places to jump-start your own adventure. I have arranged this section by chapter and topic, though some sites and books cover more than one area.

For more information, to contact me personally, or for direct links to any of the resources mentioned below, please visit the Animal Voices Web site at www.animalvoices.net.

Chapter 1: Once upon a Time . . .

To learn more about the Musk Ox Farm in Palmer, Alaska, see www.muskoxfarm.org.

Chapter 2: Becoming Doctor Dolittle

The Story of Doctor Dolittle by Hugh Lofting was originally printed in 1920. To read it (and *The Voyages of Doctor Dolittle*) online, for free, visit www.pagebypagebooks.com.

Animal Communicator Links

While there are many fine animal communicators all over the world, the following sites belong to the contributors to this book.

Kat Berard: www.katberard.com
Judi Byers: www.animalechoes.com
Carole Devereux: www.animalinsights.com
Patti Henningsen: www.animaltranslator.com
Morgine Jurdan:
www.communicationswithlove.com
Gretchen Kunz: www.animaltalker.com
Cathy Malkin: www.animalmuse.com
Rita Reynolds: www.blessingthebridge.com
Penelope Smith: www.animaltalk.net
Tera Thomas: www.hummingbirdfarm.org

Animal Communication Books

Brunke, Dawn Baumann. *Animal Voices: Telepathic Communication in the Web of Life.* Rochester, Vt.: Bear & Company, 2002. www.animalvoices.net

Curtis, Anita. *Animal Wisdom: Communications with Animals.* Gilbertsville, Pa.: Anita Curtis, 1996. www.anitacurtis.com

Gurney, Carol. *The Language of Animals: Seven Steps to Communicating with Animals.* New York: Bantam-Dell, 2001. www.animalcommunicator.net

Kinkade, Amelia. *Straight from the Horse's Mouth: How to Talk to Animals and Get Answers.* New York: Crown, 2001.

Pope, Raphaela. *Wisdom of the Animals: Communication Between Animals and the People Who Love Them.* Holbrook, Mass.: Adams Media Corporation, 2001.

Smith, Penelope. *Animal Talk: Interspecies Telepathic Communications.* Hillsboro, Oreg.: Beyond Words, 1999. www.animaltalk.net

Summers, Patty. *Talking with the Animals.* Charlottesville, Va.: Hampton Roads, 1998. www.psanimal.com

Thomas, Tera. *Opening My Wings to Fly: What Animals Have Taught Me.* Pittsboro, N.C.: Hummingbird Farm Press, 2001. www.hummingbirdfarm.org

Williams, Marta. *Learning Their Language: Intuitive Communication with Animals and Nature.* Novato, Calif.: New World Library, 2003. www.martawilliams.com

Animal Internet Groups

Some Internet sites sponsor free groups, forums, and newsletters that provide informational e-mail or allow you to interact with others who have similar interests. For example, go to Yahoo at www.yahoogroups.com and type in your area of interest ("canine search and rescue" or "animal communication"). Joining an Internet group can be an invaluable resource to learn more, share information, help others, and meet some wonderful friends.

chapter 3: magical meetings

Deepening Our Relationship with Animals and Nature

Boone, J. Allen. *Kinship With All Life.* New York: Harper & Row, 1954.

———. *Adventures in Kinship with All Life.* Joshua Tree, Calif.: Tree of Life Publications, 1990. Originally published as *The Language Of Silence.* New York: Harper & Row, 1970.

Lauck, Joanne Elizabeth. *The Voice of the Infinite in the Small: Re-Visioning the Insect-Human Connection.* Boston.: Shambhala Publications, 2002.

Ocean, Joan. *Dolphins Into the Future.* Kailua, Hawaii: Dolphin Connection, 1997. www.joanocean.com

Pogacnik, Marko. *Nature Spirits and Elemental Beings: Working with the Intelligence in Nature.* Forres, Scotland: Findhorn Press, 1996.

Roads, Michael J. *Talking with Nature.* Tiburon, Calif.: H. J. Kramer, 1987.

———. *Journey into Nature.* Tiburon, Calif.: H. J. Kramer, 1990.

Van Lippe-Biesterfeld, Irene. *Dialogue with Nature.* Forres, Scotland: Findhorn Press, 1997.

chapter 4: power animals, spirit animals— ambassadors of awareness

Working with Animal Signs, Spirits, Guides, and Totems

Andrews, Ted. *Animal-Speak: The Spiritual & Magical Powers of Creatures Great & Small.* St. Paul, Minn.: Llewellyn Publications, 1993.

Bluestone, Sarvananda. *How to Read Signs and Omens in Everyday Life.* Rochester, Vt.: Destiny Books, 2002.

Covell, Victoria. *Spirit Animals.* Nevada City, Calif.: Dawn Publications, 2000.

Houston, Jean. *Mystical Dogs: Animals as Guides to Our Inner Life.* Maui, Hawaii: Inner Ocean Publishing, 2002.

Palmer, Jessica Dawn. *Animal Wisdom: The Definitive Guide to the Myth, Folklore and Medicine Power of Animals.* London: Element, 2001.

For a great look at the teachings and wisdom of more than three hundred animals, see Shamanism—Working with Animal Spirits at: www.animalspirits.com.

Animal Cards
Sams, Jamie, and David Carson. *Medicine Cards: The Discovery of Power through the Ways of Animals.* Santa Fe, N.M.: Bear & Co., 1988.

A Shamanic Approach
Harner, Michael. *The Way of the Shaman.* New York: Harper & Row, 1990.

Lee, Patrick Jasper. *We Borrow the Earth: An Intimate Portrait of the Gypsy Shamanic Tradition and Culture.* London: Thorsons, 2000.

Matthews, Caitlín. *Singing the Soul Back Home: Shamanic Wisdom for Every Day.* London: Connections, 2002.

Scully, Nicki. *Power Animal Meditations: Shamanic Journeys with Your Spirit Allies.* Rochester, Vt.: Bear & Company, 2001.

chapter 5: animal guides and teachers

For more on the Iditarod Sled Dog Race, see www.iditarod.com.

Paulsen, Gary. *Winterdance: The Fine Madness of Running the Iditarod.* New York: Harcourt Brace, 1994.

chapter 6: animal dreams

Good Dream Books
Abadie, M. J. *Teen Dream Power: Unlock the Meaning of Your Dreams.* Rochester, Vt.: Bindu Books, 2003.

Barasch, Marc Ian. *Healing Dreams: Exploring the Dreams that Can Transform Your Life.* New York: Riverhead Books, 2000.

Bluestone, Sarvananda. *The World Dream Book: Use the Wisdom of World Cultures to Uncover Your Dream Power.* Rochester, Vt.: Destiny Books, 2002.

chapter 7: animal healing

Energy Work
Holloway, Sage. *Animal Healing and Vibrational Medicine.* Nevada City, Calif.: Blue Dolphin Publishing, 2001. Includes energy field and chakra diagrams of various animals.

Scully, Nicki. *Alchemical Healing: A Guide to Spiritual, Physical, and Transformational Medicine.* Rochester, Vt.: Bear & Company, 2003. Includes the use of animal spirits as allies in hands-on energy medicine.

Flower Essences
Johnson, Steve. *The Essence of Healing.* Homer, Alaska: Alaskan Flower Essence Project, 2000. www.alaskanessences.com.

Anaflora Flower Essences: www.anaflora.com.

Bach Flower Remedies: www.bachcentre.com and www.bachflower.com.

Flower Essences Society: www.flowersociety.org.

Green Hope Essences: See Animal Wellness collection at www.greenhopeessences.com.

Holistic Healing
Allegretti, Jan, and Katy Sommers. *The Complete Holistic Dog Book: Home Health Care for Our Canine Companions.* Berkeley, Calif.: Celestial Arts, 2003. Includes many holistic approaches, such as herbs, homeopathy, acupressure, and more.

American Holistic Veterinary Medical Association: www.ahvma.org. Includes nationwide referral list; find a holistic vet in your area!

Homeopathy

Hamilton, Don. *Homeopathic Care for Cats and Dogs: Small Doses for Small Animals*. Berkeley, Calif.: North Atlantic Books, 1999.

Walker, Kaetheryn. *Homeopathic First Aid for Animals*. Rochester, Vt.: Healing Arts Press, 1998.

Massage

Fox, Michael W. *The Healing Touch*. New York: Newmarket Press, 1990. Includes massage program for animals, with muscle anatomy and acupressure charts for dogs and cats.

Animal Massage and Therapies: www.amtil.com. Includes information on many holistic therapies for animals.

Reiki

Stein, Diane. *Essential Reiki: A Complete Guide to an Ancient Healing Art*. Freedom, Calif.: The Crossing Press, 1995.

Animal Reiki Center: www.animalreiki.com.

Tellington Touch

Tellington-Jones, Linda. *The Tellington TTouch: A Revolutionary Natural Method to Train and Care for Your Favorite Animal*. New York: Penguin, 1995. www.lindatellingtonjones.com.

Trager

Trager International www.trager.com.

Healing Transformations

Kohanov, Linda. *The Tao of Equus: A Woman's Journey of Healing and Transformation through the Way of the Horse*. Novato, Calif.: New World Library, 2001.

chapter 8:
a look at death

Reynolds, Rita. *Blessing the Bridge: What Animals Teach Us about Death, Dying, and Beyond*. Troutdale, Oreg.: New Sage Press, 2001. To learn more about animal hospice see Rita's Web site at: www.blessingthebridge.com.

Walker, Kaetheryn. *The Heart That is Loved Never Forgets—Recovering from Loss: When Humans and Animals Lose Their Companions*. Rochester, Vt.: Healing Arts Press, 1999.

Weaver, Helen. *The Daisy Sutra: Conversations with My Dog*. Woodstock, N.Y.: Buddha Rock Press, 2001. www.daisysutra.com.

The Association for Pet Loss and Bereavement: www.aplb.org.

chapter 9:
the art of shape-shifting

Kohl, Judith and Herbert. *The View from the Oak—The Private Worlds of Other Creatures*. New York: The New Press, 2000.

Murphy, Shirley Rosseau. *The Catswold Portal*. New American Library, 1992.

Pullman, Philip. *The Amber Spyglass*. New York: Knopf, 2000.

———. *The Golden Compass*. New York: Knopf, 1996.

———. *The Subtle Knife*. New York: Knopf, 1997.

The Witches. Warner Studios, directed by Nicholas Roeg, 1990.

Pay It Forward. Warner Studios, directed by Mimi Leder, 2000.

chapter 10: center Being

Books

Buckley, Carol. *Travels with Tarra*. Gardiner, Maine: Tilbury House, 2002.

Getten, Mary. *Communicating with Orcas: The Whales' Perspective*. Victoria, Canada: Trafford Publishing, 2002. www.marygetten.com

Animal Adoption and Rescue

Save a Pet: www.1-800-save-a-pet.com (or call toll-free 1-800-Save-A-Pet).

Pets 911: www.1888pets911.org (or call toll-free 1-888-PETS-911). This group also has information on spay/neutering, animal behavioral issues, pet welfare organizations and emergency animal care.

Pet Finder: www.petfinder.com.

Shelters and Sanctuaries

Best Friends Animal Sanctuary: www.bestfriends.org. This excellent site of the nation's largest animal sanctuary offers a wealth of information on everything from animal-related careers to starting your own no-kill center.

Wildlife WayStation: www.wildlifewaystation.org. Rescues, rehabilitates, and provides sanctuary to wild and exotic animals from around the world; educational and volunteer opportunities.

The Elephant Sanctuary: www.elephants.com. Natural habitat refuge for old, sick, and endangered elephants; also offers education, online newsletter, internship programs, and volunteer opportunities.

Jungle Friends: www.junglefriends.org. Refuge for abused, neglected, and unwanted primates; outreach and volunteer programs offer opportunities to learn while caring for monkeys.

Angels Gate. www.angelsgate.org. Residential hospice and animal rehabilitation sanctuary.

Spay and Neuter Groups

To find a low-cost spay/neuter program near you, visit SPAY USA: www.spayusa.org (or call toll-free 1-800-248-SPAY).

Also, see Pets 911, listed in Animal Adoption, above.

Specialty Groups

There are many excellent groups that focus on specific species in promoting mutually beneficial ways of living for humans and animals alike. A few examples:

Alley Cat Allies: www.alleycat.org. National group promoting nonlethal control for feral and stray cats.

Bat Conservation International: www.batcon.org. Devoted to conservation, education, and the finding of win/win solutions for both people and bats.

The Goldfish Sanctuary: www.petlibrary.com/goldfish. Dedicated to the universal well-being of goldfish everywhere.

Search and Rescue

National Association for Search and Rescue: www.nasar.org.

Therapy and Service Animals

Harrison, Nora Vitz. *Dear Kilroy: A Dog to Guide Us*. Sterling, Virginia: Capital Books, 2003. True stories from puppy raisers for service dog organizations.

Delta Society: www.deltasociety.org. An excellent resource to learn more about service and therapy animals, including career opportunities.

North American Riding for the Handicapped Association: www.narha.org. National group promotes the benefits of the horse for individuals with physical, emotional, and learning disabilities.

Assistance Dogs International: www.adionline.org. Training standards for service dogs and dog partners, with links to groups all over the country that train assistance dogs, many from shelters.

Loving Paws Assistance Dogs: www.lovingpaws.com. Trains service/social dogs to assist physically disabled children; promotes children and dogs working together to achieve greater independence. Volunteer and puppy-raising positions available.

Dogs for the Deaf: www.dogsforthedeaf.org. Rescues dogs from shelters, trains and places them with deaf individuals. Volunteer opportunities for foster friends, puppy raisers, and telephone interviewers.

Guide Dogs for the Blind: www.guidedogs.com. Provides free guide dogs and training to the visually impaired. Volunteer opportunities, along with information on how to become a guide dog instructor.

Animal Training
Association of Pet Dog Trainers: www.apdt.com. Articles and list of trainers who use positive-based training methods.

Clothier, Suzanne. *Bones Would Rain from the Sky: Deepening Our Relationships with Dogs.* New York: Warner Books, 2002. See Suzanne's Web site at: www.flyingdogpress.com. Site includes many articles on training and working in partnership with dogs.

To learn how to become an exotic animal trainer and work with your animals in partnership, see trainer and teacher Kayce Cover's SynAlia Training: www.synalia.com.

Wildlife Rehabilitation
National Wildlife Rehabilitators Association: www.nwrawildlife.org.

Wildlife Conservation and Habitat Protection
The Jane Goodall Institute: www.janegoodall.org. Wildlife conservation, research, and education programs to benefit people, animals, and the environment, including Roots & Shoots, especially designed for young people of the world.

The Natural Resources Defense Council: www.nrdc.org. Environmental action organization using law, science, and member support to protect wildlife and "ensure a safe and healthy environment for all living things."

BOOKS OF RELATED INTEREST

Animal Voices
Telepathic Communication in the Web of Life
by Dawn Baumann Brunke

The Thundering Years
Rituals and Sacred Wisdom for Teens
by Julie Tallard Johnson

Teen Psychic
Exploring Your Intuitive Spiritual Powers
by Julie Tallard Johnson

Teen Dream Power
Unlock the Meaning of Your Dreams
by M. J. Abadie

How to Read Signs and Omens in Everyday Life
by Sarvananda Bluestone, Ph.D.

Power Animal Meditations
Shamanic Journeys with Your Spirit Allies
by Nicki Scully

Meditations with Animals
A Native American Bestiary
by Gerald Hausman

The Nahualli Animal Oracle
by Caelum Rainieri and Ivory Andersen
Illustrated by Raphael Montoliu

Inner Traditions • Bear & Company
P.O. Box 388
Rochester, VT 05767
1-800-246-8648
www.InnerTraditions.com

Or contact your local bookseller

133.89
B   Brunke, Dawn Bau-
       mann

       Awakening to ani-
       mal voices

DUE DATE   0804   17.95

9/04

|||||||||||||||||||||
00110618
United States Marine Corps
Station Library, Bldg 298
Cherry Point, NC 28533-00009